AFTER THE RISING

AFTER THE RISING

SOLDIERS, LAWYERS AND TRIALS
OF THE IRISH REVOLUTION

Seán Enright

MERRION
PRESS

Published in 2016 by
Merrion Press
8 Chapel Lane
Sallins
Co. Kildare

© 2016 Seán Enright

British Library Cataloguing in Publication Data
An entry can be found on request

978-1-78537-051-9 (Paper)
978-1-78537-052-6 (Cloth)
978-1-78537-053-3 (PDF)
978-1-78537-055-7 (Kindle)

Library of Congress Cataloging in Publication Data
An entry can be found on request

Every effort has been made to trace copyright holders and to obtain their permission for the use of copyright material. The publisher apologises for any errors or omissions and would be grateful if notified of any corrections that should be incorporated in future reprints or editions of this book.

To the memory of
Adrian Hardiman

Contents

Acknowledgements

My thanks especially to my wife Lorna for her patience and assistance. Also, to Aideen Carroll, Davide Corbino, Matt Dempsey and Thomas Kellett.

I also thank Tom Toomey, Seán Hogan, Hugh Beckett, Pádraig Óg Ó Ruairc and Tim Horgan for kind help generously given.

I express my gratitude to Richard McCormick of the National Maritime Museum of Ireland for permission to use the photos of Karl Spindler and Captain Weisbach.

The image of men being rounded up and marched is courtesy of Pádraig Óg Ó Ruairc.

The image of Margeret Skinnider is reproduced courtesy of the Dublin City Library and Archive.

The following images are reproduced courtesy of the Kilmainham Gaol Museum: 17PC-1A-53 (Sisters of Charity feeding boys during the revolt); 18PD-1A18-15 (Eoin MacNeill); 18PD-1A18-15 (Sheehy-Skeffington); KMGLM 2015.0137(Maxwell, Birrell and Nathan); 19PC 1A46 10 (Seán T. O'Kelly at Versailles); 19PC 1A46 5 (Dáil Court); 19PO 1A33 17 (Bridie Gallagher).

The wedding photo of Captain King (CD 227/35) is courtesy of the Irish Military Archives and the picture of General Sir Gordon Neville Macready is courtesy of the National Portrait Gallery.

The image of the log for *HMS Bluebell* is reproduced courtesy of TNA National Archive. The images of Michael Collins, Dáil Éireann and the Casement submarine are courtesy of Mercier's Archive.

The following images are reproduced courtesy of the National Library of Ireland: INDH0079 (Customs House on fire, May 1921); INDH0022E (Prisoners to barracks 1916); 279885 (Auxiliary on guard duty, Dublin 1921).

The image of Major General Friend is by courtesy of the National Portrait Gallery.

I express my sincere appreciation for the assistance given by the staff of the National Archives (Kew); the National Library of Ireland.

SEÁN ENRIGHT

Dramatis Personae

The Generals

General Sir Neville Macready GCMG, KCB,1862–1946, was the last British General Officer Commanding (GOC) in Ireland. He was commissioned into the Gordon Highlanders and fought at Tel el-Kebir in 1882. Later he served at Ladysmith during the second Boer war. He led troops during the miners' strike in Wales in 1910 and went to France in 1914 as Adjutant General of the British Expeditionary Forces (BEF). He was later Adjutant General of the British Army. From 1918–1920 he was Commissioner of the Metropolitan Police and was appointed GOC Ireland in March 1920.

Shortly before taking up his new duty, he wrote to a colleague who was en route to an Ireland posting: 'I loathe the country you are going to and its people with a depth deeper than the sea and more violent than which I feel about the Boche.' He was married to an Irish woman. He was a liberal in his politics and favoured home rule and equality for women although he despised politicians. The source of his greatest pride was the reputation of the Army.

General Sir Henry Wilson GCB, DSO, 1864–1922, had his home in Currygrane in County Longford, where his brother Jemmy lived out the War of Independence. Wilson was Chief of the Imperial General Staff during the Paris Peace Conference and during the War of Irish Independence. He was a tall, gangling man badly scarred from a spear thrust on a colonial campaign. He described himself as 'the ugliest man in the British army'.

Wilson was involved in the Curragh Mutiny and is deservedly remembered for political intrigues and plotting to oust career rivals to advance his own interests.

Wilson's claim to greatness rests on his contribution to putting the BEF in a state of readiness to go to France in August 1914. As a Francophile with a good grasp of French he smoothed relations between the British and French high commands. On the question of Ireland, he seemed incapable of uttering any reasonable thought. In 1922 he resigned from the Army and became a Unionist MP. In the summer, he was murdered outside his Eton Square home. His diaries cast new light on government policy.

General Sir Joseph Aloysius Byrne KCMG, CB, 1874–1942, was Deputy Adjutant General to Sir John Maxwell in 1916. He was an able administrator. He was appointed Inspector General of the Royal Irish Constabulary (RIC) but suspended in December 1919 and dismissed without explanation the following month. Most of the rank and file strenuously objected to his dismissal.[1] The explanation for his dismissal appears to lie in his opposition to turning the RIC into a quasi-military force and a desire to open negotiations with the Dáil. He was a Catholic from Londonderry. He was later called to the Bar and served as Governor General of Kenya, Sierra Leone and the Seychelles.

General Sir Hugh Tudor KCB, CMG, 1871–1965, served with the Artillery in the Boer campaign and was wounded at Magersfontain. He later served in India, Egypt and on the Western Front where he rose from Captain to Major General. He was credited with inventing the creeping barrage. A personal friend of Sir Winston Churchill, he was appointed Police Chief in Ireland on the strength of this friendship. His brief was to militarise the RIC and stiffen the response to the insurgency.

He lived in Dublin Castle and toured Ireland in an armoured Rolls Royce, to strengthen resolve among the RIC. Reprisals by police against suspects were already underway when Tudor was appointed but he actively encouraged officers to carry out reprisals against people and property. In this way the rule of law was quietly unpicked.

Brigadier Sir Ormonde L' Épée Winter KBE, CB, CMG, DSO, 1875–1962, was an artillery officer of exceptional courage and ability. He was appointed Deputy Police Chief in the Spring of 1920 but, in fact, his actual role was Chief of Combined Intelligence Services in Ireland. In the Great War, Winter was decorated for courage and mentioned in despatches six times, although his expertise in the field of policing and intelligence was nil. But Winter seems to have realised that his moment in history had arrived. He immediately styled himself 'O' and embraced the life of a spymaster with enthusiasm and energy.

Winter was a linguist, vet and horse rider of great skill. He later wrote a light-hearted autobiography about the horses he rode, the boars he hunted and the women he bedded. After a dull time following the Irish conflict, Winter served with distinction with the Finnish Army against the Soviets in 1940.

Soldiers and Lawyers

Charles Bewley, 1888–1969, was the son of a well-known Dublin Quaker family and was one of the first, perhaps the first barrister to appear before a Dáil Court. He defended Seán MacEoin in 1921. During the Civil War he was on the pro-treaty faction and prosecuted many anti-treatyites. He was later a diplomat at the Vatican and in Berlin in the 1930s where he became an apologist for the Nazis and used his position to prevent Jews obtaining visas to emigrate to Ireland. He was an erudite but selfish man whose deeply anti-semitic views cost many lives in Germany. After the war, the Irish Government renewed his passport but under the section marked 'occupation' entered the words – 'a person of no importance'.

Sir Archibald Bodkin, 1862–1957, conducted the prosecution of Carl Hans Lody, the first German spy to be shot during the Great War. He also prosecuted the Dowling case. He was later Director of Public Prosecutions but his tenure was remarkable for his determination to eradicate pornography which included efforts to ban the work of Joyce (*Ulysses*) and D.H. Lawrence (*Pansies*). He espoused the view that lesbian sex was a cause and a symptom of mental illness. The famous line, 'that night, they were not divided', inspired a frisson of rage in Bodkin's ample frame.

John Bourke was a barrister from Cork. He defended many of the capital trials of this period, including *R v Allen* and one of the six men from Mourneabbey charged with the murder of Sergeant Gibbs during the Mallow Barracks raid. He emigrated to England after the Treaty and later became Recorder of Shrewsbury.

Sir Felix Cassel PC, 1869–1953, was a Conservative member of parliament, Kings Counsel and British infantry officer. He was born in Germany of German parents although it was rumoured that he was the illegitimate son of the late Edward VII and it was for this reason he was recalled from the trenches in 1915 to serve at the Judge Advocate General's (JAG) office. In his role as JAG, he acted as break on the martial law executions in 1921. He was JAG from November 1916 to 1933.

Lord Cheylesmore was a tall, gaunt guardsman. He had no legal qualifications but he was a pillar of the establishment and his distinguished manner resulted in him often being called to preside over high-profile courts martial. He later became the first member of the aristocracy to die in a car crash. He tried Captain Bowen-Colthurst and Eoin MacNeill, Dowling and others. Lord Cheylesmore was a notable society figure much satirised by cartoonists.

Michael Comyn KC was a slightly built man with a quiet manner. He sported a long walrus moustache. He defended on the Munster Circuit for decades and was well known for his work before martial law courts which were intimidating forums even for the lawyers who appeared. 'Shoot them if you must but try them first' was Comyn's famous retort to the president of a hostile martial law court.

Comyn was later a hefty and irascible old judge on the Eastern Circuit. The Ministry of Justice had tried for some years to retire him on the grounds of old age but the page of the parish record which showed his birth date was missing.

Major Henry Gover OBE had been in practice in the family firm at Monument Street, London Bridge, since 1911. He had joined the Royal West Kent in 1915 and served in Flanders for much of the War. He was mentioned in despatches for his service in France. He prosecuted Terence MacSwiney and most of the major martial law trials in 1921. He was appointed OBE for his work in Ireland.

Henry Hanna KC was counsel with Unionist affiliations. He prosecuted and defended in this period and espoused the view that every prisoner was entitled to a proper defence. He was counsel for the Crown in *Egan v Macready* and wrote *The Pals at Suvla Bay*, a fundraiser for the families of D Company of the 7th Battalion of the Royal Dublin Fusiliers that had suffered great casualties in 1915. He was later a judge of the Irish High Court.

Tim Healy KC, 1855–1931, author, journalist, barrister and MP, was a small pugnacious red-headed man, famous for his cutting tongue. He was a constitutional nationalist although there were suspicions that he was a long-time member of the Irish Republican Brotherhood (IRB). As an MP he was responsible for the Healy Clause in the *Land Act* of 1881, which meant that rent increases could not be levied in respect of improvements made by a tenant. He played a part in Parnell's downfall and was a long-time member of the Irish Parliamentary Party (IPP). He defended many capital cases during the 1918–21 period including the Silvermines trial. He became the first Governor General of the Irish Free State.

Travers Humphreys KC 1867–1956, Treasury Counsel at the Old Bailey for many years, was junior counsel in the prosecution of Oscar Wilde and Dr Crippen, Smith (the Brides in the bath) and Casement. Later he was a judge of the High Court, where his harsh demeanour inspired fear. He was later a judge of the Court of Appeal where he heard the appeal of William Joyce and presided over two notable miscarriages of justice: Walter Rowland and Timothy Evans.

Hugh Kennedy KC, was leading counsel for the prisoner in *Egan v Macready* [1921] I IR 265 and senior legal counsel to Dáil Éireann during the Treaty negotiations. He was later Attorney General and then the first Chief Justice of the Irish Free State, a position he held until his death in 1936.

Major Edmund Kimber DSO, b.1870, was called to the Bar at Lincoln's Inn in 1892. He married in 1913 and was then in practice in Temple. He went to France in 1914 with the 1/13 London Rifles. On the second anniversary of his wedding he was wounded at Fromelles where he distinguished himself by extricating his company from encirclement by an overwhelming enemy force. At this time the War Office were recruiting lawyers for courts martial work in Ireland. Many of these officers had been wounded on the Western Front and were unfit for frontline service. Kimber was one of these men. He was promoted Major in January 1916 and sent to Ireland after the Rebellion to do court martial work. He was later Deputy Assistant Adjutant General. He was twice mentioned in despatches and appointed CBE in 1919. He remained in practice until 1954.

Lieutenant Colonel Ernest Longworth, journalist, barrister and soldier, prosecuted some of the trials arising out the Easter Rising and was later Judge Advocate in many of the Restoration of Order in Ireland Act (ROIA) and martial law trials in this period. He retired in 1922 to take up literary interests.

Patrick Lynch KC, 1866–1947, was born in County Clare and was crown prosecutor in Clare for many years. In 1917, he stood for the IPP in the East Clare by election. He was described by one of his political opponents as a candidate who 'had defended half the murderers in Clare and was related to the other half'. In fact, in the East Clare by election, his record as a prosecutor weighed against him and he lost badly to de Valera. He was remembered by his colleagues as an honest and generous man. He was counsel for the family in the inquest into the death of Mac Curtain. He was also counsel for James Madden, Patrick Maher and one of the prisoners in the Mallow Barracks trial and in a number of trials under martial law. He was counsel in *Egan v Macready*. He was later a Fianna Fáil senator and Attorney General.

Kenneth Marshall CBE served for many years in the JAG's office. In later years, Marshall became Deputy Judge Advocate General under Sir Felix Cassel. Marshall was Judge Advocate in the trial of Hans Lody, the first German spy shot during the Great War. He sat as Judge Advocate in many capital trials in this period. Two of the last trials in which he acted as Judge Advocate in Ireland resulted in miscarriages of justice. One of these was the trial of the six Mallow men tried for the murder of Sergeant Gibbs during the Mallow Barracks raid. The second was the trial of Maher and Foley.

H.M. Meyler CBE, 1875–1929, was qualified as a solicitor but joined the Army on the outbreak of the Boer War when he served in Natal as a trooper. He remained there after the end of hostilities and became a member of the first South African parliament. He returned to England on the outbreak of the Great War and rejoined his regiment where he served in a reconnaissance role until 1916 when he joined the Royal Flying Corp. He was gassed and wounded and awarded the Military Cross, the Distinguished Service Order and the Belgian Order of Leopold. Posted to Ireland after the war, he served as a Judge Advocate in many courts martial. He was certified under the Restoration of Order in Ireland Regulations as an officer legally qualified to sit on capital trials. He took over as Legal Officer to the Sixth Division in March 1921 when the crisis was reaching its height. Meyler was a brave and able soldier but his legal rulings show the haziest grasp of the law.

After the War of Independence, he was briefly a Liberal MP and then ran a small legal practice until the Great Depression. A court order was made for the seizure of his assets. When the Sherriff came to his office to enforce the order, Meyler retreated into his office and shot himself dead.

Lord Chief Justice Molony, 1865–1949, was a home ruler. In 1916, he was a member of the Royal Commission into the death of Sheehy-Skeffington, Dickson and MacIntyre. He served as Solicitor General and Attorney General and was appointed Lord Chief Justice of Ireland in 1918 and gave some notable judgments on the application of martial law. See for instance *R v Allen* II IR 241. As a sentencing tribunal, he was known to favour capital punishment.

Sir Richard Muir, 1857–1924, was Senior Treasury Counsel at the Old Bailey for many years. Muir was an outsider, not at all from the usual Oxbridge and public school background. He was an un-showy workaholic who assembled and cross-referenced, catalogued and memorised every detail of a case. He was regarded as the most able prosecuting counsel of his generation and his cross-examination of Dr Crippen remains a remarkable feat. He prosecuted the Drumcondra trial in 1921.

Sir Charles O'Connor, Master of the Rolls. He gave the judgement in favour of the prisoners in *Egan v Macready* [1921] 1 IR 265. He issued a writ of habeas corpus and, when the order was not immediately complied with, he issued writs for the arrest of Generals Macready and his most senior commanders. He was one of the judges kept on by the Irish Free State after the Treaty. It was said, a little cynically, that he had 'acquired merit' in the eyes of the new administration. He also gave the judgment of the court in *R (Childers) v The Adjutant General of the Forces of the Irish Free State* [1923] 1 IR 5. His main source of pride was his membership of the O'Connor Clan. He would frequently bore listeners on the subject.

Michael Noyk was a solicitor who defended many prisoners tried by courts martial in this period. He was a very capable solicitor.

Henry Delacombe Roome,1882–1930, was an author and barrister in chambers in the Temple. Roome prosecuted a number of capital courts martial trials including that of Maher and Foley. He was killed in a car crash in 1930.

Sir Montague Shearman, 1857–1925, was a Judge of the High Court. He sat on the Royal Commission into the causes of the Rebellion in Ireland. Sir Montague was a founder member of the Amateur Athletic Association (AAA). As a young man he had been a gifted amateur footballer, a sprinter and Oxford Rugby Blue. His first love was football about which he wrote a notable history: *Football: It's History for Five Centuries* (1885). He later tried the two men who were charged with the murder of Sir Henry Wilson.

Sir John Simon chaired the Royal Commission into *The arrest and subsequent treatment of Mr Francis Sheehy Skeffington, Mr Thomas Dickson and Mr James MacIntyre* (Cmd 8376). He was leading counsel for the prisoners *In re: Clifford and Sullivan* [1921] A C 570. Later Lord Chancellor, he also became Chancellor of the Exchequer and Foreign Secretary.

Alexander Martin Sullivan was known as The Last Sergeant, the final holder of an ancient legal title in Ireland. A big, flamboyant advocate, he was notoriously rude to judges. Sullivan defended Casement at his trial for treason and famously suffered a breakdown during the trial. He prosecuted a number of cases arising out of the insurgency but, after he was shot at in Kerry, (he was probably not the intended victim) he left for England and set up in practice there.

William Wylie KC, 1881–1964, was from a northern Presbyterian family. In 1916, he was in practice at the Dublin bar and was also a Territorial Army officer. He was seen by the Attorney General guiding troops across Dublin and, on the strength of that sighting, appointed to prosecute the leaders of the 1916 Rising. He carried out this task with conspicuous fairness. He was appointed government Law Advisor in 1920 and held that post until his appointment to the High Court. Hook nosed, with an athletic build, he was a familiar figure in equestrian circles for decades. He became an infamously lazy judge and caused Chief Justice Kennedy to write: 'that he should sit only once a week and disport himself for the rest of the week at horse shows hunts and races is a quite intolerable situation'.[2]

The Policy Makers

David Lloyd George, was Prime Minister and war leader. He negotiated the Peace Treaty at Versailles. His record in Ireland is defined by his encouragement of reprisals against people and property.

Winston Churchill was one of the hawks in Lloyd George's cabinet. He was aware of and helped sustain the 'gunning' campaign.

Hamar Greenwood was Chief Secretary for Ireland from the spring of 1920 until after the Truce. Greenwood was one of a cabal of ministers in the administration of Lloyd George who favoured unofficial reprisals against people and property. In this he was given all assistance by General Tudor.

Lord French, 1852–1925, 1st Earl of Ypres, Viceroy 1920–21, served with distinction in the Madhi war against the Boers. He was a truly talented cavalry commander who rose to Chief of the Imperial General Staff in 1912. He was known as an avid womaniser who had several adulterous affairs which came within an ace of ruining his career. French was a very short man who, in later life, acquired a very tall mistress which provided some amusement for the public.

Like his friend Sir Henry Wilson, he was an intriguer and was forced to resign over the Curragh Mutiny. He re-emerged as Commander in Chief of the BEF but his tenure was not successful. He was replaced and appointed Commander in Chief to the Home Forces from 1916–18. During the army manpower crisis in 1918, French and his chum Sir Henry Wilson advised Lloyd George that conscription in Ireland was feasible. A Military Service Act was then passed which precipitated the war in Ireland.

He was appointed Viceroy with a brief to bring conscription in Ireland into effect. Conscription was never enforced and French chafed for a more vigorous response to the growing insurgency. He bought a house and land in Roscommon but was never able to take up residence because of the conflict. He also advocated measures to give land to soldiers returning to Ireland after the war and to provide a social structure which might keep them loyal. It was a thoughtful step which foundered in red tape. He served as Viceroy until the spring of 1921.

Introduction

The Rebellion was crushed but it gave rise to the War of Independence. At the height of the war there were 60,000 soldiers on active service and just over 15,000 police officers combating a guerrilla campaign. Lloyd George called it 'a small war': 262 soldiers were killed and 754 wounded.[1] The bulk of the Crown casualties were suffered by the Royal Irish Constabulary (RIC): 439 killed and well over 1,000 wounded.[2] There is no reliable measure of the casualties suffered by the insurgents but they too were considerable and, by the time the Truce came around, there had been forty executions. There were also forty-two men on death row and over a hundred more awaiting trial for levying war against the Crown. There were hundreds serving long sentences and there were nearly 3,500 men and women interned without trial. Perhaps the greatest suffering was borne by non-combatants: murder, bereavement, deprivation, poverty, loss of livelihood, sectarian bloodshed and enforced exile are recurring themes of this era. None of this adequately describes the seismic impact of this conflict and the long-term adverse consequences for two countries that could have enjoyed peace.

This book is the third and last of a series. Volume 1 deals with the trials arising out of the martial law era in 1921, Volume II covers the trials arising out of the Easter Rising. This volume bridges the gap. It commences after the last of the executions in 1916 and traces the deliberations of the Royal Commission into the causes of the Rebellion and the trials that took place in the months and years that followed as the criminal justice system slowly collapsed and was substantially replaced by statutory court martial.

A unique feature of this revolution was the extent to which the conflict centred on law and the legal institutions which kept the status quo in place. The government relied on the criminal justice system to suppress the growing insurrection but a crucial factor was that juries could not be relied upon to deliver convictions in cases with a political aspect. This enduring crisis in the justice system encouraged the government to revive or create special powers: banishment, internment without trial, curfews, curbs on freedom of speech and association. It also drove the executive to move trial venues from disturbed areas and to resort to special juries, special courts of summary jurisdiction and courts martial under the Defence of the Realm Act.[3] These developments were widely distrusted and the resentment they bred was exploited by the insurgents.

The crisis came to a head in the summer of 1920 when the justice system became a central part of the battleground. The insurgents introduced their own courts of justice while striving to undermine the courts established under British rule: ninety were burned to the ground during the conflict. The emerging insurgent strategy was directed towards preventing people from using the court system: judges, magistrates witnesses, staff and jurors were subjected to persuasion or intimidation. There were also many who were only too happy to give their loyalty to the emerging court system and, by the summer of 1920, the established justice system was under grave threat in the south and west of Ireland.

The failure of juries to deliver convictions in capital cases meant there was no longer sufficient incentive for the British government to maintain the justice system as it then stood and perhaps that had become impossible. The response from Westminster was to pass the Restoration of Order in Ireland Act (ROIA), which conferred much wider powers on the Army to try civilians by courts martial.

The result was that there were three concurrent legal regimes, each asserting their authority and jurisdiction: firstly, the criminal justice system under British rule which continued in the north and in an attenuated form in the south; secondly, the court martial regime put in place by the ROIA and, thirdly, the emerging Dáil courts.

As the crisis worsened in the winter of 1920, a fourth legal regime emerged: martial law was declared in the south west of Ireland and the Army brought in military courts (not sanctioned by law). Under this regime, the death sentence was available for possessing a gun or even a clip of ammunition. It was intended that trials and executions should take place swiftly and without recourse to law but the families of prisoners sought writs of habeas corpus to prevent the executions[4] and this set in motion a series of legal challenges which eventually led to the courts ruling that these tribunals were unlawful.

The second part of this book recounts some of the more significant trials. It has not been easy to decide which trials to include, if only because the number of men and women tried by courts martial during the Long

Revolution runs to at least 11,000 and many of the records have been lost or destroyed.

Such evidence as there is suggests that the Army had neither the resources nor the expertise to run a criminal justice system. The court martial process was geared up to dealing with factually simple cases: thieving from the mess fund, losing a rifle or desertion. The trials under the ROIA threw up much more difficult issues. There were a significant number of cases in which the courts martial process miscarried and some prisoners were hanged or condemned to death but saved by the Truce. This group of cases had a common denominator: they were based on visual identification unsupported by other evidence. It is now well established that visual identification is inherently fallible and dangerous but this was not known in 1921. An added factor was that identification parades were rudimentary, even by the standards of the time, and contained little if any protections for the accused.

The Truce came about in 1921 but the conflict and the courts martial process left a legacy of bitterness that endured for generations. Part of that emanated from the bitter nature of the conflict in which acts of the most wanton kind were perpetrated by both sides. Part of the residual bitterness stems from the selective application of the law: insurgents were prosecuted for capital offences but the authorities winked at murder and reprisal by police officers and soldiers.

The centenary of this conflict is upon us and there is a great deal to be learned from what took place but if these events cannot now be remembered without rancour, then we are all still prisoners of history. It might also be remembered that oppression comes in many forms. Independence brought with it the stifling influence of the Church on government and society. Religious discrimination was a fact of life, both north and south of the border. Women had played their part in the revolution but found themselves hostages in a society run by men. The last and the most pernicious consequence was the notion that any small group of men and women was entitled to claim the right to impose their wishes on society by force of arms: Pandora's box had been opened and was never shut. The result was an intermittent campaign of murder in which thousands of civilians lost their lives.

It is only as these influences have receded that we have become sensitive to other less obvious forms of oppression that have been part of the fabric of our society. In Britain, such a moment was the Stephen Lawrence Inquiry.

The setting up of the Saville Inquiry also stemmed from a recognition that the proper application of the rule of law is not selective: it is not a trump card to be played or withheld as a government pleases.

In Ireland the Ryan Commission and the Magdalene Laundries affair have proved to be revelatory events. These unacknowledged grievances and the steps taken to rectify them have been part of a transformation towards a society which protects fundamental human rights; holds the government, private individuals and institutions accountable under the law and in which justice is delivered fairly, by neutral tribunals. From this, there can be no going back.

PART I
CONTEXTS

CHAPTER ONE

After the Rebellion

Connolly and MacDiarmada were executed just before dawn on 12 May 1916. A few hours later, Prime Minister Asquith disembarked from a destroyer at the North Wall, cocooned in a fur-lined leather coat that stretched down to his ankles. He stepped off the gangway and blinked in the bright sunshine. The warm weather had arrived at Easter and would continue for many weeks.

The night before in the Commons, Asquith had signalled the end of the execution policy and his arrival in Dublin showed a politician's timing: suddenly, there was bacon and even jam for the prisoners at breakfast. Asquith moved through a crowd of prisoners shaking hands with some. He appeared oblivious to the fact that, only a few yards away, the trials continued. Most of the prisoners who had been part of the general surrender in Dublin had been tried and the Army had begun to try the prisoners from the provinces. They too were tried by Field General Courts Martial in camera, without defence lawyers.

Asquith had been disturbed about the number of executions and reports of the murder of civilians: the case of Sheehy-Skeffington and two journalists pressed most heavily on his mind. Asquith called for the list of men awaiting execution. At the top of the list was Thomas Ashe who had led the fight at Ashbourne, where eight police officers were killed and many wounded. Another was de Valera, who had been in command at Boland's Mill. Ashe, de Valera and many others awaiting execution would be allowed to live. De Valera, like many of the prisoners, had become reconciled to death. When the news was brought that his life was to be spared he was reading *The Confessions of St Thomas Aquinas*. He looked up briefly, thanked the messenger and returned to his book.[1]

In the city centre, the Saint Vincent de Paul Society had fed the hungry and, as the days passed, the lines of people queuing for food had disappeared. The rubble was still being cleared away. The sandbags protecting the windows of the Shelbourne came down and the hotel was busy again. Most Dubliners were relieved the Rebellion had been suppressed. A shop keeper in Grafton Street wrote that he had 'lost a clear fortnight's business over the troubles'.[2] A special police court sat at Dublin Castle to deal with the looters who had run amok during the Rebellion. The prisoners were brought up in batches. As the hunt for looters gathered pace, many of the slum dwellers crept out at night and, in the narrow lanes behind the cathedral, dumped fur coats, handbags, boots, umbrellas and walking sticks.

The postal service had been restored quickly but it was a mixed blessing: the week before, a gas attack near Loos had claimed the lives of nearly 600 men from the 16th Irish Division and the letters and telegrams had started to come through. Old-age pensions and separation allowances were also being paid again. The money was distributed to sub post offices by the improvised armoured cars that had appeared during the Rebellion: they looked like 'a cross between a submarine and a bread van'.[3]

The Round up in Dublin

The news of the executions and deportations had spread fast and many wounded Volunteers made their escape from hospitals all over Dublin. Patrick Morrissey had been wounded and captured during the first day of fighting at the South Dublin Union. The other men with him had been captured and held for trial but Morrissey dragged himself out of his hospital bed and onto the back of a milk cart. Others climbed out of windows or limped out on crutches. Ted O'Kelly had led the Maynooth contingent to the General Post Office (GPO) on Easter Monday and, in the desperate fighting as the GPO burned, O'Kelly was wounded in the foot and ended up in Jervis Street Hospital. Knowing that the Army was combing the hospitals for wounded Volunteers, he escaped dressed as a priest.[4]

In this small city, many men were still hiding in lofts or cellars and waiting for the knock on the front door that spelled deportation or worse. Patrick Egan from Kilmainham had been one of the men holding Roe's Distillery, on the edge of the South Dublin Union. Egan escaped the general surrender and fell in with two others who had evaded the cordon at Stephen's Green. They hid out in a loft at Aungier Street until they were able to slip away to the hills outside Dublin, where they lived rough.[5]

The Round ups in the Provinces

In the provinces, the round up had begun almost as soon as the general surrender took effect and it continued for many weeks. The process was expedited by General Maxwell who sent armoured columns into most parts of Ireland to help the Royal Irish Constabulary (RIC).

Lists of suspects were drawn up by the police, often with the help of the resident magistrates,[6] but the RIC was mainly interested in the surrender of arms. The message was put out – surrender arms or face internment. In Cork, Limerick and Kerry firearms were surrendered in significant quantities.[7] There were single shot 'Howth Mausers', obsolete Martini's, shotguns and many Lee Enfields that had been stolen or bought from soldiers on leave. The surrender of an old fowling piece caused some amusement among the RIC. Some men had gone out to fight the Empire armed only with pikes and these too were seized.

In Clare, most guns were hidden or returned to lawful owners.[8] In West Cork, rifles and shotguns were buried or hidden.[9] At Fermoy, the Kent family refused to come quietly and fought it out at their farmhouse killing Head Constable Rowe. Richard Kent was killed and David Kent wounded before surrendering.

Most men waited for the RIC to come calling. Some, to avoid a tearful scene, packed a bedroll and tobacco and trudged off to the local RIC station.

In Galway, the leaders of the Rebellion had gone on the run: Liam Mellows lived rough for some days before finding refuge in a hut.[10] Money was given over by local clergy and Ned Daly's family in Limerick. After many weeks, Mellows was driven to Cork, disguised as a nun – a very fine looking nun, his accomplices remembered. Mellows, like a few others, escaped to America by boat.[11]

Alex McCabe was hiding out in the west. Before the Rebellion he had been sent to Sligo to organise a line of escape for the insurgents if they were beaten in Dublin but, as the Rebellion fell apart, he found himself on the run moving from one house to another, one step ahead of his pursuers.[12]

Seán Hales from Ballinadee in West Cork got rid of his gun and also went into hiding. The RIC knew that time was on their side and most of the wanted men would go home at harvest time, exhausted and broke. Hales was picked up in exactly that way.[13]

Over 2,000 prisoners were gathered up from remote areas of Ireland and packed onto trains to Dublin and then to Richmond Barracks where they were chosen for trial, deportation or release. Every few days, the names and addresses of prisoners were published in the *Irish Times*. The lists ran to hundreds of names. People huddled around newspapers and gawped. A few wrote in, smugly naming prisoners who had given a false address. Others gossiped when a familiar name was found: 'I knew he would turn out bad.' But in so many towns and villages, families anxiously scanned the lists for news of a husband or a son.

Galway was worst affected, mainly Athenry. Whenever there was trouble 'Athenry was in it'. The area was 'honeycombed' with secret societies and a hot bed of Volunteer activity. When the Rebellion came, hundreds of young men had besieged the RIC barracks at Clarenbridge and Oranmore but they had been put to flight when *HMS Gloucester* appeared on the horizon and fired a few shells. In this province, over 500 men were rounded up and sent to Dublin. Over 200 men were rounded up in Wexford, 100 from Cork and 60 from Kerry.[14]

Limerick fared better than other counties. Just before the Rebellion an entire battalion from the 2nd Leinster regiment had been deployed to New Barracks and the Rebellion in Limerick had stalled. After negotiations with the Army, many rifles were surrendered by Volunteers. Many young Limerick men were rounded up and interrogated but barely a dozen were sent on to Dublin.

Those Interned without Trial

From Dublin, the internees were sent by cattle boat to prisons in Britain as far apart as Aylesbury and Glasgow. Some were released after a few weeks. One was Patrick O'Kelly from Clontarf, who had been at Jacob's factory during Easter Week. A few weeks later, an order came through for the release of a prisoner by the same name: a Redmondite interned in error. O'Kelly took his chance and walked free.[15] A few secured release by providing satisfactory references.[16] Others were freed after questions were raised in the Commons. One of these was James Kelly, a Justice of the Peace and a former High Sheriff. Kelly had been swept up with all the rest. The arresting officer was Sir Francis Vane who assured Kelly's wife no harm would come to her husband: 'I give my solemn word.'[17] Sir Francis was an honourable man but once the prisoner was taken to Portobello Barracks there was little that could be done for him. It took the authorities over three weeks to let him go. A photo taken on Kelly's release shows a gaunt, wild figure with blackened eye and crumpled clothing; there was not a trace of the fastidiously dressed man who went into captivity. This was the lot of the internees.

The Convicted Prisoners

The prisoners who were tried and convicted were a very mixed bunch. Of the 160 prisoners tried by Field General Court Martial,[18] the oldest was fifty-nine, the youngest was sixteen and only one was a woman. Among the Dublin prisoners who were tried and convicted there were four college professors, two solicitors, a handful of university students, journalists, printers, office workers, railway men, trade unionists like William Partridge and Peadar Doyle (later Lord Mayor of Dublin). There was also a Doctor (Richard Hayes) and George Irvine, a Church of Ireland Sunday school teacher. There were men like Harry Boland, a tailor's cutter, and others: plasterers, tradesmen, artisans and shop assistants.

The convicted prisoners from the provinces included thirty-three from Galway, eleven from Wexford, a handful from Cork and from Kerry and a few from Limerick: mainly farmers, agricultural labourers, a blacksmith, a few stone masons and National School teachers. One, John Grady from Athenry, gave his occupation as 'car owner'. Many of these prisoners had planned the Rebellion; others took a full part. Bizarrely, some had thought, when they marched out on Easter Monday, that they were going on a route march with prizes for shooting and the best turned-out company. A few, captured in the provinces, had just been caught up in the tide of great events.

The convicted prisoners were moved from Kilmainham to Mountjoy where they had a hot bath and a mattress for the first time in weeks.[19] They were then taken in a convoy of Black Marias to the North Wall, where families, well-wishers and dockers had gathered at the quayside.

One of the prisoners was William O'Dea, a twenty-seven-year-old Dubliner. He had been due to marry on Easter Monday. Faced with the choice of marriage or rebellion, he had turned out on Easter Monday and ended up at the Mendicity. He was tried and convicted a few days later but his death sentence was commuted to penal servitude.

Leaning against the ship rail, O'Dea spotted his fiancée on the quays, waving. He reached into his pocket and pulled out a small object that he gave to an officer and pointed at the girl. 'It's a ring!' someone said. The ring passed from one pair of hands to another until it reached the girl. The crowd was briefly silent: Would she take the ring? She did and the crowd cheered. It was not quite the public exchange of vows this couple had in mind but it had to suffice. O'Dea disappeared into the hold of the ship.[20]

De Valera and the largest group of prisoners went to Dartmoor prison where 'God is Love' was chiselled over the gatehouse. Here the prisoners were deloused. Some of the GPO prisoners had burns injuries and found their bandages prized off with little care.[21] Food was in short supply and discipline was unremittingly hard: de Valera was put in isolation for giving his bread to a very big prisoner who found it impossible to live on prison rations.[22] One of the prisoners, Willie Corrigan, complained about the thin gruel. 'I will look into it' the prison doctor promised. 'If you look into it,' Corrigan told the doctor, 'you will see the bottom of the mug.'[23] The water was heavy with iron and the prisoners' teeth began to rot. It should be said the conditions were no better or worse than for other convicts.

The other group of convicted prisoners was sent to Portland where they found a long narrow causeway jutting out into the English Channel. Here, a grim Victorian fortress stood on a rocky promontory where the guards carried shotguns and short swords. At this prison, the most dangerous prisoners in England were held: murderers, rapists and escapers. They had been sentenced to hard labour and were taken out each day, rain or snow, chained to a wagon and marched to the quarries where they cut stone. The prisoners from Ireland had been sentenced to penal servitude, which meant they avoided the back-breaking labour in the quarries. They were issued with 'blue striped shirts and brown knee breeches' and a jacket stamped with arrows. Prisoners were called by their number and never by their name. The men were put to work sewing mail sacks or 'picking oakum'. Dinner was a pint of cocoa, a twelve ounce loaf and a half ounce of margarine. The men were in bed by 8pm each night. Spells of isolation with bread and water were meted out for minor infractions. Prisoners who assaulted warders were lashed with 'the cat' but none of the Irish prisoners were punished in that way and it seems they fared rather better than other convicts. The prisoners had access to books and a chaplain and medical treatment was adequate[24] but there was still no mail from home.

Back in Dublin, raids were continuing. Army patrols occupied all major road junctions. Occasionally, in the early morning, the silence would be broken by the lines of prisoners being marched to the North Wall for deportation.

In Dublin, May was also a month of bereavement and funerals.[25] A total of 450 had been killed and over 2,600 wounded. Some were fortunate to get to hospital. One of these was nineteen-year-old Laurence Mulligan from County Westmeath who was wounded and taken to the Temple Street Children's Hospital, where the bullet was dug out of his thigh by a medical student. Gangrene set in and he died but he was not short of spiritual comfort: 'he had a most lovely death' wrote one of the nuns.[26] Others were less fortunate. Forty children were killed during the Rising.

Some bodies were moved from the street in improvised ambulances and, after a cursory search to establish identity, burial followed quickly.[27] Many were hastily buried close to where they fell, heaped in mass graves without a ceremony or a blessing: many were buried in the gardens at Dublin Castle. As the casualties mounted, the dead were brought in on carts and sewn into sheets and buried each evening after dark.[28] Later some were dug up from gardens or cellars and driven to a mortuary.[29] George Olden, manager of the Shelborne, had allowed bodies to be brought into the hotel. The bodies were held there until the surrender and then moved on to city morgues.[30] When the dust began to settle, families searched the morgues and cemeteries for loved ones and, for some, the search stretched out for weeks. For one family the search never ended. Their boy was last seen on Mount Street, giving a drink of water to a soldier. They learned their son Lionel had died from a gunshot wound but his final resting place was never found.[31]

With bereavement came hardship. For the families of police officers killed in the Rising there was a pension but for others there was nothing and for the dependants of prisoners, there was a financial crisis but no government help.[32] The fires that ravaged Dublin claimed many businesses and homes and hardship came to many. The friendship and generosity of neighbours helped to tide people over and this would soon become a national relief effort.[33] Curiously, one of the major bequests came from Tom Clarke, one of the executed prisoners. Clarke had anticipated much of the hardship and left a sizeable sum in his will 'for the relief of distress.'[34] His widow became an imposing presence on the relief committee: 'She thinks she's Kathleen Ni Houlihan' one of the other committee members complained.[35]

In May, the death toll in Dublin weighed most heavily. The rattle and clatter of horse-drawn hearses bore witness. It was much the same in England: private grief and public mourning. The casualty lists from the

Western Front were swollen by the deaths in Dublin, where the Foresters had taken the brunt of the casualties. In the last days of the Rebellion, one of the Foresters lay dying in the street. He refused the help of the priest kneeling by his side: 'Leave me. I am not of your faith. I die for my King and my country.' And so he died and was buried far from home, comforted only by his belief that his cause was an honourable one. Only a few bodies were ever repatriated, most of the men were buried close to where they fell.

In the small redbrick terraced cottages that filled Newark, Mansfield and the surrounding villages, the dead were mourned. Looking through the front window of these homes one might have seen a tidy little room with a sofa, a piano, a picture of the King and an aspidistra. But in many of these cottages the blinds were now drawn.

There was worse to come. Out in Flanders hundreds of thousands of men readied for the big push. Tens of thousands were Irish, from the north and the south. These men crouched in trenches, plagued by foot rot and lice. When the time came they went over the top. Some were fortunate to be buried in a war grave or have their name inscribed on the monument at Thiepval. The dead from the north of Ireland were remembered in Ulster. The men from the South were mourned by their families but, in the years that followed, the memorials for these men were squeezed out of public life.

The Royal Commission – Laying the Blame

The last week of May was dominated by the apportionment of blame. In the aftermath of the Rebellion the Irish executive had resigned one by one: the Chief Secretary, Sir Augustine Birrell and his deputy, Sir Matthew Nathan, and the Lord Lieutenant, Wimborne.

In the management of the Empire, the Army was occasionally called on to quash rebellion but success had been built on avoiding or managing conflict. The question at Westminster was: What had gone wrong? This was going to set in motion a fight between the politicians and the Army. In late May, the Royal Commission convened to consider 'the causes of the rebellion and into the conduct and degree of responsibility of the civil and military executive in Ireland'.[36]

CHAPTER TWO

The Royal Commission

This unexpected rising which took place without any warning, so far as I could see it was quite unforeseen by anyone.

Major General Friend, GOC in Ireland,
in evidence to the Royal Commission

Warned about a fortnight ago by GOC that there was a chance of Rising so fortunately the Curragh officers were not on leave.

Diary of Colonel Portal,
3rd Reserve Cavalry Brigade

The Commission into the causes of the Rebellion was chaired by Lord Hardinge, formerly Viceroy of India, where he had escaped assassination during a ceremonial elephant ride through Delhi. An insurgent had tossed a bomb up into the Howdah where Hardinge was perched with his wife and the elephant driver. Hardinge's wife was unhurt but the blast had killed the elephant driver and burned Lord Hardinge's ceremonial uniform into his flesh. Hardinge had firm views about insurgents. The other significant member of the Commission was Sir Montague Shearman, a judge of the High Court. Sir Monty was a stooping, emaciated figure who wore a black jacket, pinstripe trousers and sported a walrus moustache. When the Royal Commission was taking evidence at the Shelbourne, Sir Monty became a familiar sight, standing on the steps smoking a cheroot and staring out over the Green. His collection of Impressionist art was widely admired but very few knew about his much larger collection of nudes – 'all back views'. Few things in war-time Dublin were ever quite what they seemed.[1]

Some of the evidence given to the Commission was heard in private: there were sensitive issues to be canvassed about informants and intercepted German diplomatic telegrams but what came out in public was astonishing enough.[2]

The question to which the Royal Commission most wanted an answer was why no action had been taken to head off the Rising before it took place. Part of the reason lay with the system of government which the Commission found 'anomalous in quiet times and, almost unworkable in times of crisis'. At the head of the civil administration was Lord Wimborne, the Lord Lieutenant and Governor General, but his powers were ceremonial. Actual executive power rested with Sir Matthew Nathan, the Under Secretary, who answered to Sir Augustine Birrell, a member of the Cabinet who rarely visited Dublin. The system was imperfect but, as always, it was the personalities who most influenced events.

It emerged in the evidence to the Royal Commission, that the policy of Nathan and Birrell was to pursue recruitment to the Army and do nothing to spark a confrontation with the Irish Volunteers and Connolly's Citizen Army. This policy continued until Easter 1916 despite the clearest evidence that a rebellion was likely.

Wimborne had tried desperately to stir the Under Secretary into action as the events unfolded. On Easter Saturday he received news that three men had been captured after landing by dinghy in Kerry. Soon after he learned that a ship had scuttled outside Queenstown Harbour at Cork and twenty-three German Kriegsmarine had surrendered. Wimborne correctly inferred that this was the elusive arms ship about which he had only been informed that week.

Later that evening Wimborne learned that two men arrested in Tralee in connection with the arms landing were Con Collins and Austin Stack who were both well-known Volunteers. Wimborne urged the Under Secretary that there was now evidence that the Volunteers were assisting Germany and this evidence of 'hostile association' with the enemy triggered the power to arrest and intern suspects under the Defence of the Realm Act (DORA). No action was taken.

Senior army officers informed Wimborne that there were 400 troops in an immediate state of readiness in Dublin. Wimborne was not much reassured. These men were from reserve battalions, drawn from the Royal Irish Regiment, the Royal Irish Rifles and the Royal Dublin Fusiliers; they were all Irish regiments and there was a question in his mind about the loyalty of the troops. In times gone by the Empire had ensured that Irish regiments were leavened with English or Scottish soldiers. That was how the Empire functioned: English troops served in Scotland; Scottish troops garrisoned Ireland and Irish troops went to India. There were many permutations but this practice had fallen away after the outbreak of the Great War. Many Royal Dublin Fusiliers had been members of the Volunteers until Redmond's speech at Woodenbridge; they had joined the British Army to 'do their bit' in the hope of securing Home Rule after the War. They were now on standby to come out against the Volunteers and Wimborne, understandably, wondered: Would they fight?

News came into Dublin Castle thick and fast that Saturday evening: Casement was now tentatively identified as one of the men who had landed at Kerry. MacNeill, Chief of Staff of the Volunteers, issued a countermand cancelling the major manoeuvres planned for the Sunday. The countermand appeared in the papers late that night and the Viceroy guessed this was a coded message: the Rising was off.

The next day, Sunday 23 April, the Under Secretary came to Dublin Castle with the news that 250lbs of gelignite had been stolen from a local quarry and moved to Liberty Hall, headquarters of James Connolly and his Citizen Army. The significance of this was uncertain. Wimborne again urged the Under Secretary to act, without success. That night another meeting took place at Dublin Castle between Wimborne, Under Secretary Nathan, senior army officers and the Commissioner of the Dublin Metropolitan Police (DMP).

Colonel Cowan, the most senior army officer, assured the Lord Lieutenant that a raid on Liberty Hall could be launched but stressed an artillery gun would be needed and the only battery was at Athlone. On the advice of the army officers, the plan to storm Liberty Hall was deferred because there was insufficient time to get the artillery from Athlone. Wimborne told the Commission that the Military advised him that

> `'It takes about four to five hours to bring the`
> `guns up from Athlone, and they were opposed to`
> `doing so hurriedly.'`[3]

The in-lying picquets were stood down late that evening.[4] It remains remarkable that nothing was done to bring the artillery to Dublin and the mobile reserve remained at the Curragh.

Wimborne pressed for the immediate internment of the leaders but this advice was not acted on. As Wimborne later told the Royal Commission:

> `'I offered to sign the warrants and take full`
> `responsibility.'`

The Commissioner of the DMP left to draw up a list of men to be interned and the meeting broke up again without decisive action being taken.

The following morning, Easter Monday, Under Secretary Nathan phoned the Vice Regal Lodge and told Wimborne that one of Casement's companions had admitted that the Rising had been planned to begin the day before and Dublin Castle was to be attacked. At this late juncture, Under Secretary Nathan prepared to telegram London for authorisation to bring in internment without trial. He was in conference at the Castle when shots rang out and, running to the window, he saw the crumpled body of a dying policeman being carried into the upper yard.[5]

Wimborne, at Vice Regal Lodge, learned the news by telephone. He was, wrote his wife, 'very calm and very white'.[6] He was now at his wits end and penned a letter to the Prime Minister, which smacked a little of getting in his account first:

> 'If only we had acted last night with decision
> and arrested the leaders as I wanted, it might
> have been averted. The Post Office is seized
> – Nathan is still besieged in the Castle, but
> I hope he will be out soon. Almost all wires
> cut. Almost everybody away on holiday. Bridges
> blown up....'[7]

The Vice Regal Lodge was almost deserted. Most of the servants and staff had gone up to Belfast to prepare for a 'big dinner' leaving Wimborne, his wife and two aides de campe stranded at the Vice Regal Lodge, guarded by just ten soldiers. But little happened that day, save that some chickens destined for the Viceroy's table were commandeered by the rebels.[8] Later that week an artillery officer decided to fire a shell at the flag hanging over the General Post Office (GPO). Predictably, it missed the target but the eighteen-pound shell made a considerable dent in the lawn of the Vice Regal Lodge: the Viceroy was 'very annoyed'.[9] This spare, slightly built, peppery figure rattled around the Vice Regal Lodge in an old blue ceremonial jacket, heavy with gold braid. After the shock had worn off he strode up and down exclaiming: 'I shall hang MacNeill, I shall let the others off but I shall hang MacNeill.'[10] Close by he kept his plumed hat and sword waiting, perhaps half hoping for a rebel attack in which he might yet distinguish himself. In this, he would be disappointed.

His secretary later wrote that the Viceroy had 'magnified the trouble to add to his glory in coping with it' and he was crushed when he learned the government was sending General Maxwell to suppress the Rebellion. As the days passed Wimborne became a marginal figure. The Army bypassed him, even the Police Commissioner ignored him and his orders became increasingly strident: 'His Excellency commands...'[11] In the evenings, he dressed for dinner with his aide de campe and was seated at a vast dining table looking out at Dublin where the flames reached hundreds of feet into the sky. On the night air came the knocking of heavy machine guns but the Lord Lieutenant dined. While the Army fought it out on the streets, at the Vice Regal Lodge, brandy flowed.[12]

The Army had matters well in hand. The notion that the Army was taken by surprise on Easter Monday has become one of the clichés of the Rebellion. The old chestnut about army officers at Fairy House races is a vivid image but it is a misleading one.

What the Army Knew

Undisputed evidence was given to the Royal Commission that, just two weeks before the Rebellion, the Adjutant General, Macready, wrote to Sir Matthew Nathan at Dublin Castle observing that the Volunteers were openly canvassing rebellion in the press. The Adjutant General pointedly reminded Dublin Castle that, in the event of rebellion, the DORA allowed the military to try civilians by courts martial.[13] The process of suspending jury trial and ordering the trial of insurgents by courts martial could only be triggered by a proclamation by Dublin Castle.[14] The message to Dublin Castle was obvious.

Major General Friend, General Officer Commanding (GOC) Ireland, later protested to the Royal Commission that the Rebellion 'was quite unforeseen by anyone'.[15] That was hardly so, as many other sources make clear.[16] The diary of Colonel Portal, one of his senior officers shows: 'Warned about a fortnight ago by GOC that there was a chance of a rising so fortunately the Curragh officers were not on leave.'[17]

The Admiralty in Queenstown had passed on information over a week before the Rebellion that 'an arms ship was on the way' and that a rising was planned for 'Easter eve'. This information had been passed to Brigadier Stafford commander of the army in Cork. Stafford later wrote: 'On Sunday April 16 I received information that two German submarines either alone or escorting a ship disguised as a tramp steamer left Germany on 12th inst with a view to landing arms on the SW coast of Ireland. It was further stated that a rising was timed for Easter Eve.'[18]

Stafford despatched a battalion of the Leinster regiment to Limerick to guard the west. He passed the information to Major General Friend in Dublin[19] who planned a response. Friend created and reinforced the mobile reserve at the Curragh and ordered in-lying picquets to be kept on standby in Dublin.[20]

But this was the second warning given to the Army. The Director of Military Intelligence in London, Major General MacDonagh, had passed specific intelligence to Lord French, Commander in Chief of the Home Forces. The information, from 'an absolutely reliable source', showed that there would be an arms landing in the west of Ireland and a rising was planned for Easter. Major General Friend agreed, in his evidence to the Commission, that he had received warnings.[21] Even if the Army did not know the precise location of the arms landing, there were only a few viable sites. Fenit was the most obvious because it was isolated; it had a deep water harbour and a light rail link to Tralee, with train connections to Cork and Limerick. It was also a hotbed of Volunteer and trade union activity.

At sixty-four, Major General Friend was a lean, rather humourless man with one of those sparse moustaches favoured by officers at that time.[22] He had a personal engagement in London that Easter weekend, and he went on 'short leave' that Friday evening. After the suppression of the Rebellion, Major General Friend wrote to the War Office making his excuses: 'On Friday 21st April in the evening, I received information of the capture of Roger Casement and the sinking of the vessel with arms. I then left for England on weekend leave...'[23]

His explanation was untrue; the *Aud* was not sunk until the following day and the identity of the man captured on Banna Strand was not known until the Saturday evening.[24] Major General Friend's account began to unravel in front of the Royal Commission but he was never pressed on these issues and it is hard to say why. He was certainly known to the members of the Royal Commission; these men were all knights of the realm and their paths would have crossed over the years. Lord Hardinge had spent his life in the service of the Empire and Major General Friend, whatever he had done in Ireland, wore the Omdurman campaign medal that marked out the men who fought the Madhi.

Neither was Mister Justice Shearman prepared to embarrass Major General Friend in public. Sometimes the ties that bind men together are not obvious; Shearman and Major General Friend were contemporaries. In his youth, Friend had kept goal for the Royal Engineers in the 1878 FA Cup Final against their arch rivals, Wanderers. Mister Justice Shearman had been a devoted Wanderer's player. The questioning about 'short leave' remained polite and restrained:

Mr Justice Shearman: 'Was that not a little risky?'

Major General Friend: 'I may say I heard of the capture of the boat before I started.'

Major General Friend's answer must have caused a few raised eyebrows as the shorthand writer scrawled the notes. The *Aud* had been pursued by a British ship shortly after 6pm on Good Friday, about 130 miles from Queenstown Harbour, flying a Norwegian flag.[25] *HMS Bluebell* signalled the suspect ship to make for Queenstown. The *Aud* was tracked across the ocean on a moonless night as her Captain waited vainly for an opportunity to slip away. On Easter Saturday morning, a signalman on the *Bluebell* saw two German flags run up as the crew took to the lifeboats. The log for *HMS Bluebell* shows the following entry:

```
'9.28 closed on S/S "Aud" who blew the ship
up.'²⁶
```

It follows that Major General Friend could not have known the arms ship had been captured before he left Dublin on late Friday afternoon. Major General Friend may have realised his account was in danger of falling apart because he soon amended his evidence about when he had heard of the sinking of the arms ship: 'I heard it on Saturday, at the War Office.'

It was an extraordinary moment: the General Officer Commanding the Army leaving the country for the weekend, knowing that an arms ship was off the coast and that a rebellion was in the offing. Not just that but telling half-truths and lies to the Royal Commission. Major General Friend also maintained that he had heard of the capture of Sir Roger Casement before setting off for the weekend.[27] This could hardly be so because the identity of the man captured on the beach did not emerge until late the following day.

Whatever Major General Friend's weekend commitment was, it must have been a pressing one because it involved a two-way sea voyage through waters patrolled by U-Boats and a long train journey.[28] It may be that his decision to travel was simply a grave error of judgment or was he, in the crucial days before the Rebellion, kept out of the loop by senior officers?

The day before he took his long weekend the Castle Document appeared in the press. It was, on the face of it, a plan devised by Major General Friend to put Dublin in lock down, suppress the Volunteers and imprison nationalist leaders. The Castle Document caused public consternation and was denounced by the government as 'pure invention'.[29]

The consensus of academic opinion is that, 'in its final form', the Castle Document was a forgery because it elevated a contingency plan if conscription was brought about, into a plan that would be put into effect immediately. The probability is that the document was 'sexed up' by the insurgents after they got hold of it.[30]

It is now clear the Castle Document was based on a real plan smuggled out of Dublin Castle by Eugene Smith, a civil servant. Many years later Smith wrote about how he first saw the Castle Document in the course of his duties. His account carries an unwitting hint of how he may have come across this sensitive military memo:

> `'It was unusual for Major General Friend to send communications from the Castle to London, as he had a private line from his headquarters...'`[31]

Whether the Castle Document was stolen or deliberately leaked, it was intended to tip the Volunteers towards rebellion and it had that effect. The same day MacNeill ordered the Volunteers to mobilise to resist the perceived threat. Undeterred or oblivious, Major General Friend packed to go on leave the next day.

Major General Friend's adjutant was Colonel Cowan, an experienced staff officer who had been in and out of Dublin Castle all Easter weekend as the crisis deepened. As a young officer, Cowan had been wounded at the battle of Tel-el-Kebir.[32] After that, he had held a string of staff appointments finishing with a spell as aide de campe to the King before his final posting as Assistant Adjutant General in Dublin.

Colonel Cowan told the Commission about the contingency plans put in place because of the warnings of rebellion: on Easter Monday the army had 120 officers and 2,365 troops in Dublin. 'In lying picquets' of one hundred men from each of the four regiments in Dublin had been on standby for some days in readiness to turn out immediately.[33] The mobile reserve of 1,600 men from the Curragh started to arrive in Dublin about four hours after news of the fighting came through. Every twenty minutes another train load arrived. Another 600 men from the 25th Reserve Brigade were also sent up from the Curragh: 'After that the situation was pretty much well in hand,' observed Colonel Cowan.

It is certainly true that, by the second day, the suppression of the Rebellion was 'well in hand' although the Army may have underestimated the likely scale of the Rising and were fortunate that Eoin MacNeill issued a countermand. But for this, the railway link to Dublin would have been severely disrupted and the fighting much more extensive and prolonged.

The plans made by the Army in Dublin were remarkable: they were reactive not pre-emptive, unobtrusive not obvious. They depended on the in-lying picquets at Kingsbridge, the Royal Barracks, Richmond Barracks and the mobile reserves at the Curragh. There are questions about these plans; if rebellion was expected in Dublin, why place the entire mobile reserve at the Curragh? Why leave the only artillery battery at Athlone? Why not reinforce Dublin Castle and Beggars Bush Barracks which was barely occupied?

What Lies Beneath

Understanding the dynamics of these events requires a deeper analysis. The Army and the civil administration at Dublin Castle shared one vital aim in the interests of the war effort: to recruit as many Irishmen into the Army as possible. The Great War hung in the balance and the need for manpower had become desperate but there was a sharp and long-standing division of opinion about how recruitment should be handled in Ireland. The policy of the executive at Dublin Castle was based on low-key recruitment and avoiding confrontation with militant nationalists.

This approach was despised by many army officers who favoured the suppression of militant nationalist groups and conscription, which had been introduced in England only a few months earlier. The Army had warned Dublin Castle that recruitment was actively and deliberately being frustrated by the Volunteers.[34] Major Price told the Commission that the anti-recruitment campaign had cost the Army 50,000 men.[35] Major Price was well placed to give an opinion, after twenty-four years in the Royal Irish Constabulary (RIC) he had joined the Army at the outbreak of the

Great War and become Chief of the Intelligence Department at GHQ Irish Command. In this post he had access to reports from County Inspectors from every part of Ireland. Price was put forward by the Army to give evidence to the Commission and it is reasonable to infer that his view was shared by Irish Command GHQ and most other officers.[36]

The figure 50,000 men equates to four Divisions and it is a staggering number which would not have been a winning margin on the Western Front but might have been enough to stave off defeat when a crisis came. The identity of rebel leaders was well known and Major General Friend had repeatedly urged Dublin Castle to raid Liberty Hall and other known armouries months before the Rebellion.[37] It was, he told the Royal Commission, 'policy', not a lack of evidence, which prevented a pre-emptive strike.[38]

This fundamental schism between the Army and Dublin Castle emerged in sharp relief whilst Britain and the Empire were fighting for survival. The Army was facing a manpower crisis as the Somme offensive was being prepared and all this was undermined by Dublin Castle policy. The view of Major General Friend was that the activities of the Volunteers and their associates were treasonable: deliberately and seriously damaging the war effort at a time of the gravest national crisis in living memory.

The Volunteers' activities had been allowed to flourish by degrees.[39] The Royal Commission noted with disapproval that Dublin Castle's policy was to avoid enforcing the law to avoid confrontation: unlawful drilling was not prosecuted and a blind eye was turned to seditious newspapers. Encouraged by this weakness, militant nationalists began importing guns in small numbers and stealing or buying guns from private soldiers.

In the months leading up to the Rebellion, the theft of explosives was taking place on an industrial scale. In the countryside, quarries were targeted by workers who stole small amounts of explosive every week which were used to make homemade grenades.[40] In the spring of 1916, 500 weight of explosives was stolen from coal mines near Glasgow and smuggled to Ireland.

There were a significant number of prosecutions brought in early 1916 which showed what was afoot, but a single example is enough: Alex McCabe, a Volunteer organiser, was arrested with forty-two sticks of gelignite, detonators and coils of fuse wire. Two handguns were found at his address.[41] Preparations for a rising were there to be seen: 500 bayonets were seized by the RIC only weeks before the Rising and a consignment of guns bound from Dublin to Wexford was intercepted just before the Rebellion.[42]

The Volunteers were drilling, target shooting, running training camps on blowing bridges and railway lines, surprising sentries and attacking buildings. Months before the Rebellion, Major Price had seized Volunteer training manuals and brought them to the attention of Major General Friend. These were preparations for rebellion by a body of armed men that numbered about ten thousand. Major Price delivered urgent warnings to Dublin Castle but he was, as he told the Royal Commission, 'like John the Baptist in the Wilderness'.

Every morning at the Curragh and other army barracks, officers took breakfast in the mess and with the papers came news of the fighting in France and the casualty lists recording the deaths of fellow officers and friends. There was also news of seditious speeches by Connolly and other nationalist leaders. Volunteer and Citizen Army parades were increasingly aggressive and militaristic. Newspapers like the *Irish Volunteer*, the *Gael* and the *Spark* opposed recruitment to the British Army and openly spoke about rebellion. At recruitment rallies, army officers paraded Victoria Cross holders but they were booed and 'hooted' by Volunteers.

In Dublin, it was not unusual for Army and Volunteer units to pass each other in the street and the risk of armed confrontation was real. This almost came about on Saint Patrick's Day, when over 1,500 Volunteers paraded through Dublin and brought the city centre to a halt. Major General Friend and his staff officers found the road blocked by armed Volunteers. It was a moment of acute humiliation for the Army: Major General Friend's staff car reversed and found another route to the Castle.[43] The Volunteers had also staged a mock night attack on Dublin Castle involving over one hundred men, armed and in uniform. The event was widely reported in the press.

For many army officers, Dublin Castle's policy was not one of acquiescence but rank appeasement. The Volunteers and the Citizen Army were bent on rebellion and it had become blatantly obvious; it was just a question of when. The activities of the militant nationalists were continuing to damage the war effort. It is reasonable to infer that, from the standpoint of the Army, if there was to be a rebellion then, in the interest of the war effort, the sooner it came to a head the better.

There is an echo here of the Curragh Mutiny two years earlier, during which officers who were faced with a choice about going to Ulster and imposing Home Rule by force, opted for resignation. Many officers took their chance to embarrass the government, to try to stymie Home Rule[44] and even bring the country to the brink of civil war. The bottom line is that army officers in Ireland were capable of intrigue for political ends.

The Curragh Mutineers were mainly officers of 3rd Brigade of Cavalry[45] which was deployed to France in 1914 and suffered heavy casualties in the months that followed.[46] Their numbers were brought up to strength, in part, from 3rd Reserve Brigade, still stationed at the Curragh at Easter 1916.[47] Curiously, the officers who led the suppression of the Rebellion were all Cavalrymen: Brigadier General Lowe, Colonel Portal and Colonel Kennard, who would be the commanding officer in Dublin on Easter Monday.[48]

Senior army officers were only too aware that rebellion was in prospect. Since Dublin Castle formulated policy, pre-emptive action was not possible and the rebels had to be enticed into taking the field and, by doing so, the conspirators would be forced into the open.

The crucial dispositions made by the Army were made behind the scenes and were later widely praised.[49] There were officers at the races on Easter Monday but they were probably on leave from the Front, not from the Curragh or from those on standby at Templemore and Belfast. In Dublin, Colonel Cowan's 'in lying picquets' turned out within minutes of the first shots being fired.

Coincidentally, on Easter Sunday, Casement was being interrogated in London. He begged to be allowed to make an appeal to stop the Rising but Captain 'Blinker' Hall responded in typically forthright style: 'It had to come to a head.'[50]

What the Navy Knew

The part played by the Navy was even more curious. No Naval officer gave evidence to the Royal Commission because the role of the Navy was outside the remit of the Commission. Some days before the Rebellion, Admiral Bayly, at Queenstown harbour, had provided Brigadier Stafford in Cork with the clearest intimation that an arms shipment was en route. The Navy knew the size of the shipment, the date the ship was due and even the port: Fenit, in Kerry. At an early stage in the war, the Navy had acquired German naval codes. All German naval communications were routinely intercepted by 'Room 40' at the Admiralty and this gave the Navy a commanding advantage.[51]

Also, by virtue of numerical supremacy, the Royal Navy had an almost vice-like grip on the movement of all surface ships in the north sea but the *Aud*, captained by Karl Spindler, had, almost miraculously, slipped through the blockade and got to the west coast of Ireland. Spindler piloted the *Aud* to Tralee bay but failed to make contact with the insurgents.

That the Navy knew about the whole affair from the start has never been in dispute. There is even a contemporaneous diary entry of Margot Asquith, wife of the Prime Minister: 'Our Admiralty knew every movement.'[52] Another revealing source is the Captain of the *Aud*, Lieutnant Karl Spindler, who later wrote that the *Aud* had been several times sighted by Royal Navy ships and even boarded by *Setter II* in Tralee Bay where a cursory search was made and the *Aud* was allowed to go on its way. Spindler describes *Setter II* with precision and it is probable that the *Aud* was boarded simply to confirm that she was the arms ship.[53] Consequently, it was not until Spindler turned for home that the pursuit began and a number of warships joined in the chase.

The log of *HMS Bluebell* contains a reference to stopping the *Aud* at 6.15pm on Good Friday:

```
'Stopped to examine steamer S/S "Aud"'
```

The speech marks imply that it was already known that the '*Aud*' was running under a false name.[54]

There is an inference that the Royal Navy had been playing a waiting game. It was not enough to sink or capture the *Aud*, because no prosecutions could be brought against the conspirators unless they were allowed to take delivery of the guns and, by their actions, implicate themselves and their associates.

It would be surprising if the Army and Navy did not agree a joint strategy. This aspect of the affair dovetails with the actions of the Army and hints at a degree of co-ordination.

None of this was aired at the time because these issues were outside the terms of reference of the Royal Commission. Curiously, the dogfight played out between the Army and Dublin Castle before the Royal Commission was conducted in a civilised and rather languid manner. Neither the Army, the Viceroy nor the civil servants were represented by lawyers as was often the case in inquiries at that time.[55] Nor was the Commission assisted by independent counsel and few probing questions were asked. And there were some hard questions that needed to be put relating to what was done about repeated warnings of rebellion and the arms ship due to make landfall 'on Easter eve'.

There were other equally compelling questions about the Easter weekend. Only so much inaction by the Army can be explained by caution or a failure to act on intelligence.[56] Despite the Viceroy pleading for action, nothing was done. Herein may lie the explanation for the reluctance of senior army officers to take any purposeful steps that Easter weekend: Dublin Castle and other key buildings could not be reinforced without alerting the rebels. It would have been feasible to issue a proclamation to loyal citizens; to order a show of troops; bring up the reserve from the Curragh or to reinforce key points. These steps would have deterred all but the most determined insurgents. Nothing was done which might alert the conspirators and cause them to draw back from the brink.[57]

The Royal Commission finished hearing evidence in late May. Even then the view of the Commission was clear. As to the executive, Wimborne would be vindicated but Sir Augustine Birrell and Sir Matthew Nathan would emerge as the scapegoats. Major General Friend and the Army were not criticised.[58]

Ireland was quiet again. The country had been given a reminder of the chaos of revolution and the danger of German invasion but the Army had restored order and, for the moment, seditious papers and pamphlets disappeared. The vocal and strident opposition to recruitment to the Army had also been broken, or so it then seemed.

CHAPTER THREE

Conciliation and Repression, 1916 and 1917

Conciliation was the new policy, which was reflected by the way the Army dealt with the outstanding trials. One of these was the Tullamore Trial: shortly before the Rising the Royal Irish Constabulary (RIC) had tried to gain entry to a concert hall in Tullamore. In the fracas that followed some of the crowd had shot at police officers and badly wounded a sergeant. The case came up on the Thursday before Easter, when Resident Magistrate Callan remanded the thirteen prisoners while the Sergeant recovered from his wounds. The Rebellion then intervened and a few weeks later the prisoners were passed into the custody of the military and were tried by courts martial. They were convicted, significant prison sentences were handed down and the papers went to Maxwell for confirmation. Tim Healy KC then raised a legal point on behalf of the prisoners: that the offences took place before the Rebellion. The Proclamation issued on 26 April under the Defence of the Realm Act revoked the right to trial by jury but Healy suggested that this decree could not have retrospective effect. It was a bad legal point, as Healy probably knew[1] but a few days later Maxwell announced that the convictions would not be confirmed. All the men were released.[2]

Eoin MacNeill, Chief of Staff of the Volunteers, was spared execution. David Kent was convicted by court martial of murdering Head Constable Rowe; General Maxwell commuted the death sentence to a derisory five years' penal servitude.[3] Seán MacEntee (later Tánaiste) and two others were convicted of the murder of Constable Magee and the attempted murder of Lieutenant Dunville but death sentences were commuted. Of this handful of prisoners, only Casement was put to death.

There were still a handful of lesser trials that were being dealt with over the summer.[4] In Cork, five prisoners were brought to trial for sedition but after conviction it was discovered the men had been allowed to give evidence on their own behalf, contrary to the scheme of the Act.[5] The convictions were quashed: there was a new found determination to abide by due process. A handful of court martial officers were brought over to Ireland and appointed to the army commands in all the main cities.

Curbing disaffection was part of Maxwell's task although, for every disaffected person, there were others who were entirely content that the Rising had been vigorously suppressed. Irish troops at the Front showed no sympathy for the rebels. Some German troops put up placards taunting the Irish regiments about the suppression of the Rebellion. The Munster's fired until the placards disintegrated. One of the Royal Dublin Fusiliers wrote home about the rebels: 'They have brought a nice disgrace upon the old Country.'[6] There were many families entirely loyal to the Crown. Even after the Somme, one father wrote 'I am proud to think my three sons have died for their King and country...'[7]

In Dublin, the Army was still managing bad news. An inquest into the death of two men killed at North King Street during the Rising held the Army culpable for murder: the jury criticised the Army for failing to cooperate with the inquest. Dublin Castle refused permission to exhume any more bodies and no more inquests were carried out into the massacre at North King Street.[8] An army inquiry was carried out in private and the troops were exonerated but private judicial inquiries never command respect and the odour of murder hung in the air.

Maxwell strove to get the support of the bishops. He offered to decorate clergy who had shown courage during the rising: Archbishop Walsh declined permission. Maxwell again tried to enlist the support of the Catholic hierarchy to prevent people taking part in demonstrations: no assistance was forthcoming.[9] Finally, Maxwell wrote to Archbishop O' Dwyer asking him to remove two curates who had criticised the Army. O' Dwyer, who was never inclined to half measures, published a stinging refusal in the press: 'Your regime has been one of the worst and blackest chapters in the history of the mismanagement of the country.' O' Dwyer had voiced the feelings of many and it was a moment of some significance.

In mid-June 1916, Maxwell wrote to Lord French with more bad news. Confidential reports on the mail of internees showed the crestfallen tone had been replaced by defiance. In Dublin, requiem masses for the executed prisoners were heavily attended. Photos of the dead prisoners were sold in shops. Worse still, reported Maxwell: 'Recruitment in Ireland has practically ceased.' The influence of the moderate Home Rulers was on the wane and, in the event of an election, they would lose their seats 'to those less amenable to reason'.[10] Conscription was quietly shelved.

Only a few weeks before, Maxwell had been lauded in the press and cheered wherever he went but somehow the spoils of victory were slipping away. The trial of Captain John Bowen-Colthurst for the murder of Sheehy-Skeffington ended in a verdict of 'guilty but insane' and many eyebrows were raised.

Hard on the heels of this trial, was the Royal Commission into the murder of Sheehy-Skeffington.[11] Each day, an appalled public read the press reports about the final moments of Sheehy-Skeffington and his companions. After the firing squad had dispersed, the dead men were taken off for burial on stretchers. But Sheehy-Skeffington showed signs of life and the stretcher party stopped and conferred. A fresh firing party was brought up and delivered another volley into Dublin's most harmless and eccentric man.

Sheehy-Skeffington's grotesque death was not unusual by the standards of the time. In the trial records of the men executed after the Easter Rising lurked another tawdry secret: some of the firing squads had failed to shoot straight and these executions had gone badly awry.[12] Asquith had promised publication of the trial records and the families of some prisoners were pressing hard for disclosure. The potential for more embarrassment was considerable and the Army Council prevaricated and delayed until the end of the year when Lloyd George became Prime Minister. His new government consigned the trial records to the archives, not to be opened for 100 years.

The policy of conciliation was failing and disaffection emerged amongst unexpected people: Francis Ledwidge was one of the great emerging poets of his generation. He had been one of the many Irish Volunteers who joined the Army in 1914 and was later wounded at Gallipoli. Ledwidge and Thomas MacDonagh had been close and, after the news of the executions came through, Ledwidge went on a terrific drinking spree and wandered back to barracks a fortnight later. He was court martialled and reduced to the ranks. From then, until his death in Flanders a year later, he was a leaden-footed soldier.[13] For other soldiers, disaffection came in a slow burn.[14]

In this volatile climate nothing was so absurd that it could not be seized on and turned into a political issue. In the summer, Westminster abolished Dublin Mean Time and Ireland lost twenty-five minutes. The reform was disliked by many for pragmatic reasons but others 'just added stolen time to 800 years of grievances.'[15]

The Release of the Internees

There was a more pressing question for the government: what to do with the internees who were now mainly in Frongoch Camp. The Government set up a committee under Lord Sankey to investigate the prisoners still detained without trial. Each prisoner was asked to fill in a form, setting out his details and naming a guarantor for his good behaviour. Many had played no part in the Rebellion and others were country boys whose thoughts were of home and the harvest and some filled in the form.[16] Others declined to sign because they suspected an oblique motive: Irish police officers visited the camp periodically trying to build a case to prosecute prisoners.

Not all the prisoners took the process seriously. Dwyer, a Citizen Army man, filled out the form and named a Dublin Metropolitan Police (DMP) officer as a guarantor for his good behaviour. He arrested me, Dwyer explained, 'after I threw that policeman in the Liffey.'[17]

All the prisoners were sent to London to be interviewed by Lord Sankey and his committee, who were provided with an intelligence file on each prisoner.[18] Asquith's government favoured conciliation and the Sankey Committee followed that lead.[19] Interviews were held in private and no records of the Committee's deliberations can be traced. Our understanding is framed by what followed: at the end of July 1916, 862 prisoners were recommended for release and were freed a few days later. The rest remained in custody. Curiously, many who were not involved in the Rebellion were recommended for continued detention.

One distinguished historian has argued that the purpose of involving the judiciary was to apply 'a judicial veneer' to executive action, and that seems right. The prisoners were not legally represented, nor did they have sight of the intelligence records relied upon by the Committee. The Committee listened to evidence from Deputy Adjutant General Joseph Byrne and senior RIC officers but the prisoners were not present and had no opportunity to contradict or cross-examine witnesses. It was not 'due process'[20] although, in the context of the time and the fight taking place in France, it was a credible effort.

Back in Frongoch there were more trials and tribulations because the rapprochement policy had collided with the policy of conscripting prisoners who were liable to service in the British Army. Before the Rebellion, about 150 men had travelled from England to Ireland to avoid conscription and seize a chance to fight against the Empire. Many were now in custody at Frongoch and the camp commandant was required to identify prisoners liable to conscription and this led the prisoners to decline to answer their names at roll call. For this offence, the hut leaders were tried by district court martial and sentenced to twenty-eight days hard labour.[21]

A small number of prisoners liable to military service were identified and conscripted but refused to serve.[22] Seán Nunan who had fought at the General Post Office was one of these.[23] He was repeatedly court martialled and imprisoned. This culminated in a sentence of twelve months, which he served before the Army gave up on him.[24]

While these personal confrontations were being played out, the agitation for the release of the remaining internees continued back in Ireland. In the summer and autumn of 1916, there were new Defence of the Realm Regulations (DORR) permitting the Army to prohibit fairs, meetings and processions. The most significant DORR, prohibiting drilling, was implemented on 23 November: the anniversary date for the Manchester Martyrs.[25] New regulations under DORR could be created quickly but the law was struggling to keep abreast of events as people used the Manchester Martyrs as a pretext to remember more recent events.

Some things could be done to assuage discontent in Ireland. General Maxwell was transferred back to England. Redmond, the Irish Home Rule leader, was compelled to take an ever stronger lead and the new Prime Minister, Lloyd George, was equally keen to keep the Irish Home Rulers in the ascendant and the radicals on the margins. There was an international dimension to all this. Lloyd George needed America to enter the war. This was achievable but might be jeopardised if Irish-American opinion became more hostile. Therefore, the government had to be seen to be conciliatory.[26] The rest of the interned prisoners were released just before Christmas 1916. Only months before the prisoners had been abused and pelted with missiles by angry crowds as they were marched to the North Wall and herded into cattle boats. They came back to a tumultuous welcome.

Now, in the third year of the Great War, Germany began to use her U-Boat fleet to sink merchant shipping and starve Britain into submission.

For civilians on the Home Front, rationing of food and fuel were new impositions.

In Ireland, agitation for the release of the convicted prisoners continued. In February 1917, Gavan Duffy, then an unknown campaigning solicitor, organised a legal action to challenge the legality of the trials that took place after the Rising. The action was heard at the High Court in London and, perhaps not surprisingly, failed.[27] But the case marked a new development in the conflict: the insurgents used the machinery of the law where it suited but otherwise denied and undermined the legitimacy of the law.

It was here that the government policy of rapprochement came to an end. Unlawful drilling and seditious speech making had become rife. Tadhg Barry, an influential trade unionist, had made a notably inflammatory speech and he was tried by court martial, convicted and sent to prison.[28] But illegal drilling continued in the south and west and large bodies of uniformed Volunteers up to a 1,000 strong paraded in Cork, Limerick and Tralee and other smaller towns.[29]

More trials by court martial followed, mainly for unlawful drilling.[30] Some prisoners declined to recognise the court and others refused to speak English at their court martial. Edward Lynch from Tralee was one of these. The patience of the President of the court, Major Francis Bowen, wore thin as the prisoner launched into his defence in Irish.

Jasper Wolfe (prosecuting solicitor): 'He might be in pain.'

The prisoner continued in Irish.

Jasper Wolfe: 'Perhaps the court should seek medical attention?'

Major Francis Bowen: 'English must be spoken.' To which he added: 'I don't care if he is a Hottentot or a Sinn Féiner.' Tralee District Council complained about the comparison.[31]

The use of courts martial was supplemented by special criminal courts: turbulent areas were 'proclaimed' by the Lord Lieutenant. In these areas special courts of summary jurisdiction were convened before two resident magistrates who had the power to deal with drilling and public order offences and to impose severe penalties.[32] In all, 261 men were tried by special courts of summary jurisdiction in 1917. Most received terms of imprisonment.[33]

Prosecutions and courts martial proceedings were also brought for sedition: singing a nationalist song at a concert resulted in a number of trials by courts martial in Dublin and prison sentences followed.[34] In the provinces, the resident magistrates also dealt with many similar offences.

In February, Kathleen McLoughlin from Mayo was tried and convicted: her rendition of *Who Dares to Speak of Easter Week* was judged by the resident magistrates to be 'seditious'. She was ordered to find sureties to keep the peace and was of good behaviour with two months in default. It was not an isolated case.[35]

The resident magistrates were still too few in number and in recent times their role had been modest, trying cases of drunkenness, assault, poaching, trespass and other trifling matters of that kind. There were sixty-six resident magistrates scattered around Ireland. Most of these positions were filled by ex-RIC inspectors or older lawyers who had tired of the hurly burly of private practice and were looking for an easier lifestyle: their private incomes were propped up by modest pay – £475 per year.[36] Their court duties were not onerous and the post carried a degree of social respectability.[37] They were sometimes referred to as 'Removable Magistrates' because they could be sacked by Dublin Castle which did not prize independence of thought in the lowest rung of the judiciary. They were, for the most part, decent men with paternal outlooks on their district. Part of their work involved taking depositions in serious cases and sending prisoners for trial to the Quarter Sessions or Assizes. They also wrote reports on social issues and on political unrest affecting their areas. They were the eyes and ears of Dublin Castle. By 1917 they were being catapulted into the front line and tasked to deal with a growing campaign of civil disobedience. The resident magistrates were supported by a much larger body of lay magistrates but many of these were not reliable in cases with a political aspect. The legal system was creaking but not yet in crisis.

There was a much more fundamental problem developing. Some prisoners, mainly young men, were no longer cowed when they were sent to prison and had taken to insulting the magistrates. This could only be dealt with by calling on police officers to restore order and this helped foster a new dynamic: the RIC was already the focus of discontent and a significant proportion of the public began to view the RIC as the enemy.

In the summer, a series of by elections took place. Count Plunkett, father of Joseph, was elected on a nationalist ticket. Joe McGuiness, who had been one of the Four Courts garrison, won a seat at Westminster.

Lloyd George ordered the release of all the convicted prisoners in June 1917. This step dovetailed with his new initiative to convene an Irish Convention in which the future of the nation might be thrashed out. This was a generous gesture on the face of it but, as was so often the case with Lloyd George, it was all smoke and mirrors: he was already moving towards Home Rule and partition. The Lloyd George administration was a Liberal–Tory coalition, in which the influence of the Unionists was strong and the Curragh Mutiny still cast a long shadow.

America had, by now, entered the war to assist Britain but events in Ireland had acquired an unstoppable momentum. Many of the prisoners who were released went home but others went on to East Clare where de Valera was contesting a by election caused by the death of Willie Redmond, the sitting MP. De Valera, who sometimes campaigned in a Volunteer uniform, was famously elected. Liam Cosgrave, another prisoner, was also elected in Kilkenny. The Irish Convention was boycotted by many moderate nationalists and it began to stall.

The acquisition of arms was a new theme in this period. The Volunteers had surrendered their arms in the aftermath of the Rebellion. They now began to re-arm; stealing shotguns from farmers or landowners became common. In Ballinacurra, County Limerick, three men tried to hold up an armed police patrol. It was probably here that the insurgency was re-ignited.[38]

Many of the prisoners released after the general amnesty were soon back before the courts. Thomas Ashe was one. He was tried in September for sedition by a district court martial presided over by Major Swinton Browne, who was himself Irish.[39] The charge arose out of a speech he made at Ballinalee. The RIC witnesses maintained he had threatened to call out the Volunteers. Ashe denied the charge and cross-examined the police witnesses vigorously.

Ashe was asked if he had anything to say. 'I have a lot,' he replied.

Major Swinton Browne: 'I hope you won't give a long dissertation on the rights and wrongs of Ireland. We all have our views.'

The prisoner replied that all he had said on the platform was that if England was invaded and beaten at sea he would call out his men to protect the country. This provoked another exchange between the prisoner and Major Swinton Browne.

Major Swinton Browne: 'Why don't you protect it now?'

Ashe: 'That question did not arise.'

Major Swinton Browne: 'You waited too long.'

Ashe: 'I meant to protect Ireland not England.'

The logic of this argument seems to have baffled Major Swinton Browne. He and Ashe were both Irish but had nothing in common except the air that they breathed.

Amongst the crowd in the gallery sat another wanted man, Michael Collins. Ashe and Collins had become close friends in Frongoch internment camp. On the occasion of Ashe's speech at Ballinalee, he and Collins had shared the platform. Collins wrote about the trial that night: 'The whole business was extremely entertaining... the President of the court was obviously biased against Tom and although the charge is very trivial and the witnesses contradicted each other, it is quite likely that Tom will be sentenced.'[40]

Ashe was sentenced to one years' imprisonment and went on hunger strike with other prisoners. The government strategy for hunger striking depended on the judicious use of force feeding and temporary release under the Cat and Mouse Act.[41] This misfired almost immediately: Ashe died from the effects of forcible feeding. The inquest jury censured the prison governor for failing to provide proper care. Over 25,000 people attended the funeral and it was at this point that the influence of the moderate nationalists, who might have accepted Home Rule under the King, began to wane.

CHAPTER FOUR

The End of the Great War

B y 1918 there were three legal jurisdictions in force. The first regime was the court martial process.

Courts Martial under the Defence of the Realm Act (DORA)

After the Rebellion, the right to jury trial for offences contrary to the Defence of the Realm Regulations (DORR) was suspended. The suspension was never lifted and the list of regulations became longer. DORR regulations were already used to prosecute drilling, sedition and to impose censorship and restrictions on travel. DORR now intruded into every aspect of life: regulations governed early closure of pubs,[1] the keeping of meat, pigs and poultry. There were regulations governing the sale of petrol, bacon, butter, bread, potatoes and most crops.[2]

DORR regulations also authorised the creation of Special Military Areas which allowed districts to be sealed off for searching by the military. The process of searching interrupted fairs, markets and home life. Red tape and paperwork were onerous and, under this regime, army permits were required to organise a procession, leave the area, possess a motorbike or be out after curfew. DORA had become 'an itch that could not be scratched'.[3]

Contraventions of the regulations were tried by court martial although there were overlaps with the criminal law: drilling might be tried by the resident magistrates (RMs) as an unlawful assembly or by the Army as a breach of DORR.

The use of courts martial under the DORA became entrenched and extensive. The least serious trials were carried out by a District Court Martial: in the course of 1918, nearly two hundred prisoners were tried by district courts martial under the DORA.[4] The types of offences tried were sedition, unlawful drilling and possession of firearms.

These tribunals were established by law. There was no doubt about their legality. As to whether they were fair, most barristers believed they were,[5] although they were also robust. One prisoner appearing before a court martial announced he did not recognise the court. 'I don't give a damn whether you do or you don't' replied the President: 'six months'.[6]

The Criminal Justice System

The criminal justice system remained in place and, under this regime, suspects were tried by the magistrates or sent to the Quarter Sessions or the Assizes for trial. But for some years Dublin Castle had despaired of getting convictions in cases with a political aspect.[7] The Silvermines trials would be the latest prosecution to come to grief.[8] A soldier had come back to Ireland on leave from the Front and had brought his rifle with him. While he was out one night, three men raided the house looking for the rifle. The soldier's father was killed in a struggle for the gun. Three local men, all Volunteers, were charged and brought to court. The killing of the old man was widely condemned but the prosecution of these three young men brought out thousands of supporters, most set on disrupting or preventing a trial. There were running battles with the police and bloody baton charges. Major Dease, a curmudgeonly resident magistrate of the Somerville and Ross variety, sent the case to the Assizes. In the early days, Major Dease had been a senior ranking Volunteer and may have reflected on the wisdom of allowing private armies to flourish.

In England, the law decreed that the trial commenced with the swearing of the jury but there was an old adage in Ireland: the trial ended with the swearing of the jury. The prosecution could 'standby jurors' without showing cause and, in days gone by, this had been used as a means of packing juries.[9] But every prisoner possessed twenty challenges without having to 'show cause' and this weapon was also used ruthlessly. In run-of-the-mill criminal trials it was called 'knocking the brains out of the jury'. In cases with a political dimension it had become a means of ensuring that cases were determined by political loyalties.

If an appeal to political loyalty failed, the latent threat of the mob cast a long shadow. The trial and the retrial of the O'Brien brothers resulted in hung juries.[10]

This was the latest of very many cases where juries declined to convict. The justice system was no longer functioning and it was driving the Crown to place armed soldiers in court[11] to sequester juries or move trials to more favourable locations. Other tactics included simply bypassing jury trial in favour of trial by resident magistrates or courts martial under DORA.[12] Ultimately, jury trial would be abandoned in all cases arising out of the insurgency.

The Criminal Law and Procedure Act 1887

There was a third regime in operation by virtue of the Criminal Law and Procedure Act 1887 – known as the Crimes Act – which allowed the Lord Lieutenant to 'proclaim' areas and invoke the use of special juries drawn from a pool of men who had a significant property holding. The logic was that men who had a vested interest in society were more reliable than those who did not. The Crimes Act also allowed the Attorney General to move the trial to a neutral location.

Under the Crimes Act, special courts of summary jurisdiction could be convened. These courts were chaired by two resident magistrates and could impose sentences of up to two years' imprisonment. This special court of summary jurisdiction provides a crude but quite clear barometer of unrest in Ireland.[13] In the course of 1918 these courts heard 1,279 prosecutions for unlawful assembly or riot. A total of 1,140 were convicted and most of these received short terms of imprisonment.[14] Of these, 451 were required to provide sureties for good behaviour or face a significant consecutive sentence. Many prisoners were unable or unwilling to provide sureties and served the extra sentence. The law was briefly in the ascendant. Prisoners who declined to recognise the court got short shrift as the following exchange demonstrates:

Prisoner: 'I do not recognise this court.'

RM: 'But this court recognises you.'

The RMs who chaired these special courts were the visible face of government. They lived in the area where they sat as magistrates but it was no longer an attractive posting. The relationship between RMs and the Royal Irish Constabulary (RIC) was rather too close and it showed. Even in minor cases, the RMs were abused and disrespected in their courts. Lay magistrates were the subject of the same pressures and many simply withdrew from problematic cases.[15]

To the mind of the colonial administrator, the criminal process was a necessary backstop. Malefactors were prosecuted, convicted and sent to prison where they could reflect on their indiscretions. This tactic was now trumped by prisoners who invited prosecution, conviction and even imprisonment. Each stage of the trial process presented opportunities to demonstrate contempt of the court process. Young men had discovered that calculated disrespect of the court could engender a response that was objectively disproportionate and this was fuel to the fire. Prisoners refused to remove hats; they smoked, chatted with each other, turned their backs on the RM[16] or questioned the legality of the court. Some prisoners hinted at the unfairness of the proceedings: a tactic heavily used when the prisoner had no defence.

In Westport, a group of young men turned their backs on RM Milling who called on RIC officers to restore order. The resulting struggle spread into the square outside the court, where a bloody riot took place.[17] The prisoners had intended to stir the pot and they had succeeded. They would serve a short sentence and return home to a hero's welcome. Many police officers recognised that the policy of repression was failing but were unable to influence policy.[18]

The unrest and disturbances permeated every aspect of life. Part of the red tape involved in running the Great War related to the supply of food: the government policy in Ireland was to turn pasture over to tillage to feed mainland Britain.[19] As the Great War progressed, Ireland was farmed with increasing intensity. This was profitable for the big farmers but there were food shortages and many families scraped a living on tiny holdings. The plight of people living in crowded slums, the 'landless' and homeless families, is sometimes forgotten. This is an aspect of Irish life summed up by the plight of one young family evicted by court order from the pigsty in which they had taken refuge.

A campaign began to turn over pasture land to the have nots. This became a new point of conflict, particularly in Kerry, Mayo, Clare and Sligo where Volunteers redistributed land in defiance of the RIC.[20] There were prosecutions and some went to prison.[21] The most famous episode took place in Kerry, where Volunteers and the RIC (backed by a company of soldiers) were involved in a standoff over possession of Lord Listowel's lawns which ran to over thirty acres. The soldiers had been called out to deal with insurrection but the young army officer reckoned this was not rebellion, at least, not as he knew it: it was a civil matter. The officer withdrew his men and the land was ploughed.[22] Lord Listowel got an injunction for trespass but the locks on the iron gates were broken open and the land re-entered. Fourteen local leaders, including the chair of the Urban District Council, received a sentence of one months' imprisonment.[23] Gradually the RIC stopped enforcing the status quo simply because they no longer had the resources.[24] In the west of Ireland, the revival of the rebellion was being driven by poverty, sharpened by a nationalist edge.

In the south and west, the potato crop became the focus of confrontation with the law. Big farmers were netting £6 a ton for potatoes but few shared in the profit. Each month the Food Controller required farmers to make 'a potato return' under the DORR. This too proved an opportunity for civil disobedience.[25] Thomas Golden from Cork was charged with failing to make a return. Golden went before RM O'Hara and declined to remove his hat or to make a defence. He and others were ordered to pay '10/s and costs'. Golden stayed long enough to tell the RM he would not pay.[26] He was one of many. This is how the process of revolution was coming about: the courts and institutions that held society together were being ignored or undermined.

The Crisis on the Western Front

In March, Germany launched a great offensive and threatened to rout the allies. Having sent all possible reserves to France, Lloyd George introduced another Military Service Bill: a last-ditch measure permitting conscription of men aged between seventeen and fifty and up to fifty-five where men had useful skills. Lloyd George announced the new Military Service Bill would also permit conscription in Ireland. It would be implemented by Order in Council.[27] The Prime Minister's voice was briefly drowned out by the uproar from the Irish Home Rulers. Drawing breath, Lloyd George added the sweetener that he hoped would keep the Irish MPs on board: Home Rule would follow 'without delay'.[28]

'You can keep it' bellowed one of the back benchers who, until this moment, had only wanted Home Rule under the King and within the Union. The moderate Irish Home Rule party which had, until then, supported Lloyd George walked out of Westminster and out of government.

Back on the Western Front the fighting had reached a desperate pitch. Among the allied troops there were tens of thousands of Irishmen. Many had joined in the early years of the war, buoyed up by loyalty to the Empire, desire of adventure or out of economic necessity. Many distinguished themselves. In 1918 alone, four Irishmen were awarded the Victoria Cross but no one had yet been conscripted.

Lloyd George had now united in opposition the disparate political factions in Ireland: The Trade Unions, the Catholic Church, the Irish Parliamentary Party and Sinn Féin. As it turned out it was the radical nationalists that benefitted most: the Volunteer ranks were swollen with recruits.[29] Apart from the Unionists in the north, every shade of opinion in Ireland was bitterly opposed to the measure and most were prepared to resist by force. In attempting to conscript Irishmen to the Western Front, Westminster had simply triggered another war.[30]

It was known at Westminster that conscription would lead to fighting in Ireland and Sir Henry Wilson, the Chief of the Imperial General Staff, had expressed his readiness to enforce conscription at the point of a bayonet. His ready ally was his old friend, Lord 'Jonnie' French. On the day the Bill got a third reading in the Lords, Lord French was arriving in Dublin to take over as Lord Lieutenant. He brought with him a new General Officer Commanding.[31] Lloyd George also appointed others who could be counted upon: a new Lord Chancellor, a new Lord Chief Justice and a new Chief Secretary.[32] Lord French was installed as Lord Lieutenant and the government readied to impose conscription by force. Lloyd George impressed on the new Lord Lieutenant the need to ensure that the rebels were seen to fire first.[33] It was this remark, perhaps, which underpinned much of government policy that year.

The shooting, in fact, had already started and more would follow soon. The day after the Act became law, the garrison of a remote RIC barracks in Kerry was tricked into opening the door. One of the officers was hit with a baton and the rest surrendered after a hand-to-hand struggle with masked raiders. A search for arms was broken off when other officers arrived and fired into the barracks. Two of the masked attackers were mortally wounded and the rest made off. This was the first of dozens of attacks on barracks up and down the country. It was not the end of the affair in Kerry, either. Some weeks later, two of the constables appeared at the inquest at the grand old court house in Tralee, where their evidence was heard by a distrustful jury.[34] Afterwards, as the officers walked down the steps, passing the cannon commemorating the Crimea, they were shot and wounded before they could draw their weapons. The attackers threw their shotguns to the ground and made their escape on bicycles.[35] There was no strategic motive for the attack. It was revenge. The conflict in Kerry, like many rural counties, would acquire qualities akin to a bitter local feud. In the police investigation that followed, no witnesses came forward; it was a sign of things to come. The only man arrested had not been involved and was never tried.[36]

Conscription continued to dominate events and the Church weighed into the debate. The Catholic Hierarchy issued 'the Bishops Manifesto' which declared that Irish people 'were entitled to resist conscription by the most effective means at our disposal'.[37] This vague missive was repeated by parish priests with some bloodthirsty variations. The Bishop of Cashel described conscription as 'a blood tax'. One priest told his flock 'that each conscript should be able to kill at least three or four before he was taken'.[38] Many other priests were almost as intemperate. God is on your side is a dangerous message and thousands of young men joined the Volunteers and trained to fight. Thousands of pikes were made in readiness to resist conscription.[39]

This was a country in turmoil where nationalism, fear of conscription, the Spanish flu epidemic, poverty, the apparatus of the DORA and other social grievances abounded in a chaotic and sometimes frenetic atmosphere. Fear of conscription remained the driving issue: 'Death before Conscription' was a badge worn by thousands. In Kildare, a speaker extolled the principle of self-determination of nations: 'if Czecko-Slovakia can have an Irish Republic why can't we have one?' At Wexford, one of the Easter Rising veterans was introduced at the podium as 'a man who fought and died for Ireland'.[40]

On the national scene, the Trade Unions brought about a one-day general strike against conscription. Only the north east of Ireland was unaffected. Here, the Unionist community had unstintingly supplied recruits from the start of the Great War: Ulster's dead numbered many thousands and those in the north watched events in the south with increasing bitterness.

The German Plot

A few weeks later seventy-three anti-conscription leaders were arrested and interned in dawn raids. A proclamation by the Lord Lieutenant asserted that the men had been part of a plot with Germany.[41] The notion that the government fabricated 'the German Plot' to dispose of the opponents of conscription has become a historical cliché without much factual foundation.

A few weeks earlier a man had been picked up on the west coast of Ireland by a fisherman. His feet were wet but not his clothes. His name was O'Brien, he said, but his story about being torpedoed while crossing the Atlantic on *SS Mississippi* began to unravel when he was unable to name the captain of his ship. He was taken to a holding centre in west London where a formidable team of interrogators had assembled.

The interrogation was carried out by Captain Hall, Director of Naval Intelligence. Hall's lifelong facial twitch and bushy white hair gave him the air of an eccentric pensioner but he was a ruthless and innovative intelligence officer. With Hall, was the small, portly Henry Curtis Bennett, King's Counsel, one of the foremost cross-examiners of the age. He had been brought in by Sir Basil Thomson, head of Special Branch, who had a high regard for Bennett's forensic skills. A few years later, Sir Basil himself would be prosecuted for engaging in a sex act with a prostitute in Hyde Park. When he was prosecuted, he brought in Curtis Bennett again but even his skills were not enough to persuade the court to accept his client's explanation – 'I was researching a book'.

In any event, it was not cross-examination which elicited the truth from the prisoner, it was an old-fashioned threat: tell the truth and your life will be spared. The prisoner admitted he was Joseph Dowling, a prisoner of war who had joined Casement's Irish Brigade. He admitted coming to Ireland with a view to making contact with rebels and organising an arms shipment.

The affair carried an echo of other attempts by German intelligence to foment rebellion in India in 1915 and Ireland in 1916. Only a few months' later German diplomats would try to persuade Mexico to invade the southern states of America: the attempt failed. But Germany had scored a spectacular coup by sending Lenin and a trainload of communists to Moscow, which caused the collapse of the Russian government and the Eastern Front.

German intelligence had turned its attention to Ireland again. Some fishermen on the west coast of Ireland had connections with German U-boats, supplying them with fowl, water, vegetables and poteen.[42] In the spring of 1918, German High Command had tried to use this connection to land guns.[43]

The British government knew a good deal more than it could publicly admit. British Naval Intelligence had possession of the German codes and had firm information about Dowling's landing and two U-Boats, loaded with guns beating up and down the west coast looking for a chance to drop off arms.[44] Dowling had slipped through the net with coded messages sewn into his hanky but the arms shipment was prevented.[45]

Dowling was tried for assisting the enemy in time of war. He had no defence but his death sentence was commuted to twenty-five years' penal servitude.[46]

'The German plot' was real enough. At a crucial moment in the Great War, the German High Command was desperate to land guns in Ireland but the insurgents were not ready for this step. It was, even so, hugely convenient for the government to intern the most militant opponents of conscription. The Dowling affair was perceived in Ireland as a pretext to intern opponents of conscription but the government was unable to defend its actions in public for fear of compromising the source of the intelligence.

The roundup of anti-conscription activists encouraged many young men to join the Volunteers in an increasingly febrile atmosphere. One case gives the flavour of events. In the summer of 1918, J.J. Madden, a school teacher from Lismore, and Pax Whelan were charged with wearing Volunteer uniforms. The case was heard by the resident magistrate (RM) William Orr at Dungarven. At a crucial moment in the trial, one of the spectators let out a cheer and the RM ordered the court to be cleared. Pandemonium followed: 'fighting broke out between the RIC and the men in the court house'.[47] The court was cleared but, by chance, a man was passing the courthouse with a cart loaded with stones. The stones were hurled through the courthouse windows, many landing on the bench. The RIC men charged with batons drawn and the crowd hurled more stones. The fighting continued long after the prisoners were driven off to prison. Dungarvan was a quiet town not renowned for national feeling.[48]

In Clare, the conflict had already turned to shooting. Constable Johns was an active RIC detective who had carried out several raids on local Volunteers. Late one night Constable Johns was blasted with a shotgun while he was walking home from the railway station. He was fortunate to survive.[49] In Roscommon, an RIC officer was shot and wounded arresting a man for possession of arms and, in King's County, RIC Sergeant Lacey was wounded while removing a tricolour from a tree. There were half a dozen more shootings of police officers before the year was out but no prosecutions.[50]

As the crisis escalated in 1918, the use of special juries was authorised in some counties[51] and regulations were passed banning the holding of political meetings. Dublin Castle then raised the policy to a new level. Most villages had a band and they were often the focal point of disaffection or demonstrations. Dublin Castle issued an order for the destruction of 'disloyal bands'. This order was enforced by the RIC by baton charges and many dozens of bands were destroyed.[52]

In the summer of 1918, new DORA regulations proclaimed the Irish Volunteers, Cumann na mBan and the Gaelic League to be dangerous organisations. Irish classes organised by the Gaelic league were broken up by police. At a Feis in Cork an RIC Inspector stepped up to the stage and forbade anyone to speak Irish or to sing in Irish. The chair tried to make light of the situation and called on anyone who might sing in French or German. Eventually, a man stepped forward and sang in French to a bemused audience.[53]

Gaelic Athletic Association (GAA) clubs were required to obtain police permits in order to play matches. The GAA declined to cooperate and the sight of police officers and soldiers chasing footballers off pitches became one of the absurdities of the age. The standoff culminated in civil disobedience on a massive scale: 50,000 GAA players took the field on a single Sunday.

These laws proved unenforceable and made the government appear ridiculous and petulant. Dublin Castle soon gave way.

There was a belated attempt by the government to regain the initiative by demonstrating the German plot was all too real. In the House of Commons, the Chief Secretary came breathtakingly close to admitting that Britain had cracked German codes which proved 'the German Plot'. He told the House that the government had two sources of 'reliable' information: 'one of which is outside Ireland and one which is inside'.[54] It was far too little, too late.

The End of the Great War and the General Election

The Great War came to an end before conscription could be enforced in Ireland. The government had the worst of all worlds: it had authorised conscription but failed to implement it and the promise of Home Rule 'without delay' had not been met.

In the election campaign that followed, Sinn Féin ran on a manifesto pledging to boycott Westminster and set up an independent government in Ireland.

When the election took place, the moderate Irish Parliamentary Party won only six seats and their place as the dominant party in Ireland was taken by Sinn Féin which won a landslide in the south. The Unionists dominated in the north east. The demographics underlying these results would eventually dictate the shape of the political settlement that still exists today but a great deal of bloodshed and suffering would ensue before that came about.

CHAPTER FIVE

Versailles

The First Dáil convened at the Mansion House in Dublin and issued a declaration of independence. An intention to seek recognition at the Versailles peace conference was also announced. The gallery was crowded. Amongst the onlookers were two plain-clothes Dublin Metropolitan Police (DMP) men. They took it in turns to slip away to a nearby hotel where Joseph Byrne, Inspector General of the Royal Irish Constabulary (RIC) was monitoring events. Byrne took no action, probably calculating that the Dáil would wither away after some initial publicity. There was certainly publicity; the newspaper reports were carried in the *London Times*, the *New York Times* and Egypt, India and other colonies.

The sense that momentous events were in the offing was palpable. The era of protest was over and armed conflict had become imminent. Four prisoners went missing at HMP Usk. In March, Robert Barton escaped with the aid of a rope ladder and, at Mountjoy, the gaolers were held up with revolvers and nineteen prisoners went over the wall. In the summer, two of the Easter Week veterans, Beaslai, Stack and four others scaled the wall at Strangeways and disappeared. There were many other gaol breaks that year but the first to escape was de Valera, then MP for East Clare. The escape was organised by Harry Boland, MP for Roscommon and Collins, MP for South Cork. De Valera, a prudish man, walked out draped in a lady's fur, arm in arm with Boland, arriving in Dublin some weeks later disguised as a priest.[1]

This operation, which required considerable planning and resources, caused brief embarrassment for the government at Westminster. The absence of the seventy-three separatist MPs at Westminster and the setting up of the Dáil was met with curiosity or indifference but little more. Lloyd George and his new cabinet were preoccupied with getting troops home from the Front.

As the months passed, the negotiations at the Versailles peace conference would come to dominate the agenda. President Wilson's declaration of the right to self-determination echoed around the Empire. There was rebellion in Egypt and, in the Punjab, martial law and the Amritsar Massacre had been followed by executions and mass internment. Ireland, by contrast, was quiet or apparently quiet. At Westminster there was still a belief that unrest in Ireland could be contained and it was, in any event, a policing issue not a military one. This thinking may have been driven in part by the economic reality of post-war Britain: a large army could no longer be sustained. The Army that defeated the Kaiser was being dismantled, despite ongoing military commitments. The Army had a full division posted in the Rhineland, another in Mesopotamia and was also trying to extricate a large, ill-fated expeditionary force from north Russia. India and Egypt soaked up all other available units.

In Ireland, prosecutions for drilling and sedition continued as before but events were moving towards a new stage. A spate of shootings took place in different parts of the country. In Tipperary, two RIC officers were shot dead during a gelignite raid. The inquest, at Tipperary Military Barracks, was attended by the Inspector General of the RIC, the County Inspector, journalists and the families of the dead men although it was an entirely informal affair. The jurors sat around a long table and questioned the witnesses and some expressed their bewilderment. The son of one of the dead officers intervened in the questioning to ask: 'Did the police have a dog's chance?'[2]

It was the first of many such inquests and the question would resonate throughout the conflict. The jury returned verdicts of murder and offered sympathy to the family of the dead men. The funerals of the dead men were heavily attended.

Late one night in Westport, Resident Magistrate (RM) Milling stepped into the lounge of his home to re-set the grandfather clock. Silhouetted by the lamp he was holding, he was shot down through a window. Milling had handed down some tough sentences for unlawful assembly and sedition. 'Foully murdered' was the verdict of the inquest jury[3] but it was probably the last time in the conflict that a jury would add such a rider.[4]

Two more officers were killed at Knocklong during the rescue of a prisoner. A young woman, who gave first aid to a dying officer, was boycotted and abuse was shouted at the officer's widow, Catherine, on the way to church.[5]

The inquest jury found the officers had died of gunshot wounds and added a rider calling for President Wilson's principle of self-determination to be implemented. The rider also called on the government to 'cease arresting respectable persons and causing bitter exasperation' – a reference to the designation of south Tipperary as 'a special military area' under Defence of the Realm Regulations.[6]

More shootings followed soon after. In Thurles, RIC Inspector Hunt was assassinated. He had made arrests in connection with the Knocklong affair. He was gunned down in the Market Square and heckled as he lay dying.[7] At the inquest at the old Thurles courthouse police officers filled the gallery and the Inspector General attended again. The Coroner directed the jury to find a verdict of wilful murder but the foreman simply related that death had been caused 'by bullet wounds inflicted by person or persons unknown'.

'Will you not say it was wilful murder?' asked the inspector presenting the case. The foreman replied the jury was not unanimous on the point. After some argument with the inspector and perhaps cowed by the large audience of police officers, the jury returned 'wilful murder'. But only a handful of local people attended the funeral, where Kate Hunt, the dead inspector's widow, cut an isolated figure.

A close inspection of these shootings shows they were local affairs and, in the case of RM Milling, the settling of a private grudge.[8] They were all unauthorised by the Dáil, which had pinned all hopes on the Versailles negotiations.

Failure at Versailles

The primary strategy of the Dáil was to focus on securing recognition for their delegates at the Versailles peace conference and no shooting was to be countenanced which might attract unfavourable publicity on the international stage.

But, in the country, the pressure on the RIC was stepped up. De Valera issued a decree on behalf of Dáil Éireann ordering that the RIC be denied free association with the community. It was a revival of the Boycott and it was already happening in some parts of the south and west; police officers were squeezed out of community life. One of the strengths of the RIC had been the rule that no officer could serve in his own county. This rule ensured that officers were not partial in the discharge of their duties but it also meant that they could be relied upon to carry out unpalatable duties. This rule now became a weakness because it was so much easier for people to boycott officers who were already outsiders. Shop keepers would not serve them and people would not drink with them, speak to them or even share a church pew. The Boycott gradually extended to the families of police officers. Those who broke the Boycott were themselves boycotted. Occasionally girls who associated with RIC officers had their hair brutally shorn. The Boycott gradually extended to those who gave evidence for the Crown[9] and those who gave information. Within a few months the conflict would reach a new stage: those suspected of informing were removed from home at night and shot dead.

At this time the Dáil arbitration courts were established in the west and here began the first steps to replace the legal system. The first reports of refusal to pay tax to the government also began to emerge at this time.[10] These were the most potent sign of the revolution as the prospect of a settlement at Versailles receded.

President Wilson promoted the idea that the Paris Peace Conference would put an end to war but many were not invited; there was no place for the losers and, for ideological reasons, no seat for the Bolshevik government. A few minority leaders were admitted because it suited British and American policy makers: Chaim Weismann, the Zionist, got a hearing but the Irish Delegates, the Koreans, the Arabs and dozens of nationalist leaders like Seán T. O'Kelly and the young Ho Chi Minh were frozen out. In Egypt, the Governor General ordered that Zaglul Pasha and his delegation be refused permission to attend. Pasha was arrested and confined on Malta.

Wilson's idealism gave way to expediency, compromise and the self-interest of the British and French empires. The Treaty, quite remarkably, sowed the seeds of revolution and war in the Middle East, the Balkans, Africa and the Pacific and, ultimately, would provide the impetus for the next world war. There were many losers at Versailles and some were already trying to unpick the Treaty or overturn it by rebellion or war.

In Ireland, however, failure at Versailles meant the crisis had been reached. Michael Collins had been hard pressed by the G men of the DMP in the summer. A few were warned off and one was left handcuffed to railings.[11] But a few G men persisted with remarkable tenacity. Constable Smyth of G Division was one. He was shot down in the street and carried into his home by his children, before dying of his wounds.

The year before, Michael Collins had been appointed Director of Organisation of the Volunteers. He had set in motion a process of training which was still not complete. Out in the provinces thousands of men were training for war and most still envisaged a conflict between uniformed armies in the field. It would never happen. The question of belligerent status had been determined in 1916. As the conflict deepened, the uniforms would be put away and a grim insurgency would emerge.

For an insurgency to be fought, arms had to be acquired and this was another distinct theme of 1919. Up and down the country guns were being stolen or bought from farmers, landowners or soldiers on leave.[12] But here we see a shift to a much more systematic approach: in some areas funds were raised to buy guns. In Westport, this went a step further; shop keepers were required to pay a levy to buy guns.[13] Volunteers from different parts of the country went up to Dublin to meet Michael Collins who was bringing in arms from abroad. Over lunch at Vaughan's hotel, arrangements were made for payment and delivery. Then there were arms raids: one, in Tipperary, netted three cases of gelignite.[14] In March, seventy-five rifles were seized at Collinstown airfield and very soon the arms raids became more aggressive.

At Araglen, in Cork, an RIC barracks was seized while all but one of the garrison were at mass: six carbines were seized. In Kilbrittain, five soldiers were set upon and disarmed.[15] At Castlegregory a group of masked men set on two RIC men and stole their guns.[16] At Newmarket on Fergus, raiders cleared an RIC barracks of all weapons.[17] In the summer, a large haul of guns was seized at Amiens Street in Dublin. A few weeks later a group of soldiers, on the way to church in Fermoy, was ambushed by men armed mainly with sticks who made off with fifteen rifles.[18] At Lorrha, in County Tipperary, an RIC patrol was ambushed and a Sergeant shot dead before the raiders were driven off. In many county towns gunsmiths were raided. The most serious was in Cork, where over fifty shotguns were stolen in a single break in.[19]

The government at Westminster remained inexplicably pre-occupied with Europe and the Middle East. Sir Henry Wilson, who had played a key role at Versailles, went back to Ireland in the summer but it was recreation not business. He visited his long-time chum, the new Viceroy, Lord French, who told him that rebellion was 'not expected'.[20] Others, like Sir Charles Barrington of Glenstall Abbey, painted a different picture: the country was in 'a very bad state'. Sir Charles' view was well-founded: in less than two years, his own daughter would be caught up and killed in the crossfire during an ambush. Sir Charles, like many of his class, sold up and left Ireland. Sir Henry would also be murdered outside his Chelsea home: an old man tugging on his ceremonial sword as his killers closed in.

The Government Response

The policy makers at Westminster had fixed on Home Rule and this had almost imperceptibly evolved to bring about partition also. Parliament introduced the Better Government of Ireland Bill to bring this policy into effect. Westminster based its strategy on separating the insurgents from those who might support them.

At Versailles and on the diplomat circuit, the primary tactic was to shut the Irish delegation out of the Peace Conference and neutralise the influential Irish-American lobby in Washington. The British and French had invented the art of modern diplomacy and this tactic was successful.

Special Military Areas

On the domestic front, the creation of Special Military Areas was part of this policy. The constant searches and banning of fairs and markets were intended as a community punishment. It was a tactic which had worked in the colonies to separate militants from their supporters.

Making the Rate Payers Foot the Bill

Parliament passed The Criminal Injuries Act which provided compensation for police officers or soldiers killed or injured in the insurgency.[21] The compensation was paid out of the rates for the area where the incident took place.[22] It had some success; by the following year, North Tipperary County Council was saddled with a bill of just over £139,000.[23] At that time it was a staggering sum and many other counties were also burdened with heavy debts.

Censorship

Separating the insurgents from their support involved censorship of the spoken word which was achieved by breaking up demonstrations and sometimes bringing charges for sedition. Censoring of the press had been vigorously applied since the Rebellion. Mainstream newspapers that went too close to the line received an informal warning from the Censor before being closed down. There were also many small papers that were shut down: the *Cork Free Press, Mayo News, Weekly Observer* to name but a few. There were dozens of small newspapers known as 'the Mosquito

Press' – small but with a bite. As soon as a newspaper was shut down, it re-appeared under a new name. To prevent this, the Army began seizing the vital parts of the printing machinery. But these papers operated from warehouses and basements and moved as soon as a raid seemed imminent.[24]

The Suppression of Sinn Féin and the Dáil

Sinn Féin was 'proclaimed' unlawful in September – a consequence of the shooting of RIC men over the summer in Tipperary.

The attention of Dublin Castle focused again on the Dáil. For many months the Dáil had been watched but no action taken on the assumption that it might wither on the vine.[25] This stance changed in the summer when Michael Collins began raising money to fund a consular service, a civil service, a court system and the development of trade and industry, fisheries and forestation.

The significance of these events was understood at Dublin Castle: the Dáil was proclaimed unlawful and the RIC vigorously suppressed the loan,[26] seizing leaflets, tearing down posters and breaking up fundraising meetings, sometimes with baton charges. A number of newspapers that advertised the Dáil loan were summarily shut down by the Army.[27]

The Government Response to the Campaign against the RIC

The government plan was to reinvent the RIC as a heavily armed counterinsurgency force. In Britain, the government advertised for volunteers for 'a rough and dangerous task'. The new recruits, mostly ex-service men were given little training and even lacked a uniform: the recruits would not begin to arrive in Ireland until the following Spring.[28] Recruitment and militarisation were not sufficient to save the RIC. There were weaknesses, lack of weaponry, armoured vehicles and the absence of an intelligence structure to deal with a nationwide insurgency.[29]

Rebuilding the Intelligence Network

The Boycott of the RIC bit deeply and the County Inspectors' Reports show the fall in information given to the police. In Dublin, the most effective officers of the DMP's G Division had been killed by Collins' men. All other

DMP officers lived at home and could not be protected. Riddled with spies, the DMP was in danger of becoming a spent force.

In Whitehall, political infighting in the intelligence service resulted in the appointment of Sir Basil Thomson to head MI5. Sir Basil had made his name with Special Branch catching German spies during the Great War. Before his appointment, he had been a governor of a South Sea Island: a sinecure secured by patronage. He had also secured his Special Branch post through old school connections. The success of the anti-espionage campaign against the Kaiser's spies was due to MI5 but it was Thomson who took the plaudits.[30] He was described bitterly by a senior MI5 officer as 'a dirty dog' but in the shakeup that followed the Great War, Basil Thomson out-manoeuvred his rivals and became head of British intelligence.

Post-war austerity measures meant that Irish intelligence operations had been closed down and resources focused on Egypt, India and north Russia. By the autumn of 1919 the gravity of the situation had become clear to Sir Basil and plans were made to train up officers for covert duty in Ireland.[31]

The Justice System

The final strand of the government campaign rested on the use of the justice system to secure convictions and deter the insurgency. In times gone by, the justice system had always been the back stop but the supply of information was drying up; witnesses were increasingly unwilling to give evidence in criminal trials. Fifteen officers had been shot and killed during 1919 and no prosecutions had been brought.

Getting the case to court was one thing but getting jurors to convict was an insuperable difficulty. The final re-trial in the Silvermines case – the murder of an old man during a botched arms raid – ended in acquittal.[32] The failure of juries to convict was becoming an important dynamic which would contribute to the collapse of the justice system. The immediate effect was an increasing reliance on the RMs sitting in special courts and courts martial.

In the course of 1919, 528 prisoners were tried by special courts of summary jurisdiction for unlawful assembly.[33] The numbers do not quite do justice to the scale of events. The policy of the RIC was to arrest only Volunteer officers. The RIC avoided public confrontations and tried to arrest suspects at home or at work.[34] Most of the 452 convicted received short sentences of imprisonment.[35] Many prisoners declined to recognise the authority of the court and the prisons filled with men and women bent on disruption and protest.

Another significant trend relates to the prosecution of those who raised money for the Dáil loan but Collins could not be found and his grassroots fundraisers were hard to identify. Ultimately only twenty-seven people were prosecuted for soliciting money for the Dáil loan.[36] They were tried before special courts of summary jurisdiction. All were convicted and most received short terms of imprisonment including three members of the Dáil.[37]

The justice system was supplemented by courts martial. In all, 168 prisoners were tried by courts martial under the Defence of the Realm Act.[38] Most of the prisoners were tried for unlawful drilling and a smaller number for sedition.[39]

The biggest coup in the anti-insurgency campaign came in the summer at Glandore where a Volunteer training camp was discovered and surrounded. Dozens of men had surrendered but only a handful of prisoners were tried and these were sentenced to a derisory six months' imprisonment. The surrender at Glandore was effected by a single RIC District Inspector followed by an armoured car. He had walked up to the house and demanded the occupants turn themselves in, which they did.[40] The Glandore raid summed up the weakness and inertia in government: the insurgency was still viewed as a policing issue in which the Army played a subordinate role when called upon by the civil authorities. This policy was about to collide with the squeeze on the Army imposed by the post-war austerity cuts. The Army announced it could no longer provide support for the RIC in outlying areas and began withdrawing troops, leaving the RIC exposed.[41]

Dublin Castle's response to insurrection was muted. Sir James MacPherson, the Chief Secretary, was a career politician who had been appointed some months before and would soon go on to another post. He had no experience of quelling insurrection and no experience of Ireland.[42] His civil service at Dublin Castle had thirty-six departments, many of which 'were hardly on speaking terms with each other'.[43] In this chaotic environment, policy was dictated by factions and personalities. A whispering campaign began, directed against the few Catholic Irish to attain high office in the administration. Slowly these men were forced out of office or marginalised.[44] The campaign found the Viceroy ready to listen and the whisperers claimed their first scalp: Joseph Byrne, the Inspector General of the RIC.[45] Byrne had resisted the militarisation of the RIC and argued that the Sinn Féin movement had won the lion's share of the vote and the government should negotiate with them and come to a settlement. This process, he argued, would divorce them from the militants.[46]

No public announcement was made but the former Commissioner of Police for Belfast, T.J. Smith, was brought in as 'acting deputy'.[47] In Belfast, Smith was remembered as 'an Orange Lodge' man and for turning a blind eye to the Carsonite gun running in 1914. Smith signed off the order which allowed the recruitment of the Black and Tans. Smith remained 'acting deputy' until a suitable army officer was found to oversee the next step: the militarisation of the RIC.

The next phase of the conflict was about to begin. In late December, the Viceroy, Lord French, was ambushed on his way to the Vice Regal Lodge. The convoy was intercepted at Ashtown where a cart was pushed out into the road. Hand grenades were thrown and the attackers fired on the second car in which Lord French usually travelled. Quite by chance, Lord French was in the first car which crashed through the barricade and on to the Vice Regal Lodge as the fighting continued in the roadway behind. There were casualties on both sides. There was an echo here of the Phoenix Park murders forty years earlier, when the Chief Secretary and Under Secretary were stabbed to death within yards of the Vice Regal Lodge. Dublin Castle was shaken into action and, the same day, a request was sent to Westminster for the Army to be urgently reinforced.

1. The *Aud* - the Arms ship. (Courtesy of Sherwood Foresters Regimental Museum)

2. Leutnant Karl Spindler navigated the *Aud* to the west coast of Ireland but failed to make contact with the rebels. The *Aud* had been shadowed by the Royal Navy and was intercepted once it turned for Germany. (Courtesy of National Maritime Museum of Ireland)

3. HMS *Bluebell* log. The ship's log shows pursuit of the Arms ship after she failed to make contact with the rebels. Note the speech marks on 'Aud', which imply that the true identity of the ship was known to the Navy. (Reproduced courtesy of TNA National Archive)

4. Captain Weisbach, Captain of U-19 which brought Casement to Ireland. (Courtesy of National Maritime Museum of Ireland)

5. U-19 with Casement, far right on conning tower. An early selfie before going off to fight the Empire. (Courtesy of Mercier Press Archives)

6. Major General Friend, General Officer Commanding in Ireland in 1916. General Friend was warned that an Arms ship was on the way and that a rising was planned for 'Easter eve'. He went on leave to England on Good Friday. (© National Portrait Gallery)

7. Baron Wimborne, Viceroy. In the days before the Rebellion Wimborne made many futile attempts to get the Army to strike a pre-emptive blow to prevent rebellion taking place. (Courtesy of Sherwood Foresters Regimental Museum)

8. Nuns feeding boys. In inner-city Dublin food shortages were acute during and after the Rebellion. (Courtesy of Kilmainham Gaol Museum)

9. Eoin MacNeill, Chief of Staff of the Volunteers, who issued the countermand on Easter Sunday. (Courtesy of Kilmainham Gaol Museum)

10. Francis Sheehy-Skeffington, feminist, pacifist and social campaigner. He was shot to death with two journalists at Portobello Barracks. (Courtesy of Kilmainham Gaol Museum)

11. Margaret Skinnider of the Irish Citizen Army. Skinnider was wounded leading an attack at St Stephen's Green. She was later denied a government pension for soldiers because she was not a man and therefore could not be a soldier. (Reproduced courtesy of the Dublin City Library and Archive)

12. North Earl Street after the suppression of the Rebellion. (Courtesy of the Dublin City Library and Archive)

13. Prisoners being taken to barracks 1916. (Courtesy of the National Library of Ireland)

14. Men being marched to docks for deportation. (Courtesy of Pádraig Óg Ó Ruairc)

15. General Maxwell was sent to Ireland to quell the Rebellion and carry out courts martial of insurgents under the Defence of the Realm Act. (Courtesy of Kilmainham Gaol Museum)

16. Judge William Wylie, who as a much younger man prosecuted most of the leaders of the Rebellion and did so with conspicuous fairness.

CHAPTER SIX

The Collapse of the Justice System, January – July 1920

Every lunch time Colonel Edgeworth-Johnstone walked the yard at Dublin Castle, a big, stooping figure with heavy shoulders.[1] As a young man he had been a boxer: heavyweight champion of all England. In his later years he kept in shape by walking from his home in the suburbs to the Castle, where he held the post of Commissioner of the Dublin Metropolitan Police (DMP). By 1920 it was no longer safe to walk to the Castle. In just a few years, the political landscape of his country had become unrecognisable. He moved into Dublin Castle with his wife. Against the gracious lines of the Georgian state apartments, he paced the cobbles of the Upper Castle Yard each afternoon.

The DMP and the Royal Irish Constabulary (RIC) headquarters were in the Castle. There was a small intelligence outfit and cells for recently captured prisoners undergoing interrogation. The intelligence room overlooking the Lower Castle Yard became known as 'the knocking shop'. Also based at Dublin Castle was the government Law Advisor, William Wylie, and the Under Secretary and his civil service team. Wylie hunted twice a week with the Meath Hunt. The senior civil servants often hacked round Phoenix Park before starting work at the Castle. Here they were supported by a team of typists, mainly officers' wives. A propaganda office run by Basil Clarke, a former war correspondent, was soon added. Army HQ was close by at the Royal Hospital and the Vice Regal Lodge was also just a short drive. Ireland was run from the Castle but it increasingly resembled a beleaguered outpost. The postal and telephone systems were riddled with spies so communications to London were sent by coded telegram or by destroyer. Light planes were used to carry despatches to Cork, Kerry and Belfast.

Some civil servants, officers and wives lived at the Castle by choice but dozens of others 'lived in' because of the security risks. It was not a bad life; there were three tennis courts, the DMP brass band often played in

the afternoon and there were dances and drinks parties. The children of
the residents lived

> `'an arcadian existence, without lessons, without`
> `governesses'.`

It was a crowded and tight little community living behind high
walls and heavily guarded gates. Later that year a full company of
Auxiliaries would be billeted at the Castle: F Company swiftly gained a
reputation for epic drinking sprees. Inside the gates, behind the walls,
the residents of Dublin Castle were safe but outside the streets were
dangerous. The new Deputy Commissioner of the DMP was William
Redmond, a northern officer with a special brief to capture Michael
Collins and revive G Division, the unit responsible for combating
politically inspired crime. Redmond was unknown in Dublin. He was
an able police officer but he had no training in intelligence work. While
cajoling his men to greater efforts, he alluded obliquely to an intelligence
officer who was making progress in tracking down Michael Collins. G
Division was rotten with spies and Collins got the news the same day.
Before the month was out, Redmond and his intelligence officer had been
shot dead in the street.[2]

The Death of Resident Magistrate (RM) Alan Bell

Resident Magistrate Bell was also working at Dublin Castle. He had been
seconded to Dublin Castle to carry out an inquiry under the Crimes
Act to gather evidence about the attempt to kill Lord French just before
Christmas. Witnesses proved reluctant and elusive and his inquiry stalled.
As a consequence, he moved on an easier target. Dublin Castle's policy
of prosecuting subscribers and supporters of the Dáil loan had failed. In
total, £372,000 had been raised and deposited with the banks. Bell was
tasked to trace and seize the money.[3] Bell, sitting in closed session at the
magistrate's court on the Quays, took evidence from bank managers and
issued subpoenas requiring production of banking records.[4] The Dáil had
been proclaimed 'unlawful' and its funds could be forfeited. Bell was weeks
away from seizing the money and crippling the Dáil.

One morning Bell was on a tram on his way to work when a group of
men appeared at his shoulder: 'Come on Mr Bell, your time is up', said

one. Alan Bell stared straight ahead 'stupefied' and silent. 'Come on', said the man, as if he were suggesting a walk on a cold day. Bell, a frail, white-haired man in a grey suit, clung silently to the passenger rail. His fingers were prized away from the rail and he was pulled off the tram and thrown to the pavement. As tram passengers watched, he was shot in the back of the head and in the groin:[5] a few women screamed and one fainted. The attackers jogged off into the distance. In recent years a good deal has been written about Alan Bell: that he was a spy; that he was heading up an intelligence network or directing a shoot to kill policy.[6] Whatever else has come to light since, Bell was an obscure RM exercising a judicial function and he was killed for that reason.

After Bell's death, the banking inquiry into the Dáil loan was not pursued. Most of the money was never seized and the influence and authority of the Dáil flourished.[7] Dublin Castle fell back on prosecuting those who could be proved to have subscribed to the loan or helped organise it.[8]

The brutality of Alan Bell's death was matched by the killing of Tomás Mac Curtain, Lord Mayor of Cork, a few nights earlier. Late one evening a group of men sealed off the street, forced their way into Mac Curtain's home and shot him dead. Who killed Mac Curtain raised profound questions.

The Mac Curtain Inquest

The inquest took place in Cork, in the old City Hall on the Quays[9] just three days after the killing. Court sat each evening for the convenience of the jurors – all tradesmen. Each night over 1,500 men and women packed into the badly lit hall. Coroner James McCabe sat on the stage with counsel and the jury and witnesses were brought up to answer questions.[10]

The family of the dead man was represented by Patrick Lynch KC who had once been a Crown prosecutor – a fact that still dogged his footsteps as he tried to carve a new reputation. Lynch's brief was to rebut the assertion being put about by Dublin Castle that Mac Curtain had been 'murdered by his own crowd' because he was against the killing of police officers.[11] As the inquest opened, Jasper Wolfe, an acerbic Crown solicitor introduced himself to the court:[12]

'I act for the authorities.'

A juror: 'What authorities?'

Wolfe: 'The authorities.'

Lynch: 'What authorities is Mr Wolfe claiming to be acting for...?'

Wolfe: 'I appear for the same authority that for so long, Mr Lynch, was a valued and trusted...'

The opening exchanges between the lawyers set the tone of the inquest.

Jasper Wolfe could not do the case alone but all leading counsel on the Munster Circuit had declined to be a part of it, despite being offered 'a blank cheque'. Eventually William Wylie, the government law advisor, took the case himself.[13] Wylie's task was a difficult one; he was known to have prosecuted the leaders of the 1916 Rebellion. His lean figure and distinctive hawk nose made him immediately recognisable and vulnerable. Outside court hours women stopped him in the street to spit in his face.[14] At the inquest, as the evidence emerged, men pushed up to the stage. Occasionally, when Wylie made a point for the Crown, men 'hawked and spat' on the floorboards.

Wylie promised the court all possible assistance in gathering evidence to identify the killers. Simultaneously and with no regard for the subjudice rule, Dublin Castle continued to brief the press on their theory that Mac Curtain had been 'murdered by his own crowd'. This was later trumped by the jury who sent a note to the coroner inviting the Viceroy and the Under Secretary to give evidence about what they knew.[15] The invitation was not taken up and Dublin Castle's theory hung in the air.

The evidence called, strongly indicated that the killing had been carried out by a large number of police officers blocking off the street and allowing the killers to push their way into Mac Curtain's home. Wylie recalled one evening, when the anger in the crowd began to boil over:

```
'I remember saying to Jasper Wolfe that we
would be lucky if we got out alive. Jasper
agreed and asked me if I had a gun. I hadn't
and told him so and he said he had a revolver
and 2 mills bombs in his pockets and he would
have company across the Styx.'
```

The cacophony of noise quietened suddenly when the slight figure of Archbishop Cohalan appeared unexpectedly on stage. The crowd rose and stood in silence. Bishop Cohalan asked if he could see Wylie and Wolfe home:

'He took my arm, Jasper Wolfe took his other
arm and we passed safely through a sullen,
silent mob... Jasper is a Methodist. I am a
Presbyterian but we both clung firmly that
night to the Roman Catholic Church.'

The inquest jury found murder proved against, amongst others, Lloyd George, Dublin Castle and named police officers.[16]

The evidential basis for the verdict against Lloyd George rested on an interview he had given earlier that year, in which he suggested that the murder of police officers might be met by 'counter murder clubs springing up'.[17] Every government engaged in suppressing an insurgency always faces this same dilemma: to uphold the rule of law or to give a nod and a wink to illegality. Lloyd George chose the latter course.[18]

Reorganisation

In the country the insurgents attacked police barracks and ambushed small patrols of soldiers and policemen but Dublin Castle had been fighting back since the New Year. There were a thousand raids in January and four times that number in February and this remained the pattern of events.[19]

In the spring, Westminster made a renewed effort to reorganise and revive the administration by bringing in a new GOC. General Sir Neville Macready was a subtle army officer who had been Commissioner of the Metropolitan Police and also had experience of deploying troops against striking miners in Wales.[20]

A new Chief Secretary was brought in: Hamar Greenwood. Described by a colleague as a man who could cope with 'one idea at a time',[21] he was a strong Commons performer, although events would prove him to be a man who believed in the rule of law only when it was convenient to do so.[22]

At this juncture, the two most powerful dynamics in the conflict began to bite. The first was the inability of the justice system to deliver convictions and the second was the militarisation of the RIC under new leadership.

By the end of April, there were 241 prisoners interned without trial in Mountjoy, Belfast and Cork and many more in England. They were interned because the justice system failed to deliver convictions and was no longer capable of dealing with the insurgency. A hunger strike began at Wormwood Scrubs and spread to other prisons. The public mood was inflamed by lurid newspapers reports of imminent deaths. In Dublin, Mountjoy Gaol was surrounded by crowds held back by infantry supported by machine gunners.

William Wylie, the government law advisor, suggested to the Viceroy, Lord French, that the internees should be released. He reasoned that there was then no lawful power to hold them and it might take the steam out of a volatile situation. Lord French agreed to act. Over the next few weeks, 279 prisoners were released.[23] By an extraordinary act, it was not just the internees who were released. At Dublin Castle, William Wylie wrote:

> 'I almost fainted when I heard... The Viceroy let all the prisoners out. Jailbirds, political prisoners, petty thieves...'[24]

Most of the hunger strikers went home or went on the run and picked up the threads of rebellion. For RIC officers, facing social isolation, harassment and ambush in rural areas, it was a sickening moment and there was worse to come.

At this time was tried the last murder case heard by a jury during the insurgency. This case demonstrated all the difficulties in getting convictions: James Madden was tried for the murder of Sergeant Brady during an ambush in Tipperary. The main prosecution witness had made a statement which neatly corroborated the evidence of the RIC officers who survived the ambush. The case was prosecuted by William Wylie who remembered:

> 'It looked like a cast iron case to me. When I was stating the case to the jury one half of my brain registered a conversation between two police officers behind me about a second statement. When I sat down I asked the county inspector whether the witness had made a second statement. He said he had. I asked for it and read it hurriedly. It was completely different from the other one and it was made first.... I handed it over to the defending counsel.'[25]

The witness was utterly discredited in cross-examination and the prisoner was acquitted. The case was widely reported in the press and questions were asked in the House of Commons. But the case was more than a seven day wonder because the police officers involved believed a guilty man had walked free and their view was shared by very many officers who thought (wrongly in fact) that justice had miscarried.[26] Officers who found their colleagues dead by the roadside knew only too well that arrests were unlikely to result in prosecutions and certainly not in convictions. The burning anger and frustration had begun to spill over in spontaneous reprisals. These officers would soon be given a lead by the new chief of the RIC.

The Militarisation of the RIC under General Tudor

T.J. Smith, the acting Deputy Inspector General, was only nominally in charge.[27] Power had passed to Major General Tudor, the new 'Police Advisor'. It was his priority to re-equip and militarise the RIC. Tudor had been a professional soldier and an artillery commander in the Great War.[28] He was now de facto chief of the RIC. He had no experience of policing and his strategy was that of a military officer.

The decision by the Army to withdraw support for outlying RIC barracks at the end of the previous year meant that many small barracks had been abandoned. Once abandoned the barracks were burned to the ground. By the spring of 1920, 277 RIC police barracks and police huts had been destroyed by fire.[29] The RIC retreated to larger barracks in less remote areas but a state of siege existed in many areas. In the first six months of 1920 dozens of barracks were attacked and at least fourteen captured or destroyed.[30] Ostracised by their neighbours, officers were stalked and shot down while they were out walking, fishing or visiting family. Resignations were running at 200 a week and about one fifth of the RIC were in their final year of service and were just hanging on for their pensions.[31]

The RIC was propped up by the arrival of the Black and Tans but the security situation continued to deteriorate. By the summer, two soldiers and twenty-four RIC men had been killed and many wounded.[32]

Lewis guns and hand grenades were issued to RIC barracks. Tudor introduced Crossley tenders covered with chicken wire to guard against grenade attacks. And soon armoured transports were also made available allowing the RIC to carry out aggressive patrols in country areas.

Under Tudor's leadership RIC barracks were reinforced and loop-holed with firing positions. Steel shutters were built in and security lights installed. Roofs were lined with soil to dampen attack by fire and walls were fortified by sand bags and barbed wire. Barracks were supplied with Verey lights to signal for help when under attack and later, when the equipment became available, with wireless.

Tudor appointed a number of veteran infantry officers as Divisional Commissioners.[33] Their brief was to instruct and lead the RIC in a new aggressive counter-insurgency campaign. Those who did not measure up were demoted or sacked.[34] The Black and Tans were now arriving in the country and they would soon be joined by the Auxiliaries, a force of ex-army officers under an independent command.[35]

Tudor himself toured Ireland in an armoured Rolls Royce, to stiffen resolve. Under the new dispensation, suspects were to be shot on sight. Officers were promised that the law would support officers who took this line.[36] Tudor found a ready audience in some officers who had become disillusioned. As the conflict wore on reprisals became increasingly common: beating and whipping young men, mock executions, shooting suspects, ransacking homes and burning creameries. It was a chaotic and sometimes random response in which much depended on the readiness of junior officers to control their men.

The campaign of reprisal was not to the taste of many RIC men. There was a steady trickle of resignations, two barracks mutinied[37] and other RIC men ensured their safety by quietly giving their support to the insurgents or adopting a passive role.

There were wider and more complex challenges facing the administration. In the spring, dozens of tax offices were burnt out and the government's ability to raise revenue was severely compromised. Earlier that year, Sinn Féin had won a substantial share of the vote in local urban elections. The rural elections followed in June and, in these, Sinn Féin won decisively. Local government bodies began to shift their allegiance to the Dáil. These bodies began to find ways of undermining the status quo by encouraging people not to pay taxes or to use courts established under British rule which were already under threat.

The Collapse of the Justice System

There were huge difficulties in getting juries to convict in cases with a political dimension. Every ploy had been tried: moving trials to more favourable venues, empanelling special juries and a vigorous use of jury vetting.

Witnesses were often too fearful to come forward and those who did could not be protected by the police in rural areas. People who were inclined to give evidence were intimidated and sometimes boycotted and driven out of their homes.[38] Trials foundered because many jurors did not trust the justice system or decided the case on tribal loyalties.

The courts were also under threat. By the spring, forty-seven courts had been burned to the ground.[39] Court houses were burned down in towns as far apart as Donegal town and Limerick. At Dromcollogher, four young men poured petrol around the courthouse and lit the flames. The draught caused the doors to slam shut and all were burned to death. Not all resident magistrates were prepared to give up easily. The Borrisokane court house was destroyed by fire and the next day Major Dease, a hefty, old RM, convened court in the blackened ruins. Major Dease continued to sit in session, his white hair plastered to his face by falling rain. The court staff exchanged glances occasionally but no one was brave enough to say anything to the old Major.[40]

Setting fire to court houses was not the only weapon. Many councils that had transferred allegiance to Dáil Éireann found other ways to shut down the courts. Roscommon County Council served notice on landlords of court buildings that no rent would be paid because the courthouses were not required. Mullingar County Council ordered that all courthouses be closed and all court staff evicted. The Council asked that the Irish Volunteers see to it that 'no judges are allowed to enter these buildings for the purpose of holding courts which are not recognised by Dáil Éireann'.[41]

New Bridge Town Commissioners ordered that the courthouse, which had been used for over forty years, be shut. The following morning Major Thackeray, RM, found the front door locked. All cases had to be adjourned.

A more formidable problem arose in respect of jury trial. When the Summer Assizes came, the High Court judges went out to the provinces, resplendent in long red robes and ermine. By ancient tradition, where there were no criminal cases to try, the High Sheriff presented the Assize Judge with white kid gloves. This ceremony, now an ironic charade, was played out in many courts in the south and west of Ireland. The country heaved in turmoil but there were hardly any court staff, jurors and too few witnesses.[42] The crisis came suddenly in July. At Waterford City Assizes only a handful of jurors attended. Judge Gibson described it as 'an unparalleled state of affairs'.[43] He adjourned briefly to consult with the Lord Chief Justice and, a few minutes later, re-emerged to issue a fine of £100 to each absent juror.

It was much the same at other assize courts: over 1,000 jurors were fined for non-attendance[44] but there was no mechanism to enforce the fines: most of the process servers and bailiffs had resigned. The justice system was simply disintegrating.

One lay magistrate was shot and killed. His horse and trap rattled home with his body slumped over the leather seats: a note pinned to his body read 'spies beware'. A few lay magistrates were kidnapped to secure their compliance and hundreds more resigned,[45] some out of choice and many through fear.

The men most at risk were the sixty-six RMs who dealt with a heavy caseload arising out of the Rebellion. The government awarded them a pay rise and 'a war bonus' but it was dangerous work.[46] Many RMs began to carry a handgun and four were killed during the conflict.

In Kerry, RM Wynne shot and killed one of an ambush party.[47] RM Milling had been shot dead through the window of his home at Westport.[48] George McElroy, an elderly RM, moved into the Old Barracks in west Clare. In Limerick, RM Williamson twice escaped assassination and soon also moved into the RIC barracks.[49]

In Clare, Volunteers hatched a plan to steal the car of RM Lendrum; he was followed to a level crossing where he pulled up. He was challenged and when he pulled out an automatic, he was fatally wounded and carried away in his car.[50]

RM Charles Crane hung on for months barely in control of his court. It came to a head one afternoon when he found himself surrounded by 'a savage booing mob' outside his court. Crane quit his post and went back to England.[51] RM Scott-Moore was briefly kidnapped and, in west Cork, RM Brady was also kidnapped and held for some days while on the way to court in Bandon.

The Response by Westminster

The immediate response by Parliament was the Firearms Act. The 'Arms Act', as it was known, imposed a maximum penalty of two years for anyone unlawfully in possession of a gun.[52] The country was awash with firearms, mainly handguns. The 'Arms Act' was hardly a deterrent to rebellion. Although in the country many young Volunteers still drilled for fun as much as anything else, now the uniforms were put away and very many of these young men would take no part in the ambush war.

This was the unfolding situation in Ireland in the summer of 1920. The government faced a stark choice; get out or rule. Choosing to rule required further hard choices: the imposition of martial law, where all power was handed to the Army or some lesser compromise. At a cabinet meeting in the summer, the failure of the criminal justice system was at the top of the agenda. The position was exacerbated by the fact that the Defence of the Realm Act could be used to prosecute possession of arms, drilling and sedition but not to try murder cases. The Army and the police had suffered significant casualties but there had been no successful prosecutions for murder.

The pervasive nature of the threat in isolated communities made the protection of the criminal justice system a daunting task. At this critical moment the government recognised the justice system did not deliver convictions and made no effort to save it. More extreme solutions were considered.

Churchill urged the Cabinet to learn from the Bolshevik government:

> `'After a person is caught he should pay the penalty within a week. Look at the tribunals the Russian government have devised....'`[53]

It emerged in discussions that the Irish Judiciary had refused to take on non-jury trials to meet the emergency but Churchill intervened again:

> `'Get three generals if you cannot get three judges.'`

Churchill carried the day. In the longer term, government strategy was to pass the Government of Ireland Bill, bringing about the partition of Ireland and devolved rule in Dublin and Belfast. In the short term, the Restoration of Order in Ireland Act (ROIA) was passed in August to allow the Army vastly increased powers to courts martial civilians.

Those in government who doubted the wisdom of this course of action were fortified by news of the next killing. Detective Inspector Swanzy was shot dead coming out of Lisburn Cathedral. His killing precipitated an anti-Catholic pogrom and many Catholic families were driven out of

Belfast and Lisburn. Dozens of homes were burned and twenty-two people were killed.

In these crucial weeks two different trial systems emerged: one created by the insurgents and the other by Westminster. The Dáil issued a decree establishing criminal courts and 'courts of justice and equity'.[54] Parish courts were set up with a higher tier of district courts and a Supreme Court to sit in Dublin. Justices were appointed by election. The new court system was held together by volunteers who acted as registrars and police officers.

The Bar Council of Ireland prohibited barristers from appearing in the Dáil courts but this rule was ignored.[55] Some barristers welcomed the new courts but, for most, the emerging courts were simply an economic reality.

The newly appointed judges went out to the country; sometimes disguised as holiday makers or commercial travellers, they travelled under false names. Court hearings were circulated to litigants, lawyers and the press. The Army and the RIC spent much time trying to catch Dáil courts in session but trial venues were often switched at the last moment. There were many raids[56] and sometimes courts were broken up at gun point. It was one of the great absurdities of a country in turmoil. One of the new judges, Diarmuid Crowley, was captured presiding over a court. He was tried by court martial and sent to prison for two years. A handful of solicitors also went to prison for appearing in the Dáil courts: Henry Burke from Ballina and John Hogan from Loughrea were two.[57] Many others were arrested on suspicion of taking part in the Dáil courts and, where there was no firm proof, internment was ordered.

The courts martial system set up by Westminster under the ROIA became the primary method of curbing the Rebellion.

Courts Martial under the Restoration of Order in Ireland Act, August – November 1920

Some historians have equated the passing of the Restoration of Order in Ireland Act (ROIA) with a declaration of martial law. It was not that; the Army was simply being called upon to provide aid to the civil authorities. But this was an extreme development which allowed all criminal offences to be tried by court martial.[1] In addition, all breaches of the old Defence of the Realm Act (DORA) regulations could also be tried by courts martial. Furthermore, the ROIA allowed the creation of new offences by Order in Council.

The Act provided other measures to overcome the insurgency: a power to withhold government funding from local authorities who had gone over to the insurgents;[2] to move a trial venue where a court had been destroyed and to dispense with coroners courts in favour of military courts of inquiry.[3] This cured the problem caused by lack of jurors and it meant there would be no more embarrassing riders to verdicts. Power was created to order curfews and to regulate the use of cars and bicycles. All these powers were extensively used in the months that followed.

The New Courts Martial System

A court martial could impose the death penalty where the offence was so punishable under civil law. As a safeguard, every court martial trying a capital charge was required to have a member certified to be 'a person of legal knowledge and experience'. Lesser offences would be heard by courts of summary jurisdiction where two Resident Magistrates (RMs) sat together.

The system was essentially the same as under DORA. The prisoner was not able to give sworn evidence in his own defence and could not be cross-examined but he could make an unsworn statement and call defence witnesses.

No prisoner could be tried with others unless he consented. In trials where a prisoner wished to call a co-accused, there was power to sever the charge sheet and order separate trials. Where such applications were made, they were always granted.

It has been asserted by some that, under this new system, prisoners could be 'arrested, tried and sentenced' without legal representation.[4] That was not so. Prisoners who wished to be legally represented were free to instruct counsel if they had the means to pay. In this respect, suspects were no worse off than in any other part of Britain or Ireland.

Trials were generally held in open court, although there was a power to hear a case in camera if there was good reason – such as fears for the safety of a witness,[5] the likelihood of disturbance or of seditious statements by the accused.[6]

With the passing of this Act, the Army was, to a great extent, taking control of the criminal justice system. Not all cases were tried by court martial. Cases were referred to the government law advisor, William Wylie, at Dublin Castle. He made the decision 'on the papers'. Some cases arising out of the insurgency were obviously destined for trial by court martial but, where there was any doubt, it seems that it was for Wylie to say whether the case would go before the RMs or to court martial or trial under civil law before a jury. The first problems were soon apparent. In every military conflict, then or since, passing control of suspects to the military is fraught with difficulty. In the summer of 1920, the Army was charged with the investigation and prosecution of offences where their own troops were the target of the insurgents. Inevitably, suspects were mistreated and there are many well documented cases.[7] The Army privately acknowledged that 'brutal' interrogation had resulted in many unreliable confessions.[8]

In fact, the Army was not the main perpetrator of violence. Prisoners were most at risk in remote police barracks where supervision wore thin and drink was readily available. The Black and Tans were the main transgressors. Inevitably, these incidents were exploited by republican propagandists and the effect was to increase the spiral of violence and undermine the courts martial process.

The implementation of the Act involved a huge undertaking for the Army which soon had hundreds of officers tied up trying civilians. Senior army officers soon found themselves trying treason and murder and, on the other end of the scale, trying a farmer for breaching the curfew or theft of geese.[9]

A complete reorganisation of the system was needed to meet the caseload. The first step was to set up legal branches in Dublin and later in Cork, which were capable of administering the new system. The Judge Advocate General (JAG) supplied officers to sit as Judge Advocates but there was also a need to find officers to prosecute these cases. The supply of counsel from the Irish Bar began to dry up after an attempt to kill Alexander Sullivan, the Last Sergeant.[10] Only a few, like William Wylie, remained involved and he slept with a gun by the bed. In most capital cases, prosecuting counsel were brought over from England.

Also brought over from England were dozens of officers who were qualified to act as court martial officers (to prepare cases) and others who had the 'legal knowledge and experience' to act as judges in capital cases. There were difficulties finding officers who were also lawyers. There were many with legal training who had served in the Great War but 'all those of standing or ability' had gone back to private practice and so the Army had to scratch around to find men of more modest ability for work which was demanding and dangerous. Fifty-seven such officers were eventually appointed. In Dublin they lived in rented flats in the city centre. Two were shot on Bloody Sunday because they were mistaken for intelligence officers.[11] Another awoke late at night to find armed raiders creeping around his house. He was shot and wounded but pulled out an automatic and kept firing until the intruders fled.

These dangers required precautions to be taken. The public was not allowed to enter court until the officers trying the case had given their names and taken the oath. The names of civilian witnesses and officers involved in the case were removed from summaries of evidence and the press was not permitted to publish the identities of witnesses or officers. Those civilian witnesses who did give evidence for the prosecution were removed to England after the trial and usually given a resettlement grant.[12]

The Army often took responsibility for bringing defence witnesses up from the country to Dublin Castle.[13] From there they were taken on foot over to the council chamber at City Hall. It was a far cry from 1916 when few prisoners had the opportunity to call defence witnesses.

The sheer number of courts martial that took place in this period is revealing. During the course of 1920, 1,266 people were tried by courts martial. An arithmetical comparison with previous years is not helpful because the gravity of the new caseload far outstripped all that had gone before.

The new system began to secure convictions but there were unexpected consequences. The implementation of the ROIA caused many wanted men to go on the run. Some of these coalesced into flying columns: hit and run was the strategy evolving in the country.

The Trials of Insurgents

One of the first prisoners to be tried after the passing of the Act was Terence MacSwiney, Lord Mayor of Cork. MacSwiney was tried for possession of an army cipher and documents acknowledging the authority of the Dáil.[14] The prosecution was conducted by Captain Henry Gover, a courteous and quietly spoken territorial officer who had been a solicitor before the Great War.[15]

MacSwiney, a slight, fastidiously dressed figure in a dark suit declined to be represented. On the morning of his trial he had been on hunger strike for nearly four days. The prisoner's opening remarks set the tone for the case: 'I am the Lord Mayor of Cork and chief magistrate of this city and I declare this court to be illegal...'

MacSwiney refused to enter a plea and he was convicted and imprisoned for two years. Before being taken off to serve his sentence the following exchange took place: MacSwiney: 'I wish to state that I will put a limit on any term of imprisonment as a result of the action I will take. I have taken no food since Thursday therefore I will be free in a month.'

The President: 'On sentence to imprisonment you will take no food?'

MacSwiney: 'I simply say that I have decided the terms of my detention whatever your government may do. I shall be free, alive or dead, within a month.'

MacSwiney went off to prison. This was the purpose of the legislation: that offenders be tried and convicted and go to prison to reflect on the error of their ways. But the conflict now entered a new and desperate stage and this painful spectacle wore on for months.

Had MacSwiney made any other demand falling short of release it is likely that the government would have quietly given way. But, at the outset, Lloyd George recalled that the hunger strike in the spring had resulted in a mass release of prisoners and it had been followed by 'an outburst of cruel murder and outrage...'[16]

In late October, MacSwiney and two other hunger strikers died.[17] MacSwiney left a famous epitaph: 'It is not those who inflict the most but those who can suffer the most who will conquer.' It has been argued that underpinning MacSwiney's actions was a more subtle justification: under Brehon law an aggrieved might fast against another to secure redress. The cultural norms were such that if the aggrieved died, culpability attached to the wrongdoer. But the government did not give way. No government could give way and hope to survive.[18]

Tens of thousands attended MacSwiney's funeral. This cut no ice with the government; it was all 'cheap sentiment' wrote a highly placed Dublin Castle diarist.[19] The remaining hunger strikers gave up their fast and, when they recovered, they too were prosecuted.[20]

The conflict had reached a critical stage. In the course of the previous eighteen months, dozens of RIC men and a handful of soldiers had been shot and killed. By the autumn of 1920 there had been 219 successful prosecutions under the ROIA[21] but not a single conviction for murder, and it was this fact that dismayed the Cabinet most. Churchill wrote and spoke often about it:

```
'If we can get one or two of them we might
secure a confession on the steps of the scaffold
which would enable us to break up the entire
organisation of this murder club.'[22]
```

It was rather naïve to think that some hoary, old recidivist would be hanged and the Rebellion would simply fall part. In any event, real life has a way of confounding expectations: the first prisoner to stand trial for murder was an eighteen-year-old medical student from 'a respectable family'.

This young man was tried by court martial in late October for the murder of Private Whitehead of the Duke of Wellington's Regiment. Private Whitehead had been part of a squad collecting bread from Monks' Bakery in Dublin city centre. A group of young men produced revolvers and began to relieve the soldiers of their guns. Someone fired and, in the fracas that followed, three soldiers were killed. Kevin Barry hid under an army lorry where he was captured. At his trial, he sacked his lawyers and made no defence. Many appeals for clemency were made but Macready observed that three young soldiers had been killed, one younger than the prisoner. Macready confirmed the sentence and the prisoner was hanged at Mountjoy.

Until this moment many prisoners declined to acknowledge the court or dispute the facts and that now started to change as the possibility of execution became real and immediate.

The Intelligence War

While this drama was being played out, the intelligence war was also reaching a crisis. In the spring, General Macready told the cabinet that the Army had no intelligence system to speak of: 'We are at present in very much of a fog.'[23] The urgent need to produce results meant that agents were being sent into Dublin in a hurry.[24]

Brigadier Sir Ormonde L'Épée Winter was Chief of Combined Intelligence Services in Ireland.[25] Slightly built, hair oiled and swept back, he always wore a double-breasted suit, a monocle and a cigarette holder. In the Great War, Winter was decorated for courage and mentioned in despatches six times. His war exploits were the stuff of legend but his expertise in the field of intelligence was nil. Winter seems to have realised that his moment in history had arrived, however: he styled himself 'O' and embraced the life of a spymaster with enthusiasm and energy. Winter's flamboyant appearance meant he was quickly identified by the insurgents. He was stalked and later ambushed in a shoot-out near his hotel, taking a bullet in the hand. He too, like the remnants of G Division, only ventured out of Dublin Castle with caution.[26] When he left Dublin he flew a small biplane from the scene of one ambush to another.

Winter's plans revolved around interrogations, eavesdropping on prisoners and a growing network of army officers working undercover in a small city, where most could hardly pass as locals. By the late summer, Brigadier Ormonde Winter had over sixty agents in Dublin and his hopes of a breakthrough lay in this quarter.

It is too simplistic to say that Collins won the intelligence war, if it can be called that. The intelligence war in Dublin was very different to what was taking place in the country and, even there, the situation varied 'from county to county and from month to month as each side scored successes.'[27] In Dublin, though, the struggle between Winter and Collins was a critical event and there is little doubt that Collins held the initiative throughout.

Winter only came to Dublin in the spring of 1920. Collins was working on home territory and already had a grip of the postal service: telegrams and letters were intercepted and read before going on to their destinations.

Collins' willing helpers eavesdropped on phone calls and sometimes tapped phones. Collins had the army and Royal Irish Constabulary (RIC) cipher throughout the war. His army of spies: porters, barmen, dockers, chambermaids and railway men permeated every area of life. He had spies in place at Dublin Castle,[28] in the Police,[29] Army GHQ at Parkgate,[30] at Victoria Barracks Cork,[31] amongst the Auxiliaries[32] and even in Scotland Yard and the Secret Service itself.[33]

Speed of action was another important factor: Collins became known for acting decisively and swiftly on information but Winter's system for processing intelligence took days and there were significant setbacks.[34] He had some coups, capturing sensitive documents and making significant arms finds. Richard Mulcahy, the Volunteer Chief of Staff, narrowly escaped twice, the second time in a moonlit scramble across the roof tops leaving a pile of sensitive documents and a hot cup of tea. But Winter, for all his brilliance and energy, lacked the skills to run an effective intelligence outfit. He also underestimated his opponents.[35]

One of Winter's lead officers was Lieutenant Colonel Hugh Montgomery[36] who, in quieter times, batted for the MCC.[37] He was the epitome of a British army officer and his record in the Great War was a distinguished one but he had no experience of covert intelligence work. Another was Lieutenant Ames who was 6' 5" – a Grenadier Guardsman, also without experience of undercover work. Dublin was a small city and some of these operatives struggled to blend in. The available cover stories for British agents were sparse and most took jobs as mechanics and shop assistants.[38] But their cover stories were one dimensional and did not withstand scrutiny and Montgomery and his men were moving too quickly, asking pointed questions and splashing out money.

Earlier that year, a string of British agents and informers had been killed trying to identify Collins and he remained the big target. It had become a case of whether the new wave of agents found and killed Collins and his men or vice versa. Collins carried out a surveillance operation to identify the Secret Service men and strike a pre-emptive blow.[39]

Collins settled on a Sunday morning in late November for the operation to take place. At 9am that morning, in different parts of the city, groups of men carrying hammers or armed with revolvers burst into apartments where some of these officers were still in the bathroom or in bed. It was a morning of unbridled horror. Thirteen officers were shot dead.[40] Later that afternoon, an Auxiliary unit went off the rails at Croke Park: thirteen spectators and a goal keeper were shot dead and sixty spectators were wounded. At Dublin Castle three prisoners were shot dead in circumstances which have never been fully explained.[41]

The chaos continued all day. Hundreds of army officers had been living in private digs around the city. Dozens were intelligence officers but many were involved in administration or court martial work. Many were Freemasons and had used their Masonic contacts to find accommodation with 'loyal' families where they lived under aliases, sometimes with wives or girlfriends. But no army officer was safe anymore and, later that day, a long queue of cars built up around the city centre as scores of officers made for the safety of Dublin Castle.[42]

Many historians have asserted that the British intelligence operation was wiped out that day. A more measured analysis suggests that the operation launched by Collins was a serious blow. Brigadier Winter lost the confidence of General Macready and Dublin Castle. When the dust had settled a little, Sir James Anderson voiced Dublin Castle's view: 'His show is thoroughly bad and I don't see it getting better...'[43]

Collins had gained himself some time but the hunt for the men who carried out the Bloody Sunday killings became intense. This would lead to a series of contentious capital trials.

CHAPTER EIGHT

Martial Law,
December 1920

In south west Ireland martial law was declared – martial law is a misnomer because it means no law at all, just the naked exercise of power by the Army.

The immediate catalyst for martial law was a spate of ambushes in Cork, the most serious of which was at Kilmichael where sixteen Auxiliaries were killed. In another ambush at Dillon's Cross, an Auxiliary, Spencer Chapman, was mortally wounded by grenade fragments. Little could be done for him and he died slowly and in great pain in front of his comrades from K Company. There is some evidence that K Company was looking for a pretext for a spectacular reprisal and that they had made their preparations. That night they went on a spree, looting, killing, shooting at firemen and burning out a large part of Cork city centre. As morning broke, the fires still blazed and a plume of black smoke hung over the city. General Strickland ordered K Company out of the city.

Within hours, the Viceroy declared martial law in Cork, Kerry, Limerick and Tipperary. In proclamation No 1,[1] General Sir Peter Strickland was appointed Military Governor and all persons were required to 'render obedience' to his orders in all matters whatsoever. Under this regime, the death sentence was permitted for murder, rebellion, helping rebels, possessing arms, ammunition or explosives or wearing the uniform or equipment of 'His Majesty's Army, Navy, Air Force or Police' without authority to do so.

The Church agreed to allow guns to be surrendered to the clergy and then passed on to the Army before 27 December. The deadline came and went, however, and the amnesty boxes were empty: a few fowling pieces of the flared muzzle variety were handed in but not a single rifle or revolver.[2] Privately, Macready expressed the hope that some guns had been quietly dumped but in public nothing more was said about the arms amnesty.

Four more counties (Clare, Kilkenny, Waterford and Wexford) were proclaimed to be under martial law to coincide with the territory occupied by General Sir Peter Strickland's Sixth Division.[3]

Over Christmas, the Army set up military courts (unsanctioned by law or Parliament) to bring about swift trials and executions. At a meeting at the offices of the Judge Advocate General (JAG) in London, Felix Cassel advised that executions should follow quickly after the trial to avoid prisoners seeking the protection of the courts by writs of habeas corpus.[4]

As it turned out, the first prisoner to be sent for trial by a martial law court was not an insurgent but an Auxiliary from K Company, which had found a billet at Dunmanway police barracks. Two lorry loads from K Company had stopped at the roadside for a routine car check. The car belonged to Resident Magistrate (RM) Brady and had broken down on the way to court. A young man, Crowley, had stopped to help. One of the Auxiliaries, Vernon Harte, destabilised by drink and grief, shot Crowley in the face. Canon Magner, an elderly priest, remonstrated and he too was shot dead. Harte threatened to kill the RM who appealed to the other Auxiliaries for help.

'You had better clear', said one Auxiliary laconically and the RM scrambled over a hedge and began to run across the fields. It could have been just another unexplained roadside killing but RM Brady demanded an inquiry and Harte was brought to trial immediately. His counsel argued the prisoner was insane and the case was put over until the New Year for medical evidence.[5]

Back at Westminster, the cabinet was 'badly frightened' and a senior civil servant was sent to Dublin Castle to remonstrate over the inaction: 'What is the point of martial law if he is not hung already?'[6] But General Macready and the Chief Secretary 'refused to be stampeded'. Harte would be tried but there would be no short cuts.

A few days later, Macready and his generals went to Downing Street. General Boyd (commanding the Dublin District) and Strickland (Governor of the martial law area) assured Lloyd George that the Rebellion would be crushed within four months.[7] This was the news Lloyd George wanted and plans were set in motion for an election the following May, with partition and devolved rule in the north and the south. While the conference was in session, news was brought to Downing Street that, at a remote country house in Limerick, the Army had killed 5 men and over 130 prisoners had been taken at a dance. Eyebrows were raised briefly: *A Dance*? But Ireland was otherwise quiet and the cabinet discussions returned to the suppression of the Rebellion.

In the New Year, two Auxiliaries, Lemon and Brown, were given short sentences for robbery.[8] But this prosecution passed unnoticed as the press was focused on Cadet Harte's trial. Harte was tried, found guilty but insane and sent off to Broadmoor. A close analysis of the evidence suggests that the verdict was well-founded but few believed it.[9] It was the worst start to the martial law regime because it leant colour to the suggestion that the law was being selectively applied.

Official reprisals were also introduced as part of the martial law regime. Brigade commanders were authorised to destroy the homes of people who had failed to warn the Army of an impending ambush.[10] As a result of this policy, 194 homes were destroyed before the Truce. In Dublin Castle it was called 'punishing the enemy' but the reality was that these were reprisals on the civilian population.[11] And, for those home owners who knew of impending attacks, they risked their lives if they tipped off the Army and their homes if they did not.

Other measures introduced by General Strickland included an unlimited power to search, to arrest and intern without trial, to ban fairs, markets and race meetings. Home owners were required to put up lists of occupants on the door of their homes to facilitate the identification of wanted men.

The conflict was entering the bloodiest phase. Both sides would start shooting prisoners and the law and lawyers were increasingly drawn into the struggle.

CHAPTER NINE

Days of Terror, 1921

Where except in Ireland...could open rebellion, martial law, peace proposals and a general election be all running side by side at the same time?

General Sir Neville Macready,
Annals of an Active Life Vol. 2

In Dublin, a city of less than half a million people, the Army continued a fruitless search for Collins. Internment had been reintroduced and there were now over 2,000 prisoners in hastily prepared camps at Arbour Hill, Spike Island, the Curragh, Bere Island and Ballykinlar.

In Dublin the curfew was enforced robustly.[1] Every night, columns of Auxiliaries and soldiers boarded lorries and moved out of barracks in raiding parties. By midnight most troops were back in barracks with arms seizures and suspects bound for trial or internment. After midnight, the city would go quiet again.

In remote areas, the insurgents relied heavily on bicycles to cycle out and dig trenches or blow bridges to make roads unusable for military traffic. The Army met this threat by banning cycles. Occasionally fairs and markets were also forbidden until the local authority made good the roads.[2] In some areas the Army simply seized the wheels of farmers' carts until the roads were repaired.

The ambush war, as it became known, gathered pace. Ambushes were met by raids and reprisals and the Army began to carry civilian hostages on convoys. At first, this was confined to members of the Dáil or known Volunteers but the practice soon extended to civilians.[3] Hostages or 'mascots', as soldiers called them, were crowded onto lorries and handcuffed to rails to provide cover for soldiers.

Macready had two branches of strategy. The first was the military response to the Rebellion. The second was to intern or imprison those who presented a threat and to utilise the death sentence as a deterrent. Here, he perceived a weakness in his strategy. Although martial law had been proclaimed in south west Ireland, the Cabinet had resisted pressure from Macready to extend it nationwide. The policy of the government was to use the threat of martial law to bring the other side to the negotiating table.[4] This did not suit Macready. A particular bone of contention was that, inside the martial law area, the death sentence could be imposed even for possessing a clip of ammunition. Outside the martial law area – 'the nerve centre' of the insurgency – the death sentence was only available for murder.[5]

Macready sought legal advice from the Judge Advocate General (JAG), Felix Cassel, who advised that the death penalty could be extended by reviving a medieval law: levying war on the Crown.[6] This was swiftly put into effect. An ambush at Drumcondra Bridge resulted in the capture of five armed men caught running from the scene and the opportunity was used to bring charges of levying war. In this way, the execution policy was put into effect inside and outside the martial law area.

This strategy went hand in hand with a successful military campaign to crush the Rebellion by the spring and pave the way for elections.[7] This goal was not achieved and, by the beginning of May, General Macready's weekly reports to cabinet no longer speak of victory. The reports comprise lengthy summaries tracking bodies of armed men criss-crossing the martial law area.[8] Macready's emerging military strategy was to bring these columns to battle and wipe them out; their strategy was to hit and run.

While these confrontations were being played out, there were peace emissaries flitting back and forth to Ireland. One was Lord Derby, a member of the cabinet who went over under a pseudonym – 'Mr Edwards' – to meet the insurgent leaders. He was later castigated by Dublin Castle insiders for leaving his engraved cigarette case on the ferry and his coat and personal papers on a train.[9] At a Women's Institute meeting the following week Lord Derby donned a pair of spectacles: 'Lord Derby' he announced. Taking off the specs to loud laughter: 'Mr Edwards'. But while the politicians talked and sparred for an advantage, people were dying.

In late May, the elections came. In the words of General Macready, the insurgents fielded 'gunmen' in every available constituency. They won an overwhelming mandate in the south and the unionists won a commanding majority in the north. The conflict dragged on until the summer, with both sides at full stretch. The year before, the summer had been wet and this restricted army operations on poor roads and tracks in the country. The summer of 1921, in contrast, was hot and dry. Infantry sweeps, supported by convoys of lorries and spotter planes, penetrated deep into the country harrying the insurgents at every turn. Privately, Macready told the Cabinet that this effort could not be sustained into the winter without substantial reinforcements.

Propagandists on both sides were still claiming victory was imminent when, suddenly and unexpectedly, the Truce came.

During these months of crisis, General Macready's duties extended far beyond suppressing the Rebellion. The court martial system was yielding large numbers of convictions in capital cases. Part of Macready's task was to review convictions and sentences passed.[10]

Macready's policy was straight forward on the face of it: where there was evidence, the offender would be prosecuted.[11] But he had failed to grasp the nettle. Insurgents were prosecuted for capital crimes but the law stood by and winked at murder committed by police officers and soldiers.[12]

Prosecutions were only brought against police officers and soldiers where the offence was committed in the most blatant circumstances. Cadet Harte had gunned down an old priest in front of a Resident Magistrate (RM). Captain King was prosecuted for the murder of a prisoner who was removed from the cells at Dublin Castle to be killed.[13] During the first half of 1921, four officers were convicted of murder committed during pub robberies[14] which had been carried out in broad daylight in front of many witnesses. A handful of Auxiliaries who ran riot in broad daylight were prosecuted.[15] These cases were the tip of an iceberg. There are no recorded prosecutions for reprisals against people or property. The victims were either dead or too cowed to take action and there was no political will to investigate or prosecute. Auxiliaries and officers of the Black and Tans kept their silence and local army commanders were often sanguine about what had been done. The credibility of the trial process was undermined from the start and all that Macready did took place within this context.

Macready's duties involved overseeing the Restoration of Order in Ireland Act (ROIA) courts martial scheme outside and inside the martial law area. He was also operating court regimes not sanctioned by law in the martial law area.

Trials of Suspected Insurgents in the Martial Law Area

Under this regime, prisoners were usually tried within two weeks of capture. Only occasionally, where the prisoner or a witness had been wounded, was the trial delayed. The system was designed to ensure that rebels captured in arms were tried swiftly and, if need be, executed, imprisoned or interned.[16]

In the months leading up to the Truce, martial law courts sentenced thirty-seven men to death. Of these, fourteen were executed. Sentence of death was commuted in five cases[17] and two other men were able to obtain writs of habeas corpus securing their release.[18] Sixteen men remained under sentence of death until after the Treaty in December 1921[19] and thirty-three more were serving sentences of ten years or more.

In the martial law area, fifty-four summary court officers were appointed. The summary court could impose sentences of up to six months' imprisonment with or without hard labour. In Cork, a curfew officer was appointed with power to impose up to one month's imprisonment. In total 2,296 people were tried by the summary court and 549 sentences of imprisonment were handed down.

Where nothing could be proved but everything suspected internment without trial was another option. Army records show that, by the Truce, 790 prisoners were still interned in the martial law area.[20]

A feature of the martial law area was that trials under the ROIA continued for offences committed before the cut-off date. Curiously, some offenders in the martial law area were prosecuted under the ROIA even where they were alleged to have committed offences after the martial law cut-off date. In all, 398 such trials took place.[21]

The net result was that, in the martial law area, the Army was operating two concurrent trial processes: one which was not sanctioned by law and the other under the ROIA.

Trials of Suspected Insurgents under the ROIA outside the Martial Law Area

In the months leading up to the Truce in July 1921 there were 1,492 courts martial.

By the spring of 1921, there were just under 3,500 prisoners interned without trial outside the martial law area.[22] It was intended that some of these would be tried in due course but most were simply being held for the duration of the conflict.

The Process of Confirmation of Conviction and Sentence

It was for Macready to confirm or overturn convictions and for him to uphold or vary sentences. But before the papers went to him, they went to the JAG who reviewed all convictions. It was for the JAG to say whether a conviction was lawful and the sovereign took his advice on issues of law. The JAG also advised Macready on factual matters and, though his advice carried great weight, it was not binding on General Macready.

A two-tier system developed. In cases arising from the martial law area, death sentences were imposed for possession of a gun, wearing an army uniform or trenching a road or knocking down a bridge. In cases arising outside the martial law area, the position was less clear cut.

In capital cases, Macready always considered whether the evidence was sufficiently strong to justify execution. This might seems a little strange, since the test for conviction was beyond reasonable doubt but the correspondence of the JAG and General Macready frequently touch on the question of whether the evidence was strong enough to justify 'an irrevocable step' as opposed to a long prison term.[23]

A review of the decisions made suggests that Macready often disregarded the facts found by the court martial and imposed his own view. This implies a lack of confidence in the courts martial process and a degree of care on his part.

Intelligence about the prisoner was an important factor. Further considerations related to the personal attributes of the prisoner: intellect, youth and prior good character of a positive kind. In one case, two prisoners had been severely ill-treated in custody and death sentences were commuted so that they could give evidence against their captors.[24]

Subject to these considerations, the rule of thumb was that prisoners who killed, wounded or fired on members of the Crown forces were executed. Prisoners under the age of eighteen were always spared execution.

Even after this process was complete, there was a final avenue of appeal for a prisoner condemned to die. The Viceroy could still invoke the prerogative of mercy, although Macready asserted this power no longer existed in trials conducted under martial law.

After the New Year, the cases came up for consideration by Macready in a steady stream. The first was Joseph Murphy who had been court martialled for the murder of Private Squibbs of the Hampshire Regiment just before the cut-off date for martial law. A hand grenade was thrown into the back of an army lorry where soldiers were huddled together and Squibbs was killed. Murphy denied throwing the hand grenade but he was convicted and sentenced to death. A good deal of legal wrangling followed over whether defence cross-examination had been improperly curtailed:

the case was 'full of holes' a Dublin Castle diarist wrote.[25] Sentence was commuted to twenty-five years by General Macready on the grounds of 'the repeated postponements of his execution and the distress of mind that had been caused'.[26]

The Row between Macready and the Judge Advocate General

The first death sentence under martial law caused a political row at Westminster. The prisoner was Cornelius Murphy, a farmer's son from Kerry, who had been convicted of possessing a revolver and a clip of ammunition. The court martial officers observed that Murphy was a man of 'limited education' and, although they passed the death sentence, recommended a reprieve. His sentence was stayed while General Macready and the Judge Advocate General argued.

The Judge Advocate General, Felix Cassel, was based in London and he insisted on personally reviewing all death sentences. Macready demanded Cassel delegate this power to a subordinate in Dublin so that executions could follow swiftly in the martial law area. Cassel refused and the row spread with cabinet members taking sides. Cassel asserted that his duty to advise personally arose because his powers were granted by the sovereign: 'the Letters Patent which I hold...'[27]

The row was a legacy of the 1916 Rebellion when the Army had bypassed the JAG and rushed to execute prisoners. In 1916, the JAG was Sir Thomas Milvain, who was dying, and Cassel was then deputy JAG. It is likely that Cassel felt unable to press the issue at that time because of his German birth and the fact that the Rebellion had been assisted by Germany. But by 1921, Cassel was firmly established as JAG and the Cabinet backed Cassel.

A few days later, Cassel confirmed the conviction was lawful but advised the recommendation for mercy made by the court 'should carry very great weight'. Cornelius Murphy lived for a few more days while Macready considered the papers before confirming sentence. Cornelius Murphy was then shot by firing squad.

Almost immediately there was another case from the martial law area. John Allen, a boot maker from Tipperary town, was convicted of possessing a revolver and ammunition and was sentenced to death by firing squad. His supporters sought a writ of habeas corpus to test the legality of courts that had not been sanctioned by law. Allen was held for execution while the High Court considered the arguments.

In Dripsey, the Army got wind of an ambush and carried out a flanking movement which overwhelmed the ambushers. Seven were captured and, of these, two were wounded. Five were tried by a martial law court martial and convicted of levying war against the Crown. Macready telegrammed the JAG informing him that he 'proposed to carry out the sentences forthwith unless you give your opinion that I cannot legally do so'.[28]

The JAG replied tersely: sentence could not be carried out until the High Court had ruled in the case of John Allen on the legality of military courts. Macready again complained bitterly to the War Office that trials in the martial law area were being reduced to 'a farce'. Nonetheless, and with great reluctance, he stayed his hand.

Throughout this stage of the conflict, Macready was intermittently engaged in a dispute with the JAG and the courts over a range of issues: the fate of prisoners convicted under martial law courts; the legality of official reprisals[29] and alleged improprieties in ROIA trials.[30]

At first, Macready was vindicated when the High Court finally ruled in Allen's case. The Court held that a state of war existed in the martial law area and, therefore, the courts were unable to intervene.[31] Allen and the five Dripsey men were shot by firing squad a few days later.

Of the two prisoners wounded at Dripsey, one died from his wounds and the other, Denis Murphy, was tried and sentenced to death but this sentence was commuted by Macready to twenty-five years' penal servitude. It is likely that Macready took the view that five men from the Dripsey area had already been executed and that was sufficient for the purposes of deterrence.[32]

Outside the martial law area, there were just as many capital cases coming up for confirmation. One concerned a Belfast taxi driver, John Leonard, who had been convicted of the murder of District Inspector Swanzy. The killing had triggered an anti-Catholic pogrom in the north and there had been many fatalities. Of the five men involved in the killing of Inspector Swanzy, only Leonard had been brought to trial. General Macready commuted Leonard's death sentence to a mere two years with hard labour when the JAG voiced doubts about the safety of the conviction.[33]

The number of prisoners on death row was rising quickly. The convicted men were held at Kilmainham, a grim eighteenth-century gaol, where the image of snakes entwined is carved in stone above the main gate. Kilmainham had been the worst kind of Victorian gaol, with men, women and children huddled together in damp, candle-lit cells. The occasional hanging took place until the prison fell out of use and became derelict at the end of the nineteenth century. It became a place of execution again in 1916, when the leaders of the Rebellion were held there for the firing squad.

Five years on and death row was full again. Among those condemned to death were the men who had been convicted of the Bloody Sunday killings: Potter, Conway, Teeling, Whelan and Moran and five others convicted of levying war (the Drumcondra Ambush). Here the convicted prisoners waited to hear their fate. A contemporary press report related that the condemned prisoners 'enter into games and pastimes with the zest and hilarity of school boys'.[34] It was, of course, not so. For these men, the hours and days passed in uneasy dread. One prisoner described a death row inmate as 'broken and his eyes were sad and bewildered'.[35]

The fate of these prisoners was constantly argued over in different forums as execution approached. Vincent Rice, junior counsel in the case of Potter and Conway, submitted a report to the Attorney General relating an attempt by the prosecution to suppress alibi evidence vital to Conway. Soon after, the Attorney General, chancing upon Rice at the Four Courts, all but promised a reprieve for Conway:

'And what about Potter?'

'You have nothing to do with Potter.'

Vincent Rice threatened to swear an affidavit and bring a motion in the King's Bench to expose an attempt by prosecuting counsel to suppress an alibi.

'The King's Bench have no power to interfere' replied the Attorney General.

'But the newspapers have the right to publish what I swear.'

The case had the capacity to cause considerable embarrassment and a campaign for reprieve gathered wide support. General Macready was visited by a high powered delegation including churchmen and other distinguished Dubliners.[36] As the date for execution approached, a different sort of deputation was sent to the quays to meet each passenger boat. A group of Collins' men scrutinised the passengers for sight of the hangman, Ellis, a slim, bald man with a heavy moustache – it was the only description they had. But Ellis slipped through the net without ever realising that he had been hunted.

A last-ditch attempt was made to save one of the other prisoners (Whelan) by a writ in the King's Bench, asserting that no 'certificate of legal knowledge' of a member of the court was read into the record as required by the Regulations. The application was resisted by counsel for Macready and was refused.

At Dublin Castle a report was prepared on each condemned prisoner by one of the older civil servants: 'Whiskers'.[37] The report and the trial transcripts were circulated among senior civil servants, General Macready, the Chief Secretary and the Viceroy. The senior civil servants would stay up late after dinner, loosen black ties and read over the evidence. The surviving diaries and memos do not suggest any rush to judgment.

Nothing could be said for Teeling because he had been wounded and captured at the scene of one of the shootings with his revolver close by. Teeling stayed in his cell at Kilmainham for the most part. He emerged occasionally to limp around the stone breaker's yard where the leaders of the 1916 Rebellion had been shot. Just a few years later, Teeling would become a Lieutenant in the National Army, people vied to buy him a drink and he quickly slid into belligerent alcoholism and, in the bar of the Theatre Royal, he shot a man dead in a row over a bag of tomatoes. For that crime, he was convicted of manslaughter and sent to gaol. But, in 1921, he was just twenty years old, a quiet, well mannered, good-looking young man. The gaolers were touched by his fortitude in the shadow of the hangman's noose.[38]

Events on death row then took an unexpected turn: one of the other prisoners in Kilmainham was Ernie O'Malley who had been captured weeks before. O'Malley, like many of the other prisoners, was routinely brought out for identification parades that might link him to some 'outrage'. O'Malley was a resourceful young man who engaged the help of a soldier at Kilmainham. The soldier was persuaded to smuggle in bolt cutters and a Smith and Wesson.

At this time, the last Bloody Sunday trial was still underway. One of the prisoners being tried was Patrick Moran but he declined to go with O'Malley: 'I won't let down the witnesses who gave evidence for me.' O'Malley escaped that night, taking with him Simon Donnelly, one of the Easter Week veterans, and Frank Teeling. O'Malley later wrote that the Drumcondra prisoners, who were awaiting execution, were in a punishment cell and could not be brought away.[39]

The escapes were a blow for the administration but the process of review was carried forward with some care. The JAG recommended that 'no irrevocable sentence be confirmed' in respect of Potter because of the evidential shortcomings.[40] A final review by a senior civil servant recommended 'respite and commute' for both prisoners.[41]

The sentences on both prisoners were commuted to twenty-five years' penal servitude although, ultimately, the reasoning related not to a recognition of the frailties of the identification evidence but a general unease about the political ramifications of executing these two men when Teeling (who was undoubtedly involved) had got clean away.

As to the other prisoners awaiting execution for the Bloody Sunday killings, Moran was hanged. Macready was influenced by the fact that there had been an attempt to kill the main witness just before the trial. This was seen as providing some additional support against Moran although it had not formed any part of the prosecution case. Whelan who, it is now generally accepted, had played no part in the killings was also hanged. On the same morning, four of the five prisoners taken at Drumcondra were also hanged. The fifth, O'Sullivan was spared on account of his age (seventeen).

Two weeks later, Thomas Traynor was convicted of the murder of an Auxiliary in Dublin. The evidence, which was overwhelming, showed participation in an organised ambush in which two cadets were killed and three others wounded. Traynor was hanged soon after.[42]

There were more cases from the martial law area. The Army cornered an Irish Republican Army (IRA) column at a farmhouse near Clonmult. The siege was broken when an army officer climbed onto the roof and set fire to the thatch and hurled mills bombs into the farmhouse. Many of the insurgents were killed. Four prisoners were tried and convicted but the youngest was spared because he was seventeen. Another, Sonny O'Leary, aged nineteen, had sustained a head wound which knocked him unconscious and left him with a deep furrow across his forehead. The JAG observed that it had 'not been definitely proved' that O'Leary had fired on the troops.[43] This reasoning was generous to the prisoner and he was spared by Macready.

A last-ditch legal challenge was mounted for the remaining two Clonmult prisoners but it raised no fresh point of law and the men were shot by firing squad with two prisoners captured in an ambush at Mourneabbey.[44]

Macready began to focus his attention on the martial law area, where the challenge to the Army was greatest. He appears to have finally persuaded the JAG to delegate the review to his deputy.[45] Macready wrote to the Chief Secretary at Dublin Castle reinforcing his view that 'Executions should take place within two or three days of the fight.'[46] And that is what began to happen in the martial law area. Patrick Casey was captured on 1 May: he was tried and executed the following day.[47] Daniel O'Brien was captured on 10 May and executed six days later.[48] Thomas Keane's execution was expedited as part of this process.[49] Each of the prisoners had fired on the troops and, although they had inflicted no casualties, it was not for want of effort. Although General Macready continued to be plagued with challenges to the legality of the military courts convened under martial law, he was now getting his way.

Outside the martial law area, Ned Foley and Patrick Maher were tried and convicted of the murder of two police officers during the rescue of Seán Hogan at Knocklong railway station. General Macready confirmed sentence and Maher and Foley were hanged in June: the last men to be executed during the insurgency.

In early June, the Mallow Barracks trial ended. Some months before, a group of some fifty raiders had tricked their way through the front gate of the Barracks and shot a sergeant who had resisted. Two machine guns and two dozen rifles were seized. The Barracks were set on fire and the raiders made off in a convoy of cars. Five of the six prisoners were convicted and sentenced to death. The JAG indicated that the trials had been conducted according to law and sentence could be confirmed. Applying his usual criteria, sentence was confirmed by General Macready.

Edward Carmody and John Lenehan were awaiting execution for the murder of Inspector Tobias O'Sullivan. The JAG approved the lawfulness of the trial and sentence was confirmed.[50]

One other trial is worthy of note. Seán Mac Eoin was convicted of the murder of District Inspector McGrath in mid-June. Mac Eoin was one of the very few senior insurgents in captivity and, after the trial, General Macready, driven by curiosity, went to see him in hospital where he was being held. Macready later recalled the prisoner was unaccountably 'cheery' despite his imminent execution.[51] Curiously, Macready continued to go back to see Mac Eoin and formed an attachment.

While awaiting trial, Mac Eoin had been elected to the Second Dáil and peace talks were already informally underway. There was also a letter written by the mother of Inspector McGrath, and her three sons shown to Macready asking for the prisoner to be spared: 'the sorrow and loss sustained by us will be all the greater should it entail the loss of a single additional life.'[52] General Macready stifled his personal feelings. Mac Eoin, he wrote, was a murderer and must pay the price. He confirmed sentence but Mac Eoin's execution was stayed by the Truce and he was later released by the government to take part in the Treaty talks.

Looking back on Macready's case load over the preceding months, it can be said with confidence that three prisoners were convicted and executed for killings in which they played no part: Moran, Whelan and Maher. When the Truce came, a handful of prisoners were also awaiting execution for offences they had not committed: two of the Mallow Barracks prisoners and Carmody and Lenehan, who had been convicted of the murder of District Inspector Tobias O'Sullivan. It is likely that there were others but the records for this period are incomplete.

These convictions all had a common denominator: all were based on visual identifications entirely unsupported by other evidence. At that time, the dangers of visual identification evidence were not at all understood.[53] It is now acknowledged that, during this era, there were a significant number of miscarriages of justice in Britain and America based on visual identification. It is now well recognised that visual identification is an inherently unreliable and potentially dangerous form of evidence. The admission of such evidence is now rigorously scrutinised for precisely these reasons. These considerations cannot offer a complete explanation about what took place but they provide an important insight. There are two final observations. Firstly, most advocates of this period acknowledged that a General Court Martial was as fair a tribunal as it was possible to find. But it is not possible to say how the officers trying these cases might have been influenced by the pressure for convictions when the conflict was at its height. Secondly, in the last months of the conflict, the Army was briefing court martial officers on the prevalence of false alibis in Ireland and this too may have influenced events.[54]

One final chapter of the conflict was still to be played out. It concerned the legality of the trials conducted under martial law and the fate of the very many men awaiting execution.

CHAPTER TEN

Stepping Back from the Brink

When the Truce came, there were still forty-two men on death row and over a hundred more were awaiting trial for levying war.[1] Some had been caught in failed ambushes but dozens had been captured during the last significant engagement: the burning of the Customs House, in May. While plumes of smoke were rising up over the Liffey, a heavy armed Auxiliary unit had driven past the Customs House by chance; they rounded up seventy-seven prisoners. Preparation to bring these men before a court martial halted when the Truce came[2] and there were no more Restoration of Order in Ireland Act (ROIA) trials or trials under martial law.[3]

Policy at Westminster shifted over the summer. Either the Truce held and acceptable peace terms were negotiated or the re-conquest of Ireland would begin with martial law of the most draconian kind.

Macready was now gearing up for a resumption of hostilities. Westminster had promised sixteen battalions of infantry and as many cavalry units as could be spared. Macready had issued instructions to his senior commanders to be ready to re-take and occupy areas under rebel control; to subdue the cities and then begin intensive sweeps in the country and the hills with cavalry.[4] Prisoners captured in arms would be tried and executed on the spot.[5]

Macready also intended to execute the men on death row and begin trying the very many other men awaiting trial. In the final act of this conflict, the lawyers were also gearing up for a legal challenge to the power of the Army. In this chaotic and febrile situation all depended on the Truce continuing to hold. There were also two crucial legal cases that were still being played out.

The first was *Clifford and Sullivan*: two young men who had been convicted of possession of hand guns. They had been tried by a military court and sentenced to death but, with considerable ingenuity, Michael Comyn KC had got their case before the Court of Appeal (where he lost) and up before the House of Lords on a jurisdictional point. The executions of these two men were stayed pending the ruling of the Lords.

Another prisoner, J.J. Egan, also convicted by a military court of possessing a quantity of ammunition, had also been sentenced to death but his lawyers had got his case before the Master of the Rolls on a different legal point.

In some respects, General Macready's difficulties were never more acute. Egan's case had its origins in the martial law area but Dublin, seat of the High Court, was not under martial law. General Macready needed to win the case to maintain the credibility of martial law but, on the other hand, he could not publicly acknowledge the supremacy of the Civil Court without endangering the whole edifice of martial law.

The primary argument advanced for the prisoner, Egan, can be distilled into a few lines: the Crown had released the prerogative power to wage war in Ireland to Parliament by passing the ROIA to deal with the Rebellion and, therefore, only Parliament could embark on new measures. It followed that the whole edifice of martial law was unlawful. Precisely this argument had been argued before Chief Justice Molony in the Clonmult case a few months before.[6] Molony had dismissed the application as unworthy of argument. Nothing had changed save that the prisoners had got the case up in front of the Master of the Rolls who was known to be open to argument on the legality of martial law. The hopes of the lawyers rested with him.

Counsel for General Macready argued that the court should simply follow the decision of the court in the case of John Allen[7] and the Clonmult case.[8] At the end of the second day of legal argument, the Master of the Rolls reserved judgment and, turning to counsel for Generals Macready and his commanders, he asked:

'What is to become of the prisoner in the mean time?'

Counsel: 'I have no instructions one way or the other.'

'I will make an order for the arrest of the execution of the prisoner until judgment.'[9]

Judgment in *Egan v Macready* was reserved while the Master of the Rolls considered the law. The Truce remained in force but the fate of the men awaiting execution was uncertain.

The position was further complicated by the fact that the House of Lords delivered their speeches in *Clifford and Sullivan* on 27 July: the prisoners lost the case.[10] They, and many other prisoners in the martial law area, were at risk of immediate execution.[11]

The following day, *Egan v Macready* came back before the Master of the Rolls who ruled that the military courts were unlawful and ordered that the writs of habeas corpus would be issued and the Crown must produce the prisoner at court on Friday 29 July.[12]

General Macready was in London when the news came though. He telegraphed Dublin GHQ with orders to disregard the writ.[13] The confrontation between the Army and the courts threatened a constitutional crisis of some gravity.

Egan v Macready was relisted again before the Master of the Rolls the following day. Counsel for the Crown, Henry Hanna KC, pressed for more time: 'An appeal lies,' Hanna argued, 'and notice of an appeal having been served, the Crown did not propose to produce the prisoners or release them pending the appeal.'[14]

The Master of the Rolls: 'I will not listen to any such answer to the writ. The writ must be answered in the ordinary way. Has the writ been obeyed?'

Lynch KC (for the prisoners): 'No, my Lord.'

The Master of the Rolls: 'Then I will order a writ of attachment to issue against the three parties for whom Sergeant Hanna appears.'

Writs were then issued for the arrests of General Macready, General Strickland and General Cameron. The news travelled swiftly around the world: 'Writs out to seize the Generals'[15] was the headline in the *New York Times*. In London and Dublin the news created a sensation. General Macready's weekly report to Cabinet tersely recorded events and finished with a veiled rebuke: 'the situation will have to be cleared up as it affects the power of the British Army all over the world'.[16] This was only a slight exaggeration; at that time the British army was enforcing martial law not just in south west Ireland but Egypt, Mesopotamia, Constantinople and occupied Germany.[17]

The next day, the Government at Westminster gave way and ordered the release of Egan. One final hearing took place in *Egan v Macready* when the Master of the Rolls, Sir Charles O'Connor, was informed of the release of the prisoner and he then stayed the writs for the arrests of Generals Macready, Strickland and Cameron.[18] The crisis was averted.

General Macready's next weekly report to Cabinet recounted, with barely concealed fury, the release of Egan and also a number of imprisoned members of Dáil Éireann, freed so that they might take part in the treaty debates: 'It might have been useful had I also been informed.'[19]

There were no more trials by Military Courts and there were no more trials under the ROIA in respect of offences connected with the insurgency. Those interned or in prison awaiting trial remained in custody and the fate of the many men awaiting execution or trial hung on the Truce continuing. The Truce held and, for a time at least, it seemed there might be peace.

PART II
THE TRIALS

Trials 1916

CHAPTER ELEVEN

Eoin MacNeill

MacNeill was a forty-nine-year-old professor of Early Irish. The formation of the Volunteers had been his brainchild – a response to the formation of Carson's Ulster Volunteers in 1912. MacNeill became Chief of Staff of the Volunteers and, in the year preceding the Rebellion, he had espoused an increasingly militant anti-conscription campaign. He was unaware that Pearse, Clark, MacDonagh and others had hijacked the Volunteers and steered them towards rebellion. Only a few days before the Rebellion he became aware of what was afoot and he issued the famous countermand order which was published on Easter Sunday. The Rebellion went ahead, although the turnout was hugely reduced as a result.

MacNeill took no part in the Rising but he wrote to General Maxwell after the surrender, inviting a discussion about how further bloodshed could be avoided. The letter came before Major Price, the Intelligence Officer attached to Irish Command. Price could hardly believe his luck and sent a car for MacNeill who accepted the invitation to go to Dublin Castle where he was arrested. It was a fantastically naïve step by MacNeill which was typical of this slightly unworldly man. MacNeill was held at Arbour Hill for some days while the other prisoners were being tried. He wrote an account of being allowed out to exercise in front of a line of soldiers ostensibly engaged in weapons training but shooting rather too close to the prisoner. After this he was interviewed by Major Price and offered his life in exchange for a statement that incriminated the Home Rule MPs Dillon and Devlin.[1] MacNeill gave his wife a note about the interrogation the next day which she was able to smuggle out.

On 9 May he was brought up to Richmond Barracks in a cab. In a famous encounter, he turned to leave the cab and found himself face-to-face with Seán MacDiarmada, one of the signatories of the Proclamation, who had been tried and convicted only minutes before. MacDiarmada refused his handshake. Leaning on the shoulder of Harry Boland, who had also just been tried, MacDiarmada limped off under escort to Kilmainham Gaol where he and James Connolly were shot two days later.[2]

General Maxwell decreed that MacNeill be tried by General Court Martial (GCM). He did so in response to a letter by MacNeill's lawyers and replied on 12 May. This was a significant day. The night before, Asquith had signalled to the House of Commons that the last two executions were due to take place that night and he hoped there would be no more.[3] That night Connolly and MacDiarmada, the last two signatories of the Proclamation of Independence, were executed.

The same day, MacNeill was charged with rebellion with intent 'to assist the enemy'. An alternative charge of inciting disaffection was also preferred.

Until this point all the prisoners had been tried by Field General Court Martial (FGCM) and denied legal representation as part of that process. Where lawyers came to the barracks, they were turned away. Maxwell, as it happens, was 'perplexed' by MacNeill's case and he wrote to Westminster 'I believe he did try and stop the actual rebellion taking place when it did.'[4]

It was in these circumstances that Maxwell acceded to a request that MacNeill be tried by GCM, which carried with it certain protections for an accused, such as the presence of a Judge Advocate and legal representation, albeit at the expense of the prisoner.

Years later, MacNeill wrote that he had foreseen that executions might follow the Rebellion and that this would cause revulsion in Ireland and so 'I determined to use what means I could to delay the court martial proceedings.'[5]

This was no more than MacNeill rewriting history. He had no influence over when he was tried or how he was tried. It was simply his good fortune to be tried after the execution of all the signatories to the Proclamation of Independence and after Asquith had told the House of Commons that the execution policy was to be discontinued.

Maxwell, however, was determined that the trial would be in camera. Trial in public 'would have a most serious effect and would cause danger to the public safety'.[6] It had become the practice in war-time Britain to conduct courts martial in private.[7]

MacNeill was tried on the standard charge of rebellion with intent to assist the enemy. He also faced twelve counts of attempting to cause disaffection[8] and committing acts likely to prejudice recruitment.[9] These charges were signed by Maxwell and dated 22 May, the morning of

MacNeill's trial.[10] This appears to have reflected the view of the prosecutors that the charge of rebellion was unlikely to succeed.

The Army brought over a lawyer from the War Office to act as Judge Advocate: Major Edmund Kimber. In peace-time Kimber had scraped a living at the criminal bar in London. He had been a territorial officer for many years and, when the Great War broke out, he went over to France with the British Expeditionary Force (BEF). This slightly built, quietly-spoken man was anything but ordinary. In the battle of Fromelles, he held his company together for many hours in the face of overwhelming odds. At the end of the day, despite his own wounds, he had extricated the remnants of his company from encirclement and brought them back to safety. This was a turning point in his career when his qualities of 'coolness and conspicuous ability' were recognised.[11] He was decorated and posted to the War Office and then to Ireland. He was the first of a stream of legal officers that began to arrive in Ireland as the courts martial process became entrenched and extensive. These officers were all veterans of the Western Front. Most had been wounded and were no longer fit for front line service. In time, these officers came to hold the whole courts martial system together.

MacNeill's trial took place at Richmond Barracks on 22 May and ran for three days. General Blackader and twelve officers sat in judgment.[12]

MacNeill was prosecuted by Lieutenant William Wylie KC who had prosecuted most of the trials by FGCM and had been scrupulously fair to the unrepresented prisoners. This trial was different, Wylie remembered. This prisoner had 'done more than anyone else to mislead the youth of the country and he had made the rebellion possible'.[13] The prisoner was represented, he reckoned, and so 'the gloves were off'. The evidence spoke for itself and very little of the prosecution was actually in dispute. The charges of causing disaffection focused on acts that were a matter of public record and could not be denied: creating the Volunteer movement; attending executive meetings; editing *The Irish Volunteer*; inspecting the Volunteers on Saint Patrick's Day; ordering the display of Volunteer recruitment posters and speaking at Volunteer rallies. The charges of committing acts likely to damage recruitment to the Army followed a similar pattern.[14]

Wylie called evidence linking MacNeill to the arms landing. Only days before the Rising, a Citizen Army man, William Partridge, had gone down to Fenit in Kerry to meet the arms ship.

Partridge's instructions were to land the arms and, using trade union labour, commandeer trains to get the guns to Cork, Limerick and Dublin. When the arms landing failed, Partridge went back up to Dublin and reported the failure to Connolly.[15] This sequence of events tied in with the timing of MacNeill's countermand and allowed the prosecution to argue, wrongly, that Partridge answered to MacNeill, who had only issued the countermand because the arms landing had failed.[16]

MacNeill was in a desperate bind. The truth of the matter was that he was not the prime mover, nor was he even part of the inner circle that planned the Rebellion. He could fairly say that the Army had shot all the principal witnesses that might have helped his case: Pearse, Connolly, Plunkett and Clarke, in particular. A few others, who had witnessed the deception played on MacNeill, were lying low or scattered in prisons and internment camps in England.

MacNeill later recalled that his position was made worse by Major Kimber, who, time and again, added his weight to the prosecution.

MacNeill's position, already precarious, worsened when his lawyers called a series of witnesses to speak on behalf of the prisoner and to detail the circumstances in which the government had allowed private armies to spring up all over Ireland. It would seem the nuances of what took place were entirely lost on the Court.[17] The officers on the court martial probably took a robust view of the connection with Germany and the arms landing: in their minds Germany's assistance to Irish rebels was the same as the rebels intending to assist Germany.

Wylie later wrote that he had difficulties establishing a connection with Germany because the intelligence services had intercepted Casement's letters to MacNeill and, therefore, they could not be used against the prisoner. In fact, Casement, who was awaiting trial at Pentonville, wrote to MacNeill's lawyers offering to give evidence. He said MacNeill was 'not in the confidence' of the planners of the Rebellion.[18] There was no other witness who could prove that Pearse and his confidantes had hijacked the Volunteers and manoeuvred it into rebellion. MacNeill's counsel wisely took the view that they could not call Casement. There is no doubt, as history has shown, that Casement was entirely truthful but, as a disgraced knight of the realm, his credibility before a court martial would have been nil. What matters is not chiefly how a witness stands after his evidence but how he stands after cross-examination.

MacNeill was acquitted of rebellion but convicted on all the lesser charges and the court added a rider that the accused had committed all offences 'with the intention of assisting the enemy'.

MacNeill was sentenced to penal servitude for life and sent to Dartmoor to serve his sentence.

CHAPTER TWELVE

Captain John Bowen-Colthurst

With dark features and a grand moustache over a long face, he was prone to stooping on account of his immense height.

The Colthurst family owned Dripsey Castle in Cork and much farm land: there had been a family pew in the church at Magourney since the seventeenth century. Colthurst held a commission with the Royal Irish Rifles, he had served in the Boer War and Tibet but, despite his long service, he had not progressed beyond the rank of captain.

During long winter nights on the frozen plains of Tibet, he had slowly drifted away from the Church of Ireland and become 'a bible Christian'. He was briefly aide de campe to the Lord Lieutenant and, in 1914, when it seemed that Home Rule must come to pass, Colthurst joined the Curragh Mutineers – the group of army officers who offered their resignations rather than go to Ulster to face down Carson's Volunteers.[1] The crisis in the Army began to blow over as the threat of war with Germany loomed and Colthurst went to France with the British Expeditionary Force (BEF). He was briefly relieved of duty for disobeying a command and ordering his company to advance on the German Army. He was restored to his post and badly wounded in the chest. As the BEF fought a magnificent fighting retreat, Colthurst and many other wounded men were crammed into the back of a horse-drawn cart that bumped and jolted its cargo of bloodied, sweating young men across France.

He made a recovery but his psychological difficulties were more profound and his commanding officer judged him unfit to command troops on active service. He was stationed at Portobello Barracks with a reserve regiment and the Easter Rebellion marked his return to active service.

On the second day of the Rising, Colthurst's volatile personality surfaced with a vengeance. In front of many witnesses, he ordered a private soldier to club seventeen-year-old James Coade to the ground. As the boy lay unconscious on the ground, Colthurst shot him dead.

On the third morning, Colthurst arrived at the guard house at Portobello with a detail of seven soldiers. He had three prisoners brought out and invited to walk to the end of the yard. When they turned at the far wall, Colthurst ordered his men to fire and they did so, before the prisoners realised what was taking place.

One of the three men shot dead was Francis Sheehy-Skeffington, one of Dublin's great eccentrics, a bespectacled, bearded, 'slightly ridiculous figure' in knickerbockers sporting a 'votes for women' badge.[2] On the first day of the Rebellion he had gone to the aid of a wounded soldier despite the firing sweeping the streets. On the evening of his arrest, he had been walking home after trying to raise an anti-looting force among the citizens of Dublin. Behind him, a crowd of young children ran and skipped along, chanting his name. Inevitably he was picked up by the Army and he was held at Portobello Barracks.

Colthurst had collected up two other prisoners. One was James MacIntyre, a journalist who ran a small newspaper – a front for right-wing industrialists. The other was Thomas Dickson, a middle-aged Scot, a tiny wizened figure with a hunchback condition. A contemporary described him as being about four foot six, a grotesque figure in a black coat with curious eyes.[3] Dickson was not an insurgent. He was the editor of *The Eye-Opener*. Sex in the city was a favourite theme in his magazine. Under the surface of buttoned-down war-time Dublin, sexual infidelity and forbidden romances abounded. Dickson ran a small salacious rag that wrote about the affairs of married men and woman.[4] He had a knack for discovering the identity of couples illicitly sharing rooms at the Shelbourne or walking on the sea front. Sometimes it was enough to hint at the identity of the couple 'walking at Clontarf' to bring them to Dickson before the next edition. On payment of a suitable fee, the story was 'buried'. Financial scandals were another speciality of Dixon's. Just before the Rising, he had targeted a leading Dublin businessman and this time he had bitten off more than he could chew: he was charged with criminal libel.[5]

The shooting of these three men had far-reaching consequences. It seemed for a time that nothing would be done but for a coincidence of two factors. Sheehy-Skeffington's wife, Hannah, was a formidable woman, the sort that no one trifled with, and her father was a well-known Home Ruler Member of Parliament.

Sir Francis Vane, another of Dublin's great eccentrics, was also stationed at Portobello. Vane, a red-faced, portly fifty-something, learned of the shootings but, despite his remonstrations, Colthurst remained on duty at Portobello. Another officer recalled Colthurst's increasingly bizarre appearance: 'great black circles hung under his eyes'. He carried a rifle, a revolver and a bag filled with grenades. His giant stooping figure raged along the walls of Portobello Barracks. Occasionally, he led a raid on a suspected rebel household and his men remembered him because he showed not the slightest trace of fear. There is evidence that he carried out at least one other killing.[6]

A day after the shooting, Sir Francis noted the arrival of a detachment of Royal Engineers. They repaired the damaged bricks on the wall where the three men had been shot. It was night time, half the city centre was in ruins, snipers made any journey across Dublin dangerous, and it was an odd time to carry out a minor repair, Vane observed.

Vane's complaints were ignored at Portobello Barracks and he was soon relieved of his duties which were assigned to Colthurst. Vane went to army HQ at Parkgate but failed to get an interview with General Maxwell. He was told to speak to Major Price, the intelligence officer, who brushed him off with a brief aside: 'men like Skeffington were better off out of the way'.[7]

Sir Francis crossed over to London and saw Harold Tennant, Under Secretary for War. Only the day before, Tennant had told the House of Commons that the rumours of men being shot without trial were untrue. Vane was taken to see Lord Kitchener, Chief of the Imperial General Staff, who quickly began to lose his temper when the affair was related: 'Why is this man not under arrest?' It was this episode more than anything else that caused Asquith to curb the executions of insurgents in Dublin.[8]

Colthurst was put under arrest and preparations were made for trial. There was little enthusiasm in the Army for the prosecution of Captain John Bowen-Colthurst. General Maxwell had little choice but to convene a court martial and did so, although his private view was that Colthurst's history suggested 'madness'.[9] Maxwell inexplicably described Sheehy-Skeffington as 'a very poisonous person'.[10]

General Maxwell faced another battle to ensure that the prisoner was tried by the Army and not by a jury. There were doubts that a soldier could legally be tried by court martial for murder and steps were put in place to amend the Defence of the Realm Regulations (DORR) to cure this problem.[11]

Wylie, who had prosecuted most of the trials arising out of the Rebellion, declined to take the case for 'private reasons'. Wylie and Colthurst were part of the Irish ascendancy: both army officers; both hunted and both lived in Dublin and it is likely that they knew each other. The prosecution was taken over by Major Kimber.

Another officer who had just arrived in Dublin was Lord Cheylesmore, who had been sent to act as president in the forthcoming round of trials by General Court Martial (GCM). Lord Cheylesmore was a grenadier guards officer, a tall, gaunt figure and a well-known socialite. He had acquired a wealth of experience of courts martial work. Although he was not a lawyer, his grand manner brooked no dissent. A few years later he would achieve the dubious distinction of being the first peer of the realm to be killed in a car accident. During his stay in Dublin, he lodged with General Maxwell, the officer convening trials. They were gentlemen and, by the standards of the time, it was not thought improper.

The Trial

The trial was heard at Richmond Barracks in June 1916.

Lieutenant Samuel Morgan, adjutant of the Third Irish Rifles told the court that Colthurst had come to see him on the Wednesday of the Rebellion and reported that he had shot three prisoners.[12] He added that he had done so because he feared they would be rescued 'by armed force'. The accused added that he had lost a brother in the war and that 'he was as good an Irishman as the men he had shot'.

None of this evidence was disputed. Defence counsel, James Chambers KC, simply stressed the number of army casualties in Colthurst's battalion: an officer had been shot dead, four wounded and sixteen other ranks had been killed. The men in the barracks had been on duty for three days continuously. Lieutenant William Dobbin was called. He was still a teenager and only just commissioned. He testified that he had been in charge of the guard house when Colthurst arrived and said, 'I am taking these men out of the guard house and I am going to shoot them.' Colthurst added: 'I think it is the right thing to do.'

Sergeant Aldridge of the 10th Royal Dublin Fusiliers related what happened next:

'Captain Bowen Colthurst told the three men to go to the farther end of the yard, which they did. He then told all the men to load. To pull off the catch and pull the bolt out of their rifles. Then he told them to "present" and to "fire".'[13]

Lieutenant Dobbin went out into the yard and saw the bodies. Sheehy-Skeffington showed signs of life. He sent an orderly to report this and soon enough received orders to fire again.

'What did you do?'

'I stood by four men of my guard and I complied with the order.'

Colthurst gave no evidence in his own defence. His counsel called Colthurst's former commanding officer Major General Dent Bird, DSO. During the retreat from Mons, Bird had taken over the Royal Irish Rifles when his colonel had been killed. Later, after the Front had stabilised, Bird was wounded and lost a leg and had gone on to become a highly regarded staff officer.

Bird described Colthurst as 'eccentric'. At the battle of Mons, Bird had held his battalion in line but every time he moved away he found that Colthurst's company advanced on the enemy. When he asked the reason there was no reply. Finally, as he turned away, he heard Colthurst giving the order to advance in 'a weak voice'. He decided Colthurst should be suspended forthwith: 'he was quite broken down and unfit to lead troops'. Colthurst later returned to duty and was wounded some days later.

Bird ventured the opinion that 'when unusually fatigued and in a state of excitement' Bowen-Colthurst was 'not quite responsible for his actions'.

Another officer, Captain Edward Kelly, recalled seeing Colthurst at the barracks the night before the killings. 'He was half lying across the table, with his head resting on his arm. He looked up occasionally and stared around the room and then fell forward again with his head on his arm.'

Everyone who knew Colthurst reckoned him very odd.[14] And the defence called some of these people to give evidence. Major Goodman gave evidence for the accused, who he described as a kindly man capable of eccentric acts. Asked by the President of the Court, Lord Cheylesmore, to give an example, Major Goodman recounted that, while serving in India with Colthurst, they had been kept up all night by a howling dog. In the morning, Colthurst had gone out and shot the animal. He had not killed it but 'it was sufficiently wounded to die'. Having placed this endearing cameo before the court the character witness departed.

Four doctors gave evidence for Colthurst. One, Dr Parsons, had seen Colthurst in November 1914 when he returned from the Western Front. He was recovering from a wound and was in a state of 'marked nervous exhaustion'. He saw him again in February 1915 and he was still not fit for duty.

Dr Parsons saw Colthurst again a few days before the trial. He recounted that Colthurst was restless and excited. He did not appear to realise the serious nature of the charges against him and spoke about the fighting at Mons and the great retreat.

Colthurst also told Dr Parsons about the killing of the three men. He said he had gone to bed at about 3am and read his bible and came upon a passage which seemed to exercise 'a very powerful influence on his mind':

```
'And these my enemies which will not have me
to rule over them, bring them forth and slay
them.'
```

Colthurst told the Doctor that he had done his duty and that 'in any other country it would be recognised as right to kill rebels'.

Parsons concluded that 'his condition was far from normal' and that 'he was unbalanced'. Another Doctor who had sat in on the examination confirmed the findings of Doctor Parsons. Two army Doctors gave evidence concurring.[15]

The Verdict

Colthurst was found to be guilty on all three counts of murder but insane. The legal test for insanity was a high one: every man is presumed to be sane, and to possess a sufficient degree of reason to be responsible for his crimes until the contrary is proved; and to establish a defence on the grounds of insanity, it must be clearly proved that, at the time of committing the act, the accused was labouring under such a defect of reason, from disease of the mind, as not to know the nature and quality of the act he was doing or, if he did know it, that he did not know what he was doing was wrong.[16]

The key to this case is that the defence called four distinguished medical witnesses to testify that Colthurst was insane. The two army doctors called by the defence were originally instructed by the prosecution but, on examining the prisoner, found him to be insane. These witnesses were then 'given away' by the prosecution and called by the defence. The officers sitting on the court martial were presented with a fait accompli: the medical evidence was not contradicted by prosecution evidence. A verdict of guilty but insane became inevitable.

The Bowen-Colthurst affair has often been paraded as an example of the brutality employed by the British Army in suppressing the Rebellion and a whitewash afterwards. In fact, the actuality is far more subtle. Bowen-Colthurst was Irish, as were nearly all of the men and officers in Portobello Barracks and all of those who took part in the firing squad. As to the verdicts, all four doctors who gave evidence were distinguished practitioners and they were all Irish. The description of Colthurst was quite compelling: a man on the eve of his trial for murder rambling on about the retreat from Mons.

After the Rebellion, four soldiers were tried by GCM for murder. Each was represented by Kings Counsel and given every opportunity to prepare a defence. The contrast with trials of the prisoners tried in the aftermath of the Rebellion was not lost on the public.

What of the others bound up in this affair? In the summer, Lord Kitchener was drowned at sea and, after his passing, Sir Francis Vane found himself without friends in high places. He became a pariah and was quietly squeezed out of the Army.

Mrs Sheehy-Skeffington secured a Royal Commission into the death of her husband. She had significant political connections and used them to full effect and was vindicated by the Royal Commission.[17] But there were so many people killed by soldiers in the vicinity of Portobello Barracks, North King Street, Eden Quay and elsewhere. For these people there would be no Royal Commission.

The Colthurst family was boycotted and forced off their estates in Cork. Colthurst had been due to inherit Oakgrove House near Dripsey but this was burnt to the ground in 1920 to ensure he never returned. Colthurst was held at Broadmoor, where he had many visitors and was allowed to cycle around nearby villages. He fathered a child while in 'confinement'. In 1921, he was released and emigrated to Canada. Many years later he was recognised and hailed by a Cork émigré who recalled that Colthurst reached for his jacket pocket.

CHAPTER THIRTEEN

Sir Roger Casement

He stood alone in the sand dunes holding a sword stick in his hand and was drawing the blade in and out as he spoke. 'If you take that out,' said Constable Reilly, 'I shall have to fire my rifle.'[1] Casement surrendered. Many hours earlier, the dinghy had tipped over in the surf and he had come close to drowning. His clothes had dried slowly in the chill wind. He was unshaven, thirsty and he had not eaten or slept.

Many who saw him in better times turned to stare at this immaculately dressed and singularly graceful man. He had been a career diplomat in the British Consular Service. His exposure of human rights abuses in the Congo and atrocities against the Putumayos in South America gained international acclaim and the King conferred a Knighthood. In fact, although Casement's work brought him fame and a knighthood, it also shattered his settled outlook on life. He became an opponent of the Empire that lionised him: 'Charity begins at home but imperialism begins in another man's home' was one of his sayings.[2] He began to focus on Ireland, the country of his birth. When the government urged Irishmen to join up and fight Germany in the Great War in return for Home Rule, Casement described it as: 'a promissory note payable on death'.[3] It was in these circumstances that, in 1915, he went to Germany to organise a rebellion.

Casement and two companions left the port of Wilhelmshaven on 12 April 1916. They were aboard U-boat U-20 which had sunk the Lusitania some months before. U-20 encountered mechanical difficulties and returned to port. Casement and his companions, Bailey and Monteith, embarked on U-19 and made a crossing in wild seas round the Shetland Islands and down the west coast of Ireland.

Their progress was tracked by the British Fleet. The operation had been rumbled weeks before when British Naval intelligence intercepted communications to the German Embassy in Washington. One of the intercepted signals read:

'Between two or three steam trawlers could
land 20,000 rifles and 10 machine guns, with
ammunition and explosives at Fenit Pier in
Tralee Bay. Irish pilot boat to await the
trawlers at dusk... at the entrance to Tralee
Bay, and show two green lights close to each
other at short intervals...'[4]

The plan was monitored as it developed. When Casement left Wilhelmshaven, the Royal Navy knew and they knew about the arms ship and knew it would make landfall at Fenit in Kerry. They even knew the date of the landing.

In the early hours of Friday 21 April, U-19 surfaced in Tralee Bay two miles off Banna Strand. It was a cold moonlit night. A ship was moored about two miles away, close to the shoreline and it was believed to be the arms ship.

The mountains of the Dingle peninsula rose up to their right and before them lay a shadowy coastline rising out of the sea. The Kriegsmarine officers looked down from the conning tower as they edged ever closer to the shore. Here and there, the darkness was broken by the flickering lights of Saint Elmo's fire.

Casement and his two companions were given a small dinghy. They asked for an engine but this was refused in case the engine noise might alert a Royal Navy patrol. Captain Weisbach, the U-boat commander, reckoned the sea was calm enough and the three men were invited to row to shore. After they set off, Casement discovered that the oars were different lengths and the little boat travelled in circles until the men were exhausted.[5]

On that stretch of coastline the slow but powerful Atlantic swell is not apparent at sea. But closer to shore it often ends in boiling surf and, as they closed with the beach, the boat tipped over, Casement almost drowned and the three men came ashore exhausted. They attempted to sink the dinghy to cover their tracks but the tough rubber hull was resistant to every knife thrust.

This was the moment when the rebels' plans started to come undone. The *Aud*, the arms ship, had arrived an hour or so earlier and moored close to Castlegregory.[6] It failed to make contact with the Volunteers. The *Aud* turned for home and later that day was intercepted by British warships that had shadowed her for some days.

Four men had been sent down from Dublin to make contact with the *Aud* by radio transmitter. In the darkness, the car went off Ballykissane pier and three of the four men drowned. It was another needless tragedy because the *Aud* did not even have a wireless.

Casement was picked up by the Royal Irish Constabulary (RIC) within hours of landing. He gave a false name and kept his silence. He was moved to Dublin the next day and then to London where he was interrogated at New Scotland Yard on Easter Sunday by Basil Thomson, the Assistant Commissioner at New Scotland Yard, and Hall. Casement made full admissions and expressed no regret. Knowing that the Rebellion was hopelessly compromised, he asked to be allowed to make a public appeal to stop the insurrection. Captain Hall declined.

Casement's flat in Chelsea was searched and some locked trunks were found. 'There's nothing in them' Casement said but Basil Thomson had been tipped off that Casement had diaries which might be dynamite and his officers were already looking for them.

A few weeks later, Casement was committed for trial by the Grand Jury. He knew that his life was all but lost and he was resigned to that but he almost lost his composure when his counsel informed him the diaries were in the hands of the prosecution. He did not deny writing the diaries and did not suggest forgery. Casement intimated that, if the subject was brought up in the trial, then counsel should argue they were 'the manifestation of distinguished genius'.[7]

In the weeks before the trial the Attorney General, F.E. Smith, tried to persuade Casement's counsel, Sergeant Sullivan,[8] to inspect the diaries: they were available at the Home Office 'day and night'. Sullivan knew that the prosecution was anxious to get the diaries before the jury because the prejudice against homosexuality was so strong that this would discredit Casement and all those associated with him. But the diaries were not admissible to prove the prosecution case. In these circumstances, F.E. Smith hoped to persuade Sullivan to introduce the diaries himself, to argue that Casement was insane.[9] On the morning of the trial the prosecution tried again and sent junior counsel Travers Humphreys down with a full copy of the diaries. Sullivan refused to look at them and the jury never saw them.

Casement was tried at the Royal Courts of Justice on the Strand by Lord Chief Justice Reading and two High Court Judges with a jury.[10]

It is a curious irony that Casement had helped raise the Volunteers as a counter to the Ulster Volunteers. The Attorney General F.E. Smith, had joined the Ulster Volunteers as 'a galloper' and was ready to fight a rebellion against the government in 1914.[11] Both the Irish Volunteers and the Ulster Volunteers were illegal organisations but, by a fluke of history, it was the Irish Volunteers not the Ulster Volunteers who were pitched into rebellion.

So it was that F.E. Smith now prosecuted Casement. F.E. Smith, a tall, thin figure, addicted to alcohol and the demonstration of his own brilliance, cultivated a contemptuous manner and finished his opening with a flourish:

```
'the prisoner has played a great hazard. And
he has lost. Now the forfeit is claimed.'
```

Casement faced a charge under the *Treason Act* of 1351.[12] It alleged that he had tried to raise an Irish Brigade to fight against Britain and, while in Germany, he had organised the arms landing that would coincide with the Rebellion. In the quaint language of the indictment:

```
'intending to aid and assist the said enemies
of our Lord the King against our Lord the King
and his subjects, did traitorously adhere to
and aid and comfort the said enemy in parts
beyond the seas without this realm of England,
to wit, in the empire of Germany...'
```

Casement's capture near Banna Strand was related to the jury along with the finding of a dinghy, three Mauser pistols and some maps. On his way to the RIC station, he was seen to discard a piece of paper which contained entries in a crude code. One of the entries read:

```
'Send more explosives.'
```

Another:

```
'Cannons with plenty of ammunition are needed.'
```

In Casement's pocket was found a railway sleeper ticket from Berlin to the port of Wilhelmshaven, a notable U-boat base.

His connection with the arms shipment was proved by leading seaman Sidney Waghorn of *HMS Bluebell*. Waghorn related the interception of the *Aud* on Good Friday coming from Tralee. The ship was scuttled the following morning as it was being escorted to Cork harbour.

Waghorn was cross-examined up hill and down dale about the time the *Aud* had been intercepted, its location and the course taken by *HMS Bluebell*, along with other matters of that kind. To all these questions he could give no answers. In a case of this gravity one might expect the Navy to send an officer to give evidence.[13] However, the fact that the Royal Navy had access to German codes was a military secret of huge importance and it had to be concealed. If the Navy sent an officer to give evidence, he might be asked some difficult questions: how did the Navy know about the arms ship? When did the Navy know about the arms ship? Had it been the Navy's intention to allow the shipment to land? So the Navy sent leading Seaman Sidney Waghorn, who could only tell the bare facts.[14]

A Navy diver, John Dempsey, told the court that he had dived and found the wreck in over seventeen fathoms. There was a large hole in the hull and he had seen rifles and ammunition scattered on the sea floor.

He retrieved one of the rifles which he produced to the court. The rifles were obsolete, single-shot, Russian guns seized on the Eastern Front. Even if distributed in numbers they would not have posed a threat against the British Army.

The rest of the witnesses were former prisoners of war who had been repatriated to Britain during a prisoner exchange. Corporal James O'Connor was one. O'Connor was from Wexford, he was in his forties, a veteran of the Boer War. He had gone to France in August 1914 with the BEF and lost an arm in the retreat from Mons. He was taken prisoner. O'Connor described Casement's efforts to recruit prisoners of war to join an Irish Brigade. Many of the prisoners 'booed and hissed' Casement when he came on a recruiting drive. The prisoners were deliberately starved to induce them to join Casement's Irish Brigade. For months their captors dangled the prospect of good food and warm clean uniforms and it became a cruel test of fortitude and loyalty. But of the 2,500 Irish prisoners at the camp, only fifty-two took up Casement's offer.

Corporal Robinson related how Casement was 'shoved' by a prisoner and, as an ugly incident threatened, 'the German guard got him away'. A Dragoon Sergeant who called Casement a traitor was removed for punishment. Some of these prisoners of war were disabled by war service and their accounts speak of intense hunger, cold and loyalty.

As the evidence emerged, it became clear that Casement had no factual defence to this charge and there was little cross-examination. At the close of the prosecution case Sergeant Sullivan launched a legal argument which challenged the indictment. Sullivan's submission recognised that, when the statute was passed into law, many of the Barons had lands in France and England and owed allegiance to both monarchs of England and France. The Barons were called upon to supply troops to both in time of war. The statute, argued Sullivan, did not intend to encompass those who gave comfort to the King's enemies while outside the realm: all the overt acts of treason relied on by the Crown had been done outside the King's realm.

The submission lasted for many hours and traversed many ancient legal cases. Ultimately, it would all turn on the punctuation and meaning of a single phrase of an ancient statute in Norman-French.

Lord Chief Justice Reading was not impressed by the argument. His view was expressed succinctly: 'If a British subject does an act which strengthens or tends to strengthen the enemies of the King in the conduct of a war against the King that in law is the giving of aid and comfort to the King's enemies.'

Casement made an unsworn statement from the dock. He did not deny trying to bring about rebellion in Ireland. He denied that the Irish prisoners of war had been given less food than others to persuade them to join the Irish Brigade: food shortages were the result of the British Navy blockade. Finally he stated: 'the rebellion was not made in Germany, and that not one penny of German gold went to finance it'.

Sullivan's closing speech rambled far and wide. He even touched on the Ulster Volunteer Force (UVF) arms landing which kick-started the whole affair. The Attorney General, F.E. Smith, rose at once and objected that there was no evidence about the UVF arms landing before the court. What is evidence in a criminal trial and what is in fact true may be very different. F.E. Smith was right that there was no evidence about it and that was just as well because he himself had been complicit in arming the UVF.

Sullivan collapsed on the final morning of the trial. In Dublin, he was a very big fish in a small pool but he had found this trial an overwhelming strain. He would not recover for some months. His junior counsel took over but it was a lost cause.

Casement was convicted. He was given a chance to speak before sentence and did so. He told the court that his involvement in the Volunteers was a matter of principle but he taunted the Attorney General over his involvement in the UVF and stated bluntly that it was

```
'a path to the woolsack'.
```

F.E. Smith was a man incapable of personal embarrassment but it was hardly wise to bait him while he still had some influence over whether Casement lived or died. The Lord Chief Justice donned the black cap and sentenced Casement to be hanged.

A few weeks later, the Court of Appeal dismissed Casement's appeal. The trial and the appeal were conducted according to law and no complaint can be made about that.[15] At that time an appeal to the House of Lords could only be made if the Attorney General gave his consent. The Attorney General, F.E. Smith, had prosecuted the case and he now withheld his consent.

A campaign was gathering pace to have Casement reprieved. It was put about by his supporters that he had come over to stop the Rising. The Kriegsmarine would hardly have brought him to Ireland if that were the case. In fact, he had come over to meet the arms ship and he was equipped with a gun, a flag and codes to allow him to send for munitions. The overwhelming inference is that he came to fight but his conduct, once arrested, suggests that he realised the Rebellion would fail and attempted to stop it taking place and asked his captors to allow him to make a public appeal. The Cabinet authorised a discreet press campaign to put the government case before the public.[16]

The diaries were already circulating in the press and were shown to opinion formers. It is not clear who made the decision to use the diaries in this way but it was sufficient to undermine the campaign for a reprieve and Casement was hanged at Pentonville Prison on 3 August.[17]

Trials 1918

CHAPTER FOURTEEN

Joseph Dowling

He became known as the man in the submarine. The prisoner had been picked up on Crab Island on the west coast by a fisherman. His feet were wet but not his clothes. His name was O'Brien, he said. His story about being torpedoed while crossing the Atlantic on *SS Mississippi* began to unravel when he was unable to name the captain of the ship. He was brought over to London and, during interrogation by Captain Hall of Naval Intelligence, he admitted that his real name was Joseph Dowling of the Connaught Rangers. He had been a prisoner of war until he joined Casement's Irish Brigade. He had been sent over by submarine to make contact with the rebels and organise an arms shipment.

His capture had triggered the German Plot which resulted in seventy-three leaders of the anti-conscription campaign being arrested and interned. Dowling was sent to the Tower of London to await trial. There was no operational need to put him in the Tower; it was just an old-fashioned way of telling the prisoner he was in a great deal of trouble. There was still a difficulty about proof. The admissions that Dowling made during interrogation had been secured by a promise that his life would be spared if he 'came clean'. What he said under interrogation could not be used in court so an inspector of police eavesdropped on his conversations with family visitors at the Tower.

The government wished to give the widest audience to this trial, to demonstrate that the German plot was real and not simply a device to intern opponents of conscription. Unlike many courts martial of this period, the proceedings were in public and in a court that was readily accessible to the press: the Guildhall court had the largest public gallery in London and was centrally placed on the edge of Westminster Square. Here, the prisoner was tried by General Court Martial (GCM).[1] Lord Cheylesmore presided.

The prisoner was thirty-two, slight in build, of medium height, a man with a 'wide awake' look. He was brought into court cuffed to a soldier and escorted by a non-commissioned officer holding a revolver.

He faced three charges: voluntarily joining a hostile force, namely Casement's Irish Brigade; voluntarily aiding the enemy by persuading others to join and going to Ireland in a German submarine with the intention of aiding the enemy. To these charges he pleaded not guilty.

He was prosecuted by Sir Archibald Bodkin, now remembered for prosecuting the brides in the bath murders and Carl Hans Lody, the first German spy to be shot in the Great War. Bodkin was a man born to prosecute – he never took defence work. A burly figure with an overbearing manner, he could not quite be described as top flight but he was famous for his meticulous preparation. In 1918, he was Treasury Counsel at the Old Bailey when he was called upon to prosecute Joseph Dowling before a GCM. No special skills were required for this prosecution because the evidence was overwhelming.

Thomas Lynch, a fisherman from Doolin, told the court that they had found him on Crab Island and taken him to the mainland where the prisoner gave them five shillings.

William Healy, a clerk at the National bank at Enistymon, said that the prisoner came to the bank and changed wet discoloured silver from a canvas bag to the value of £31. 'The stranger' bought some clothes and was soon picked up by the Royal Irish Constabulary (RIC). He gave the name O'Brien and said he was working his passage on *Mississippi* from Baltimore to Liverpool when the ship was torpedoed. He climbed aboard a small boat and was washed up at Crab Island.

Major Charles Williams was called to disprove this account. He told the court that his inquiries showed that there were two ships registered as the *Mississippi*; one was French and one British and both were currently in dry dock.

Alexander Ford, chairman of the Ford Boat Company, told the court that the dinghy found was a hastily improvised boat which was not made in Britain or America.

Inspector Parke of New Scotland Yard related that, while the prisoner was awaiting trial in the Tower, his brother was brought to see him and, during the visit, the inspector eavesdropped. He heard the prisoner say to his brother 'I had a fine trip on a submarine – some trip.'

Evidence was given by Irish soldiers who had been held at Limberg prisoner-of-war camp. One, John O'Sullivan, told the court that they had arrived at Limberg 'falling on our knees with hunger'. They were brought to see Dowling and two officers in a room. On the table between them were cigars and beer. Those who were prepared to join the Irish Brigade were given a uniform, good food and accommodation. He and most of the others gave these men short shrift.

One ex-prisoner, John Cronin, related that Dowling had been assaulted by other soldiers and ran to his German captors for protection.

Dowling gave no evidence in his defence and made no statement from the dock. His counsel, Holman Gregory, Kings Counsel, had little to say in closing.[2] Dowling was convicted and sentenced to death. Sentence was commuted to penal servitude for life.

Dowling was the very last prisoner released after the conflict. He remained inside during the War of Independence and the Civil War that followed. When he emerged, the world had moved on.[3] Dowling's erstwhile prosecutor, Sir Archibald Bodkin, had become Director of Public Prosecutions and was defending civilisation against other potent threats, notably obscene literature.[4] His wrath was greatest against lesbian tracts which he viewed as a cause and symptom of mental illness.

Trials 1919

CHAPTER FIFTEEN

The Silvermines Case

Metal ores have been mined in the Silvermines Mountains since the fourteenth century. Just north of the mountain range is the small village to which Henry Sheahan, of the King's Own Yorkshire Rifles, came home on leave from Flanders. He brought his rifle with him as was the custom of the time. He went out for the evening leaving his elderly father and mother at home. What took place there became known as the Silvermines tragedy. The prosecution of three young men for the murder of an old man gripped the nation for many months.[1]

On the night of 2 January 1918, three masked men entered the Sheahan house and old George ran to secure the rifle. He struggled with one of the attackers for possession of the gun and, in the fracas, three revolver shots rang out. Sheahan died from a wound to the stomach and another to the forearm which bled profusely. The three raiders ran.

The O'Brien brothers were arrested. Pat and John were national school teachers who lived a few miles away. William worked at the post office where his father was post master.

They were brought to the courthouse at Nenagh where their supporters massed outside. The murder of Old George Sheahan was widely condemned but the prosecution of the three young men brought huge crowds to the court house, where there were running battles with the police. Finally, the Royal Irish Constabulary (RIC) cleared the street with a series of bloody baton charges.

To avoid further disorder, the committal hearing was convened at the governor's office at Limerick Gaol before Major Dease[2] a curmudgeonly Resident Magistrate (RM) of the Somerville and Ross variety. The RMs' pay was slim but the duties were light: assault cases and trespass actions were the lot of an Irish RM. All that had begun to change: the office of RM no longer carried respect; it was just an unpleasant and increasingly dangerous post. Major Dease himself, in the early days, had been a senior ranking Volunteer.[3] Now, the country seemed to be tearing itself apart.

The prisoners were brought in on stretchers having gone on hunger strike. Widespread disorder was imminent and Major Dease took the only sensible step: he adjourned the case back to a courthouse and the hunger strike was brought to an end.

John and William O'Brien were tried at Cork at the summer Assizes.[4] Mr Justice Dodds summed up for a conviction but the jury hung and, at the re-trial, the next jury also hung. The Attorney General certified the re-trial should take place in the north of Ireland where juror demographics favoured the Crown. This was resisted by the defence.[5] The High Court ended this tug of war by ordering a trial at the Four Courts before a special jury, qualified to serve by ownership of property.

At the start of the re-trial, the prosecution asked that John and William be tried for a third time and that the case against Patrick be put back again. Tim Healy KC resisted this, pointing out that Patrick had been waiting his trial in custody for eighteen months. Chief Justice Molony declined to split the defendants and the prosecution promptly offered no evidence against Patrick: there was no evidence against him. Healy shook his head: 'Eighteen months in gaol and no trial.'

The trial against the other two men turned to the empanelment of the jury. In England, the trial commenced with the swearing of the jury, though there is an old adage in Ireland that twisted this to quip that the trial ended with the swearing of the jury. The prosecution could 'standby jurors' without showing cause and, in days gone by, this had been used as a means of packing juries.[6] But every prisoner possessed twenty challenges without having to 'show cause' and this helped redress the balance and, in cases with a political dimension, it had become a means of ensuring that the outcomes were determined by latent political loyalties.

This tactic had been pursued by the prosecution and the defence during the trials at Cork. Both prosecution and defence could inspect the jury panel list which included names, addresses and occupation of jurors, details which were usually enough to determine the affiliations of jurors. Where there was any doubt, it was often dispelled by the demeanour of the juror at court, the newspaper he carried, the clothes he wore or the badge in his lapel.

When the case was transferred to Dublin the position was rather more difficult for the defendants because a panel of 300 special jurors had been summoned from County Dublin. The panel was far too large for the defence to vet and that might have been the point in summoning so many.

In any event, these were special jurors: men with land and money and a stake in the status quo. One special juror was probably much like another.

Healy challenged the entire array of jurors on the grounds that the Sheriff had improperly summoned the panel. The challenge was a technical one and the complaint was without substance and smacked a little of desperation.

The prosecution was able to rely on the RIC to supply information about the jury pool and, in accordance with the usual practice, 'stood by' eighty-nine of the jurors in the selection process that followed, including all those of Jewish extraction – of which there were a surprisingly large number. The decision to 'stand by' these jurors probably arose from a perception that most Jews supported the Zionist cause which had received much publicity at Versailles. It was thought that Irish Jews were, therefore, likely to support the principle of self-determination and, therefore, favour the prisoners.

Both defendants used their full complement of challenges to remove forty jurors. The evidence then began. The widow Sheahan described the raid by three masked men. Two of them 'middling tall', their coats and caps had been turned inside out and one carried a bike lamp. She told the court her husband had been killed trying to hold onto his son's rifle.

RIC Sergeant Daughton visited the Sheahan address after the killing. He found a piece of tweed in the bedroom where the old man's body lay. Fragments of a bike lamp were found.

He also found a cap and a watch and chain which he said he knew belonged to John O'Brien who lived only a few miles away. John O'Brien was picked up at home. He was not wearing his usual watch and chain, the officer noted. John O'Brien told the officer he 'would not say anything that would implicate others. He knew he was a marked man but he was innocent.'

Close by the house the officers found blood on a stone and in a ditch, the imprint of five fingers left when the attackers made off. A boot print found in the ditch was a perfect match for the left boot of John O'Brien.

Lord Chief Justice Molony: 'How was it you did not take a wax impression of the footprint?'

Sergeant Daughton: '…the ground was very soft by this little stream and the footprints were on a slope…'

Lord Chief Justice Molony: 'You had the wax at Nenagh?'

Sergeant Daughton: 'Yes.'

William was also linked by forensic evidence. The piece of tweed found at the house was a good match for a torn area of his coat pocket. When questioned, he told the officer he 'had not been out after ten'. A search of his house revealed two bikes but only one bike lamp: it was an inference that the other lamp had been damaged in the struggle and discarded. Also found concealed behind some trunks was a mask.

Old George Sheahan made a statement before he died but it was not established that he knew he was dying and the evidence was ruled inadmissible by Lord Chief Justice Molony.

There were other shortcomings in the Crown case: there was no evidence that either prisoner had any injury and nor was their clothing stained with blood. A wool merchant was called to prove the tweed left at the scene had come from William O'Brien's coat but it transpired that the witness had a government contract to supply police uniforms. His credibility finished at very low ebb.

The defendants gave no evidence: the law in Ireland did not permit a prisoner to give sworn evidence on his own behalf.

In his closing speech, Healy barely touched on the evidence. He asserted the prosecution had wasted much public money by summoning so many special jurors for the trial and challenging off eighty-nine. He hinted, without blushing, that the prosecution had manipulated the trial process by seeking a special jury and by standing by jurors of independent mind. The question obliquely posed by Healy was: Are you independent?

Whether this argument proved persuasive cannot be known. There were other factors at work. Molony's reputation as a 'hanger' was well-known and, in the mind of some, the charge smacked of manslaughter by one prisoner, not murder by two. Ultimately, the jury failed to agree. The O'Brien brothers spent some more months in custody before the prosecution finally dropped the case.[7]

In later years, Patrick O'Brien wrote a very full account of his trial for murder, implying but never stating his innocence: he railed against the perfidy of the prosecuting authorities and perjury by police officers. Curiously, O'Brien admitted to others that he and his brothers had carried out the raid and he himself had fired the fatal shots.[8]

This case had a wider significance. It had become impossible to secure convictions in cases arising out of the insurgency. This case was one in a long series of such trials. Where the charge was murder, the law required the case to be tried by a jury. In order to avoid a stalemate, the prosecution was increasingly driven to ask for a special jury or a change of trial venue. Even these steps were insufficient.

In non-capital cases, the charge could be formulated in such a way as to avoid jury trial altogether. This could be done by framing a charge under the Defence of the Realm Act so the prisoner could be tried by court martial. Alternatively, the case could be brought before by an RM which was a safe tribunal but the penalties were far less.

The reluctance of juries to convict had two consequences. Firstly, it was driving the authorities to use special tribunals but this tactic caused resentment and was exploited for propaganda purposes by prisoners and their supporters. Secondly, as the conflict intensified, the failure to secure convictions in serious criminal trials helped foster a new dynamic: police reprisals against people and property.

Trials 1920

CHAPTER SIXTEEN

John Madden

Late on the night of 2 September 1919, a three-man Royal Irish Constabulary (RIC) foot patrol was passing through the small village of Lorrha in north Tipperary. A man stood up from behind a stone wall and shot Sergeant Brady dead.[1] Men hidden behind the wall called for the surrender of the other officers and both sides opened fire. Constable Foley was wounded and staggered off. The third constable, McCormack, opened fire with his carbine and drove off the attackers.

John Madden was arrested for complicity in this ambush. The Madden family was from Galway, where the father had been a herdsman. He retired and took his family to live in Tipperary. The son, John, was twenty-eight years old, a labourer and lived with his parents. Like tens of thousands of other young men, he had been involved in the Volunteers.

Madden was taken before the court at Nenagh where depositions were taken before Resident Magistrate (RM) Dease. He was identified by Constable Foley as one of the men who had appeared behind the wall and fired. In a field close by a loaded shotgun was found and the ammunition in the gun resembled the pellets found in Sergeant Brady's chest. Madden was sent for trial at the Tipperary Assizes.[2]

This case was marked by the usual pre-trial manoeuvring. The prosecution sought and obtained a change of trial venue to Belfast, where the demographics of the jury pool were plainly unfavourable to the defence. The defence objected and the case was transferred to Dublin to be tried by Lord Chief Justice Molony.

By this time, another witness had come forward, namely John Gilligan, an ex-soldier who had allegedly been present with the ambush party. Now, in addition to implicating Madden, he named his nephew James Carroll, as one of the ambushers. Like many informants, Gilligan was a malleable man, without land, a job or a trade.

The case was prosecuted by William Wylie who had just finished the Mac Curtain inquest. Against him was the same opponent, Patrick Lynch

KC. The trial took place in the old Green Street Courthouse. Built in the late eighteenth century, the neo-classical columns in white Portland stone had become blackened with soot and grime. Over the decades, the court had hosted many famous trials: the United Irishmen, Emmet, John Mitchel and the Young Irelanders, the leaders of the 1867 uprising. In years to come, the courthouse would be used to try insurgents captured in the Civil War and, later, in the 1970s, it would become the home of the Special Criminal Court. In 1920, the courthouse was used to try John Madden for the murder of Sergeant Brady.

Madden, a slightly-built young man, arrived at court for the trial in an open-topped army lorry, handcuffed and guarded by soldiers. A detachment of armed soldiers lined one wall of the court.

Constable Foley told the jury that after the first volley he had turned and saw a man shouting 'hands up'. He was able to get a good look at this man and recognised him as Madden before he, Foley, was wounded.

Foley's view was enhanced by a full moon, although evidence was adduced that the full moon had set at 10.22pm, over an hour before the ambush. Foley readily agreed he had been drinking before going on duty: eight pints that day. He knew Madden because they had been vying for the affections of the same girl. Constable Foley asserted that he could also recognise Madden because, a few weeks before the ambush, he had issued him with a summons for failing to show a light on his bike.

John Gilligan was then called to give evidence. He had made a full statement setting out the detail of the ambush in a way which dovetailed with the evidence of the officers. It emerged that this was his second statement and that the officers investigating the case had suppressed his first statement which set out a very different account. Prosecuting counsel William Wylie recalled:

```
'It looked like a cast iron case to me. When
I was stating the case to the jury one half
of my brain registered a conversation between
two police officers behind me about a second
statement. When I sat down I asked the county
inspector whether the witness had made a second
statement. He said he had. I asked for it and
read it hurriedly. It was completely different
```

from the other one and it was made first....
I handed it over to the defending counsel.'[3]

Wylie was an old-fashioned prosecutor who believed that he had a duty to disclose to the defence material which undermined the prosecution case. He handed the statement over to his opponent, Patrick Lynch, who cross-examined Gilligan into the ground.

Lynch called Madden's mother and father. Thomas Madden and his wife Anne established an alibi that their son had been at home on the night of the shooting. Lynch was able to argue to the jury that the evidence was tainted by investigators who had concealed evidence which might exonerate the accused. Gilligan, he told the jury, was 'a contemptible specimen of humanity' who could not be relied upon.

Lord Chief Justice Molony summed up even-handedly, inviting the jury to disregard Gilligan's evidence. The case, he said, rested on Constable Foley's identification of the accused which was unsupported by other evidence. Madden was acquitted after less than half an hour.[4]

The police officers involved in the case thought that Madden was a guilty man who had walked free. Their opinion was shared by many other officers who criticised the investigating officers for mishandling the investigation.

Had Madden been convicted there is little doubt that he would have been hanged because this was a premeditated murder of a police officer carried out in order to steal arms to further the insurgency. Here, however, is a vital detail: Madden had not been present at the ambush. This reflects another of the complexities and ambiguities of the time: he was a Volunteer but tens of thousands of young men had been Volunteers. Many young men enjoyed the uniforms, the parades, the camaraderie and the social life but most took no part in the insurgency. He was also a garrulous and self-opinionated young man. The ambushers were all local Volunteers but Madden was not in their confidence and there is no doubt that Madden was not present at the ambush.[5]

The RIC had the greatest difficulty in finding witnesses to come forward and support prosecutions. In their anxiety to convict a man that they believed to be guilty, the police had subverted the law. The attempt to suppress evidence that favoured a man on trial for his life got the widest publicity.

The justice system was falling apart because witnesses would not come forward and, even where there was evidence, juries would not convict. The collapse of the case against Madden coincided with the decision of the Viceroy to free hundreds of prisoners on hunger strike. RIC men were left exposed by the weakness of the government and the shortcomings of the justice system. These events were fuelling police reprisals which became a crucial dynamic in the conflict.

CHAPTER SEVENTEEN

Michael O'Rourke

Michael O'Rourke was tried in late November 1920 at what was then Marlborough Barracks for the murder of a soldier, Private William Rogers of the Machine Gun Corps.[1]

The trial arose out of an ambush on 29 July 1920. An army cycle patrol, under the command of Lieutenant Wilkinson of the Machine Gun Regiment, was ambushed near Bruree in Limerick. Private Rogers and Constable Murray were at the head of the line when a shot was fired. Rogers fell wounded and the rest of the party took refuge in a nearby cottage. The ambushers disappeared before army reinforcements arrived[2] and arrested O'Rourke at his home.

Constable Murray, who had been close to Private Rogers at the time of the shooting, did not identify the accused but the court admitted a dying declaration from the dead soldier who had identified the accused: 'That's the bloke that shot me.' Another soldier, who had survived, also identified O'Rourke. The prisoner had been arrested at home but no arms or ammunition were found there. The case rested on the identification evidence.

The prosecution case closed on Saturday 20 November and resumed on the Monday when the court heard that Captain Baggally, who had prepared the case, had been shot 'and foully murdered in front of his wife'. Baggally had been one of the many officers killed that weekend.

Opening the case for the prisoner, Michael Comyn KC remarked: 'We meet on the morrow of the slaughter.' The officers killed on Bloody Sunday were colleagues of the officers trying the case and some would have been acquainted.

The prisoner's case was that he lived close to the scene of the ambush with his widowed mother, brother and sister. He had been 'saving hay' in the meadow and hearing the shots looked over the hedge at the ambush in progress. He asserted that he was not a member of any illegal organisation.

His mother gave evidence that her sons were saving hay when she heard shooting. She sent her daughter to bring the boys in and they came into the house. The Army arrived soon after. She told the officer: 'The handcuffs are going on an innocent boy.' The officer replied: 'If there is nothing against him then you will have him home again.'

A lay magistrate gave evidence for O'Rourke. He told the court that the identity of those involved in the insurgency was well-known in his area and the accused was not one of them.

Counsel Michael Comyn KC later recalled that despite the events of Bloody Sunday, he received a patient and fair hearing.[3] O'Rourke was acquitted.[4]

CHAPTER EIGHTEEN

Countess Constance Markievicz

Constance Markievicz was tried in November 1920 at the Royal Barracks.[1] For centuries the Royal Barracks had been the main garrison for British troops in Dublin. Wolfe Tone was tried there in 1798. Troops from the Royal Barracks had fought the Fenians and later turned out on Easter Monday 1916 to lay siege to the Mendicity and the Four Courts.

Markievicz was charged with conspiring with other persons to promote Fianna Éireann which was alleged to be concerned with the murder of policemen and soldiers, the unlawful drilling of men and the carrying of firearms.[2]

The trial record shows:

> 'The accused was accommodated at a table, and behind her sat an armed guard and a wardress. When asked to plead, Madam Markievicz declined to recognise the court and a plea of "not guilty" was formally entered.'

The Army lacked officers with legal skills to prosecute these cases and members of the Irish Bar were no longer prepared to take the work. Quite a number of Old Bailey counsel were brought over to prosecute cases arising out of the insurgency. This trial was prosecuted by Travers Humphreys KC who appeared before the court martial in wig and gown, as was the custom of the time. Humphreys was a slim, tall figure. He had made his name prosecuting big cases at the Old Bailey, including Oscar Wilde and Casement. It was not loyalty or national sentiment that brought Humphreys and other advocates over from London: it was money. Prosecuting these cases was dangerous work but well paid. Counsel were brought over to Dublin by destroyer and billeted at army

HQ at the Royal Hospital and ferried back and forth to the court martial by armoured car.

As the conflict wore on, officers trying these cases no longer gave their names in court, as was customary. The names of prosecuting counsel were blotted out of the trial record. The rule against taking photos in court had not yet been introduced but, in these cases, the press was forbidden to use cameras or name witnesses.

Markievicz had been on the wanted list for some time and, although Dublin was a small city, it was a labyrinth to the Army. Markievicz was only picked up by a fluke: a car was stopped for 'not showing a tail light'[3] and she was found to be a passenger and her address was traced.

An unnamed Lieutenant gave evidence that, on 6 September, he took a 'raiding party' to 25 Nassau Street, Dublin and, on the top floor, discovered a large trunk. He identified a number of documents which he found in the box. One was headed 'Fianna Éireann' and was signed 'Constance de Markievicz'. He also identified a certificate which was signed by the accused. It expressed appreciation of the work done by a person 'who was in action in 1916'.

A minute book, which a witness found on the floor beneath, was also identified. Some of the minutes were signed 'Constance de Markievicz'. Among the documents was one which included reference to the establishment of Fianna Éireann. Its object was declared to be the re-establishment of an independent state. Another seized document stated that the aim of the organisation was to have 'always ready a well-trained body of Boy Scouts, who could take their place on the field of war'.

Other documents referred to company and infantry training. One stated: 'We have found this game of dodging the soldiers is in itself the best possible training we can give the boys.' The document also stated that their aim was to train their boys as infantry scouts.

Another army officer stated that he was in charge of a patrol on September 27 when he found that the accused, with three men, had been taken into custody by police. He took her to the Bridewell. While the men were being searched he had a conversation with the accused and she was rather free with her comments.

Prosecuting Counsel Travers Humphreys KC: 'Were they all voluntary observations?'

'Yes. She said that she shot a soldier, and the last time she was captured by a policeman he was "put away".'

Replying to a member of the court, the witness said that he had understood by this that, in using the phrase 'put away', the accused had meant that the policeman had been shot.

Continuing, the witness said that the accused also stated that: 'If every Englishman had three necks she would cut them all.' While being escorted to the Bridewell she said that British soldiers, or the majority of them, were always willing to sell their rifles.

When Madam Markievicz rose about to address the court, she was asked by the President if she would care to have her table removed to where the sun would not be in her eyes. An opportunity for drama had arisen and she seized her chance: 'I rather like the sun. I have not seen it in two months'.

She continued: 'I am only one woman against a dozen men.'[4] In point of fact, she appeared unrepresented by choice. Her solicitor was in the public gallery. If she needed representation or legal advice, it was readily available.[5] Throughout her trial she was afforded every courtesy.

She emphasised her resentment against having words put into her mouth, saying that she believed they were calculated to incite people to murder her. Already she had received some documents signed by the 'Black Hand Gang', threatening her life.

'With emotion' the accused repudiated the suggestion that she was responsible for the shooting of some policeman who arrested her. No policeman ever treated her like the officer who arrested her, she declared. When first he questioned her she thought he was a spy, then she thought he was ashamed of himself, or a fool or that he was drunk. She was dead tired at the time, having had nothing to eat. 'I admit being nervous' she said, 'and I answered the questions to put him off.'

The Judge Advocate then summed up and the court closed and found her guilty. After a short adjournment, the court re-opened and counsel produced evidence of prior character: a conviction in May 1916 for rebellion. Then, the death sentence had been commuted to penal servitude for life but she had been released under the general amnesty. In this trial, the court imposed two years' penal servitude.

Brigadier Ormonde Winter, who interrogated her after her arrest, wrote that she was 'hard and unrepentant but loquacious'.[6] All of that seems right. She had learned that, in order to make some young men fight, one must first make them hate the enemy. It is probable that, during her trial, she disavowed killing only because of fears for her own personal safety. Markievicz had been in custody for two months awaiting trial and, in that time, Dublin had become a frightening city. Only weeks before, many officers of the British Secret Service had been killed by Collins' men. Nearly every day people were being shot down in the street or in their homes. Sometimes it was not possible to say why some were gunned down or who had shot them. Earlier that year, the Lord Mayor of Cork had been shot in his home late at night and the Lord Mayor of Limerick would soon be killed in similar circumstances as well. The Igoe Gang and the Cairo Street Gang walked the streets terrorising and killing. There had arisen other shadowy groups like the Black Hand Gang: a front for disaffected policemen who shot down those the law could not touch. Markievicz and her comrades had unravelled the law and no one was safe.

There have been so many criticisms of Markievicz: that she was a snob, that she was not a countess or that she shot down Michael Lahiff, an unarmed policeman stationed at Saint Stephen's Green on Easter Monday. There is something in all these points: she was a snob and was certainly not a countess by birth or marriage. She had certainly given away much of her personal wealth. She was at Stephen's Green on Easter Monday 1916 when she was armed and wore a dramatic uniform:

'A wide awake hat whose leaf was pinned up on one side by the flaming badge of the red hand – the insignia of Larkin's union: on her left breast was an immense tara broach of beaten silver.'[7]

But here legend collides with what can be ascertained: there is no evidence that she shot Constable Michael Lahiff, although he was undoubtedly killed by one of the rebel party occupying the Green. A bronze to Madame Markievicz now stands on the Green but there is nothing at all to remember Lahiff.

Famously, William Wylie, who prosecuted the 1916 trials, recounted in his memoir that she had begged for her life: 'I am only a woman, you cannot shoot a woman. She never stopped moaning the whole time...'[8] This version was put about by Wylie after the trial and was written up in the diary of Elsie Mahaffy, the daughter of the provost at Trinity. Historians have used one source to corroborate the other although both versions came from Wylie who had been living at Trinity during the Rising and knew the Provost and his family well. Wylie hated Markievicz and all she stood for. The trial record, written up contemporaneously by General Blackader, contradicts all of what Wylie said. If the prisoner had begged for clemency he would surely have recorded that.

She is venerated by some as a champion of the poor and the first woman to be elected to Westminster. But for others she remains 'a self indulgent blood thirsty show off who brain washed children into thinking they must die for Ireland'.[9]

CHAPTER NINETEEN

Father Patrick Delahunty

F ather Delahunty was tried by court martial at Waterford Barracks in December 1920. He was charged with 'possessing seditious documents issued by an illegal organisation, namely Dáil Éireann'.[1] The accused was not represented by choice. A not guilty plea was entered by the court.

An officer told the court that he had ordered a search of a house at West Street, Callan, where the accused had a room. An Auxiliary Cadet told the court that the search took place on 3 September and a great deal of correspondence was found, much of it from the Finance Department of Dáil Éireann in respect of the loan raised by the Dáil. The letters showed that Father Delahunty was coordinating the fundraising in Callan. One letter stated 'you will be glad to know that at the time of writing the Loan exceeds £262,000'. The letter was signed 'Michael Collins'.

At the close of the prosecution case, the accused told the court 'he had nothing to say'. He was found guilty and imprisoned for two years.[2]

The context of the trial concerned the national bond raised by the First Dáil. The Finance Minister was Michael Collins and, under his leadership, citizens were invited to loan money to the government on the security of a bond. The government at Westminster had declared the First Dáil an illegal organisation. In order to suppress the Dáil, it was necessary to cut off funding. It was an almost impossible task because a wide cross-section of society subscribed to the Dáil loan. Most did so out of conviction but a small number subscribed because they thought it was prudent to have a foot in both camps or because it might secure their safety from the insurgents.[3]

The Royal Irish Constabulary (RIC) broke up fundraising meetings – baton charges were not uncommon. A secondary tactic was to prosecute those who organised the bond. By late 1919, this policy had failed and the attention of Dublin Castle turned to seizing the Dáil funds from the banks. This inquiry ended with the killing of Resident Magistrate (RM) Bell in the spring of 1920 and the banking inquiry stalled. Prosecutions again focused on organisers of the Dáil loan. There are no reliable statistics on the number of prosecutions or sentences imposed for these cases but there were very many.[4] Suppressing the Dáil loan was part of the wider policy of suppressing the institutions of the new state. Prosecutions were brought against those who acted as officers of the Dáil:[5] clerks of the new courts,[6] judges of the Dáil courts,[7] police officers[8] or those possessing documents acknowledging the authority of Dáil Éireann.[9] Where there was suspicion but insufficient evidence, then internment usually followed.

Quite a number of the clergy were active supporters and organisers of the Dáil loan[10] but proving involvement was difficult. Delahunty was the only priest prosecuted for raising money for the Dáil.

At the time of his trial, Father Delahunty was forty years old, a native of County Kilkenny. He had been a founder member of the Volunteers. When the Great War broke out, he followed the Redmondite faction and urged men to join up. After Easter 1916, his view changed. He was soon faced with yet another life changing choice: following the instructions of the Catholic hierarchy to condemn the Rebellion or leading his parishioners in an armed conflict; he chose the latter course. He was not so much at odds with the Catholic Church; he simply went his own way. He took a full part in the War of Independence in Kilkenny.[11]

After his capture, he was one of many prisoners held in prison until the Dáil ratified the Treaty with Britain. After the Truce and before the Treaty was ratified, Father Delahunty and forty-six other prisoners tunnelled their way out of Kilkenny Gaol. According to a reliable account, Father Patrick was the first man through the tunnel: out of the darkness and into the light.[12] None of the prisoners was recaptured.

After the Civil War, the Catholic hierarchy moved Father Delahunty to America, where he became prison chaplain at Kansas Gaol. He became the confidante of death row prisoners, many of whom had learning difficulties. He attended many executions in that capacity.

CHAPTER TWENTY

Father Michael Ahern

This trial arose out of an ambush on an army lorry near Leary's Cross, County Cork on 10 December 1920. Leary's Cross stood in an isolated rural area at the junction of five roads. A group of Volunteers spotted the lorry by chance. As the lorry turned at the junction and began to gather speed, a small number of Volunteers were able to fire on the lorry bringing it to a halt.

About fifteen soldiers decamped and took up firing positions in the hedges by the road. A few appear to have frozen and remained crouched in the lorry.[1] The fighting lasted for over an hour. One soldier, Gunner Cambridge, was killed. Two soldiers were wounded and the rest retreated across country. A local man, Daniel Daly, was later arrested and sent for trial. He escaped soon after and was not recaptured.[2] The only other person tried was a priest who had come to the scene and given assistance to the wounded.

Father Michael Ahern was tried on 9 March 1921 at the Old Barracks, Fermoy, by Field General Court Martial. He was charged that 'knowing of an ambush by rebels on His Majesty's forces, he did deliberately fail and neglect to give full information to the competent military authority when required to do so'.[3]

The prisoner had been held in custody for three weeks. It seems that he had been arrested because the rebels had trenched the road near his house to disrupt military transport. The view of the Army was that citizens could not remain neutral: everyone had to render active assistance where it was possible to do so. Father Ahern had not reported the trenching of the road to the Army and was brought in for questioning.[4] After questioning a new and more serious charge was framed.

The substance of the charge against the prisoner was set out by an army officer who told the court that the accused had gone to the scene of an ambush and given aid and comfort to wounded soldiers. He was asked to tell an investigating officer what he knew about the ambush. He told the officer there was an armed man at the scene and he told him to go away:

'Have you not done enough?' The army witness stated that Father Ahern failed to state what must have been obvious: that he had seen the ambush party leaving the scene.

A soldier gave evidence that he was one of the army patrol ambush at Leary's Cross on 10 December. He had been wounded and, after the ambush, he had crawled over to another soldier who was also wounded. About four minutes after the ambush he saw the accused come riding up on a horse.

'He had water brought to us...and brandy.'

Question: 'What followed?'

Answer: 'Accused asked my religion and I replied Church of England. He asked my wounded comrade the same question and got the same reply. At that time there were about eight of the ambushers proceeding away towards Castlelyons.'

Question: 'Where did you first see those ambushers?'

Answer: 'They were on the road and were still armed. As they passed they raised their hats to the priest.'

Question: 'How were they armed?'

Answer: 'They had bandoliers and some had rifles.'

Question: 'Where was the accused then?'

Answer: 'My comrade and I were lying with our heads towards the road and the accused was leaning over my wounded comrade when the eight men passed.'

Cross-examined, the soldier told the court that the ambush had lasted over an hour and that his patrol had been gradually surrounded. When challenged, the soldier maintained that Father Ahern had cantered up only four minutes after the fighting ceased. He accepted that the accused had done everything possible for him and the other soldier: he remained there until the other soldier died.

A local man gave evidence. He told the court he lived four miles from the scene of the ambush and he was with the accused when they heard the shots.

Father Ahern's housekeeper gave evidence that, on the day of the ambush, Father Ahern had been at home when he learned of the ambush; he went straight out to the scene.

A final witness told the court he had come upon the aftermath of the ambush and seen two wounded soldiers. He saw Father Ahern go down on his knees and try to help the two men. He told the court that he had seen a man with a gun standing over Father Ahern who said 'Go away. You have done enough.' He said there were no other armed men there.

A lieutenant colonel gave character evidence for Father Ahern. The lieutenant colonel was an unusual character witness: he acknowledged he had only known the prisoner since his remand in custody. He told the court that the prisoner was held in high regard by his parishioners. This was, one suspects, an oblique way of telling the court that they were barking up the wrong tree.

According to the law, the accused was unable to give evidence on his own behalf. He made an unsworn statement reiterating what he had told the officer investigating the ambush. Father Ahern was acquitted.

The prosecution of a priest may seem incongruous but it was not unusual. A number of priests were prosecuted or interned during the war. Many were threatened and assaulted by Auxiliaries in particular.[5] At least two were killed by Auxiliaries.[6] Ireland was an intensely religious country and there were many republican propagandists who made capital out of these events. The full picture was rather more complex.

Most of the hierarchy of the Catholic Church squarely condemned the insurgency. Archbishop Cohalan roundly criticised the excesses of the Auxiliaries and the Black and Tans. With equal clarity and vigour he condemned the 'ambush war' and his priests spoke against violence from the pulpit. Cohalan excommunicated all those who took part in the conflict. He was joined by others like Archbishop Gilmartin of Tuam. Not all priests shared the official line and they gave their support in varying degrees to the insurgents. This support was not limited to acting as confessors for condemned men. Many priests gave food and shelter to wanted men or turned a blind eye to those who cared for men on the run. Occasionally they used their clerical status to disguise their activities.

All too often, priests were on hand before an ambush to give a blessing. Occasionally, priests appeared to administer last rites after an ambush.

Sometimes their arrival was all too timely. Father William Kennedy, of Newmarket on Fergus, witnessed the killing of one unfortunate man. He later told the court of inquiry that he had been stopped on his journey and brought to hear the confession of an informant before he was shot.[7] Eyebrows were raised amongst the Royal Irish Constabulary and Military. This was the context of this prosecution.

Trials 1921

CHAPTER TWENTY-ONE

Caherguillamore House

In the depths of County Limerick, Caherguillamore House was one of those grand old houses that graced the west of Ireland. The house was set in heavy woods at the end of a long drive: a mansion with an imposing Georgian facade. The lady of the house died in 1919 and after this, there were no more house parties and the ballroom that was once lit up remained quiet. The shutters went up and the widower, Lord Fermoy, moved away. The Bruff battalion of Volunteers decided to hold a dance at this secluded house on Saint Stephen's night of 1920.[1]

Few people were told of the exact venue. Guests were asked to go to designated locations from where they were brought to Caherguillamore. Sentries were placed around the House in case of a raid. As a diversion a rumour was put about that a ceili was to be held at Herbertstown some miles away. In fact the Royal Irish Constabulary (RIC) knew the precise arrangements for the dance. According to one account, a local police sergeant, Fred McGarry, tipped off the organisers but the dance went ahead.

Just before midnight, hundreds of soldiers, RIC men and Auxiliaries were driven in lorries to drop off points around Caherguillamore and from there, they began to close in on foot. It was a bright Christmas night and some of the sentries outside the house saw figures moving in the distance and raised the alarm.

Martin Conway and the O' Dwyer brothers[2] emerged from the house and saw an army lorry freewheeling silently towards them. They ran into the darkness and through the fields. The army lorries rolled to a halt and fixed searchlights snapped on. Machine guns opened up on the figures running through the fields. Conway was killed and the other two got away.[3]

There was an exchange of fire with sentries. Constable Alfred Hodgson was killed. He had served in the Great War with distinction as a motor torpedo gunner before coming to Ireland with the Black and Tans some weeks before. A regular RIC man was also wounded.[4] Five Volunteers were killed or mortally wounded as the Army approached the house.[5] Flares were fired into the sky, the raiding party fired on the house and crashed through the front doors. According to John Regan, the senior RIC officer, one of the men in the hall approached in a brazen way and

```
'demanded to know our authority for being
there. This was the last straw, with one of
my men shot dead. He was hit and there was a
very rough house for some time.'6
```

It was hardly an accurate description. Dr Michael O'Brien gave first aid to the dying Constable Hodgson. Following this O'Brien received a sustained beating from which he never fully recovered and he died two years later. All the other male prisoners were forced to run a gauntlet of police officers during which they were beaten with gun butts, stair banisters and whips. A number of prisoners sustained life-changing injuries.[7]

The following morning about 138 prisoners were moved in open-topped lorries to New Barracks, in Limerick. Most of the prisoners had significant injuries which were obvious to passers-by.

The first batch of sixty-two prisoners was tried on 7 January. They received short sentences of a few months' duration.

On 11 January another batch of men was tried. Major Ralph Eastwood presided.[8] Fifty-nine men were tried and sentenced to ten years' penal servitude, reduced on confirmation to five years. This batch of prisoners was moved by destroyer to England.[9]

No trial record survives in respect of any of these prisoners. However, for reasons which are not clear, the trial of two prisoners was delayed for some weeks.[10] On 23 February 1921, John Mulcahy from Herbertstown and Thomas Conway from Fedamore were tried by Field General Court Martial at New Barracks Limerick.[11]

They were charged that while at Caherguillamore House on 26-27 December 1920, they assembled together with others and armed sentries and committed an act likely to cause disaffection. The prisoners were represented by counsel, Patrick Kelly, a local man. So far as can be established, these were the only two prisoners who were legally represented.

The evidential case against these men was that they had been sentries at the dance. Counsel for the defence, Patrick Kelly, tried to pass the affair off as a Christmas dance of the sort common in the area. But the Army called the caretaker, Tom O'Donoghue, a most unwilling witness. O'Donoghue named no one and gave a brief but revealing account. He told the court that, on the evening of the dance, about six men came to the house and demanded the key. They told him they were going 'to have a bit of a dance'. Their faces were blackened and one had a revolver. His daughters had gone to the dance but he had remained indoors on the instructions of the men, he added unconvincingly.

Inspector John M. Regan recounted approaching the house at about 1am. The house was surrounded on three sides. About 200 yards from the house he saw a civilian with a rifle on sentry duty, who fired on the police. The civilian fired first and the police returned fire at him. The police then advanced and found him seriously wounded and he was taken into custody. A little while later another civilian was seen crouching in the bushes. He was called upon to halt and, not responding, he was fired upon and shot dead. A revolver was found close by.

Another RIC officer recounted that he led other officers up the driveway. The House was quiet and in darkness. The shutters were up. It was later discovered that clothing and paper had been inserted into gaps in the shuttering to prevent any light escaping. The officers burst through the front door and found the ground floor lit up and 'people were standing as if a dance was in progress'.

He told the court that no shooting took place inside the house but there had been some disorder. There were about 140 men and 40 women in the house. The accused were present in the house. They refused to say who had invited them or who had organised the dance. He continued: 'The police were anxious to find out if there were any dupes there, but being unable to get any satisfactory answers, all the men were arrested.'

Mulcahy and Conway were convicted and sentenced to ten years' penal servitude.

The operation at Caherguillamore was described by the Sixth Divisional GHQ Staff as 'One of the most successful operations of the year'.[12]

CHAPTER TWENTY-TWO

The Bloody Sunday Trials

In the three months that followed Bloody Sunday, over 310 revolvers were seized in Dublin. The raids were directed at suppressing the Rebellion, not securing evidence. Little thought was given to linking the guns to the shootings. Ballistic technology existed but was only used once during the conflict and not at all for the Bloody Sunday investigation.[1] Nor was there any attempt to link the guns seized to prisoners in custody. Even at that time, the Dublin Metropolitan Police (DMP) routinely relied on fingerprint evidence but the Army had effectively taken over the prosecution of capital trials and rarely ever sought or relied upon forensic evidence.

In these months 1,745 men were arrested[2] and, of these, hundreds were interned without trial but there was a dearth of information as to which of the prisoners might be involved. The intelligence rooms at the Lower Castle Yard were known as the 'knocking shop'. Interrogations were brutal but this was intelligence gathering as opposed to collecting evidence. Admissions could not be used in evidence because they were not voluntary and, in any event, most prisoners kept their silence.

The hundreds of young men interned in the aftermath of Bloody Sunday formed a ready pool of suspects. It seems that almost by accident all the prosecutions came to rely solely on visual identification evidence.

The identification parades which were conducted reflected the Army's lack of experience in this field. No initial descriptions were taken from witnesses to provide a point of comparison with suspects picked out and no arrangements were made to record what witnesses said when carrying out identifications. Sometimes witnesses picked out prisoners in the presence of other witnesses which compromised the evidential value of identifications.

Witnesses to the Bloody Sunday shootings were driven to Marlborough Barracks, Arbour Hill and half a dozen other prisons to view line ups of prisoners. At Arbour Hill, the windows of an old wash house were covered in sheets and witnesses crowded in to peer through the cracks into the yard where prisoners walked back and forth. As a consequence of this chaotic process, eighteen prisoners were picked out and eleven were sent for courts martial.

A curious detail is that not a single witness in all the trials that took place mentioned any suspect having any distinguishing features, save for James McNamara who had red hair and was said to have an odd gait (he also had a rock solid alibi and was later acquitted). Boyce also had 'a boxer's nose' but he too would be acquitted. All the prisoners sent for trial favoured the usual dress style of the period: three-piece suits, coats and scarves. They were pale young men with short hair, sometimes obscured by flat caps. None of them were heavily built and none especially tall or short. The prosecution evidence, therefore, rested essentially on facial recognition carried out in difficult circumstances.

It is well recognised now that visual identification evidence is inherently unreliable and that an apparently reliable witness or witnesses may be mistaken. The admission of such evidence is now rigorously monitored and scrutinised for precisely these reasons. At that time, the dangers of visual identification were still not at all understood.[3] The judge advocates who handled these trials can hardly be criticised on this count.[4]

Another common feature of the trials is that all the prisoners claimed to have alibis: that they were at mass or returning from mass or were home in bed. All the prisoners had a raft of witnesses in support: some truthful and many not.

Teeling, Potter and Conway[5]

City Hall was fixed on by the Army as a venue for the trials. This fine old edifice, with its Portland stone columns, remains one of Georgian Dublin's most enduring architectural works. In more barbarous times, felons were whipped on the steps and, on one occasion, the balustrade gave way and many of the crowd that had gathered to watch the prisoner bleed toppled over the edge and were crushed to death.

The Army took over City Hall, turned out the aldermen and lined the front steps with sandbags and barbed wire. Soldiers stripped out the gilt-edged mirrors and furniture from the main council chamber. Bare tables and functional chairs were installed.

City Hall was chosen for these trials in part because it was possible to move prisoners and witnesses securely from the Lower Castle Yard and from there into a side entrance and up a curving cantilevered stone stairway to the council chamber. The grandeur of Thomas Cooley's designs may also have leant a certain authority to the process and the implicit message was that the secret trials of 1916 were of a bygone era. What was being done was being done in public and for the benefit of all. And so the public was admitted although most of the gallery was taken up with undercover officers.

The first prisoners to be tried were Frank Teeling, Edward Potter and William Conway.[6] These three men stood trial for the murder of Lieutenant Angliss, who had been living under an alias at a flat on Lower Mount Street.[7] Another officer in the flat upstairs had built a makeshift wall of furniture across his bedroom door when he heard a commotion downstairs. The raiders fired through the door but he escaped death. He was never called to give evidence and his identity remains a mystery.

The first morning of the trial was marked by an ominous event. As defence counsel walked through Dublin Castle up to City Hall, they had to pass a group of Auxiliaries gathered in the yard. One of the Auxiliaries stepped forward and pointed out leading counsel to his friends: 'That's Brown' and then, pointing to junior counsel: 'That's Rice'. The meaning of this became very clear at the end of the trial when it seemed likely that some of the prisoners would be acquitted. The Crown Solicitor approached defence counsel and passed a grim message: 'Do not stay in your own homes tonight.'[8]

The Auxiliaries and the Black and Tans had been given a certain licence and now many were entirely out of control. Father Griffin had been shot dead by Auxiliaries only weeks before and the Loughnane brothers, taken prisoner by an Auxiliary unit, were found dead and grotesquely mutilated. The week before the Bloody Sunday trials, two prisoners were removed from Dublin Castle and taken out onto wasteland and shot dead.[9] Earlier that same week, two prisoners, Patrick Blake and James O'Neill, had been acquitted by a court martial at City Hall and travelled back to Limerick by train before taking different roads home. Both were intercepted by groups of armed and disguised men who asked for them by name. O'Neill was shot dead. The attackers intended to kill Patrick Blake but shot his brother by mistake. In Cork, Resident Magistrate (RM) Brady was put on extended leave. He had given evidence against an Auxiliary (Harte) charged with murder. Dublin Castle thought there was a risk that the Auxiliaries would kill the magistrate by way of reprisal.[10] Some solicitors had taken to hiding acquitted defendants for fear that they would be killed.[11]

No one was safe and some King's Counsel with nationalist affiliations had quietly made themselves unavailable to take defence work. Most of the briefs went to counsel with unionist connections. This was the context of the Bloody Sunday trials.

The evidence in the trial of Teeling and the others had two distinct strands. The raid on Lower Mount Street had been interrupted by a maid screaming. Some passing Auxiliaries opened fire on the raiders, who ran out of the back. They scrambled over a garden wall with Auxiliaries shooting from the house behind them. Teeling was wounded in the ankle and fell into the roadway.

Brigadier Crozier arrived on the scene to find one of his men pointing a revolver at Teeling's head and counting down to zero. Crozier knocked the gun away and Teeling was spared for trial. His recently fired gun was found on the ground close by. He had no answer to the charge.

The other evidence came from a maid and also a young officer referred to in the press as 'Mr C' – Lieutenant Connolly. He was not a special branch officer nor was he an army agent. He was still getting treatment for shell shock sustained during the Great War. When called upon to give evidence, it was learned he was in Portsmouth and he only came back to Dublin because he was forced:

'Are you under armed escort?'

'Yes.'

'Were you arrested in Portsmouth?'

'Yes.'

He was Irish and may have been afraid that his name would become known. There was rather more eating away at this young man's well-being, however: he was a homosexual and he had been asleep in bed with Angliss when the raiders broke in.[12] There were few more heinous crimes in the Army and he must have agonised over whether this secret would emerge in evidence. It did: he was accused of being 'a drunk and a coward if not worse'.

When the shooting started, he rolled under the bed and much of his view of the killers came from that vantage point. Lieutenant Connolly was not a good witness. The other witness was the maid, Nellie Stapleton, who picked out Potter as a figure she had seen on a darkened landing.

The identification parades were gravely flawed even by the standards of the time: both Connolly and Nellie Stapleton were together when they identified Potter.

The prisoner, Conway, lived only doors away from the shooting but he had given an alibi when he was arrested that he had been at mass at Westland Row. It so happened that the officer preparing the court martial had discovered that a young girl, Nellie Finnegan, could support the alibi. The defence team, Brown and Vincent Rice, got wind of this and saw the mother and child waiting with the other witnesses on the morning of the trial. They noted that, after the first morning, the girl and her mother no longer appeared at court with the other witnesses.

Leading counsel Brown hatched a plan to embarrass the prosecution. He began to ask some pointed questions in court about whether the prosecution had alibi evidence which might support the defence case. He named the missing witness. Prosecuting counsel, Travers Humphreys, and his junior remained silent. After a long pause, the officer who prepared the case, Captain Martin, came forward and whispered urgently to prosecuting counsel and pointed out a statement in counsel's brief which was heavily underscored. It was a curious thing that it was an army officer who was prepared to ensure fairness rather than counsel brought over from London.

At this crucial moment the Attorney General Denis Henry KC walked in and, learning what was taking place, went over to prosecuting counsel's table and tore the witness statement out of the brief and passed it to defence counsel. Nellie Finnegan was never actually called as a witness. Defence counsel simply submitted her statement to the court as an exhibit. He had secured his client's position, on review at least.

Potter maintained he had been in bed and he called his mother to say how difficult it was to get him up on a Sunday and other supporting witnesses.

The summing up by the Judge Advocate was a barely concealed invitation to convict both prisoners. One observation, which caused dismay, was his direction on the main witness, the maid, Nellie Stapleton: 'the court is bound to act upon the evidence of that witness if they are satisfied she is an honest witness'. Her honesty had never been in issue because the defence case had been put squarely on the basis that she had been mistaken in her identifications.

As to the defence witnesses, the Judge Advocate finished with some pungent observations about the ability of murderers to find witnesses 'willing to help them to carry out their designs by coming forward to give evidence which they know to be untrue'.[13]

Potter and Conway were convicted and sentenced to death. Their sentences were commuted to twenty-five years' penal servitude.[14]

Thomas Whelan, Patrick Boyce, Michael Tobin and James McNamara[15]

These four men were charged with the murder and, as an alternative, manslaughter of Captain Baggally at Lower Baggott Street. They were tried at the end of January 1921 at City Hall.[16]

Identification evidence came from an officer who lived in the flat below Baggally's rooms. Attracted by noise on the landing, he had stepped out into the hallway where he was held up at gun point by men he identified as Whelan and Boyce. He told the court that Whelan kept him prisoner at gun point while Boyce went to and fro and, after a while, he heard shooting in Baggally's flat. Identification evidence was given by Private Snelling, an Army Service Corps motorcyclist. He had been on an errand that morning but he had taken his bike for a spin on the way and he chanced on the shootings. He also picked out the prisoners as having been running from the scene or milling around in the aftermath. He told the court that McNamara and Tobin had held him prisoner briefly and Whelan, he said, seized his bike.

Whelan was convicted and the others acquitted. The conviction of Whelan was criticised as being capricious and internally inconsistent but there was logic behind the verdicts. Tobin was identified by only a single witness after a brief observation and the case against him was dismissed on a direction from Kenneth Marshall, Deputy Judge Advocate General. Marshall appears to have followed the usual practice in such cases.

Private Snelling had identified McNamara as 'a bandy legged' man who ran in a curious way. McNamara had red hair but this was hardly compelling in a city where so many young men had red hair. McNamara offered to run to demonstrate his gait and, although the offer was not taken up, the point had been made. He also had a very solid alibi from a DMP officer and an ex-soldier who had seen him at mass at Dun Laoghaire on the morning in question and so McNamara was acquitted.

Boyce had been identified by a single witness who had a less than full opportunity for making a proper observation. Boyce also called alibi evidence and he was also acquitted.

In respect of Whelan, the observation by the main witness took place over a period of many minutes in a reasonable light and it was supported by Private Snelling, although his view was far less satisfactory.

Whelan, then aged twenty-two, was a talkative and excitable young man from the west of Ireland who had settled in Dublin. He had made a statement on arrest, setting out an alibi that he had been at church. His counsel called witnesses in support of his alibi and transcripts do not suggest the defence witnesses had failed to come up to proof or been inconsistent but they were disbelieved. It is as well to remember that the identification parades were lamentably unfair, with no protections for a suspect. Whelan was sentenced to death and his case was put over for confirmation by General Macready. He was executed. There is no doubt that he had some limited involvement in the insurgency but it does not seem that he was involved in the killing of Captain Baggally.[17]

Patrick Moran and Joseph Rochford

Moran and Rochford were tried by General Court Martial[18] for the murder of Lieutenant Ames at Upper Mount Street. Manslaughter was charged as an alternative.[19] Both were represented by leading counsel.[20]

Again, the evidence came in large part from Army Service Corps motorcyclist, Private Snelling, who had seen armed men near Number 38. He had been held up by a man he identified as Moran. He was forced to go into Number 38 where he saw many other armed civilians and a tall man in 'night attire' with his arms raised. He saw this man shot.

The trial had barely opened on the second day when the President announced that one of the witnesses had been shot in a nearby cafe and the case would have to be stood out. This witness was Major Carew, a special branch officer who had been working under cover. Even after Bloody Sunday, Carew continued on duty. On the morning of the trial, he had been in a Dublin Bread Company café in Dame Street, while he waited to go before the court. A group of men who were also 'taking tea' at a neighbouring table opened fire on him. Carew, helped by another undercover officer, fired back. One of the other group was wounded and they were driven off. A few days later Carew was well enough to attend court with his arm in a sling.

The identification of Moran was supported by a qualified identification by Major Carew who had been living in a house opposite the shootings. Living under cover in Dublin was difficult and dangerous work but Carew

17. Sir Thomas Milvain was Judge Advocate General (JAG) with responsibility for reviewing all capital trials by court martial and advising the Army on whether conviction and sentence could be confirmed. In 1916 Milvain was terminally ill and the JAG was bypassed in the trials following the Rebellion. (Courtesy of the Office of the Judge Advocate General)

18. Sir Felix Cassel, appointed Judge Advocate General in October 1916. When the insurrection reached a crisis in 1921, Cassel acted as a brake on the execution policy. (Courtesy of the Office of the Judge Advocate General)

19. Sir Augustine Birrell and Sir Matthew Nathan: the Chief Secretary and Under Secretary and head of the British government in Ireland. The Royal Commission into the causes of the Rebellion in Ireland castigated Birrell and Nathan. (Courtesy of Kilmainham Gaol Museum)

20. The First Dáil Éireann in session at the Mansion House. (Courtesy of Mercier Press Archive)

21. Seán T. O'Kelly shut out of Versailles Peace Conference. (Courtesy of Kilmainham Gaol Museum)

22. Michael Collins collecting money for the Dáil loan. (Courtesy of Mercier Press Archives)

23. Army raid on Dáil offices 1920. (Courtesy of the Irish Military Archives)

24. Dáil Court in session. (Courtesy of Kilmainham Gaol Museum)

25. Bridie Gallagher, a refugee from war in the summer of 1920. (Courtesy of Kilmainham Gaol Museum)

26. Chief Justice Molony had a reputation as a 'hanger' but juries declined to convict in capital cases arising out of the insurgency. (Reproduced by kind permission of the Honourable Society of Kings Inns)

27. Patrick Lynch Kings Counsel, who acted for the Mac Curtain family and in many other notable trials of this era. He was remembered by his colleagues as an honest man. (Reproduced by kind permission of the Honourable Society of Kings Inns)

28. Captain King, F Company Auxiliaries.
(Courtesy of the Irish Military Archives)

29. The Customs House burned for days in May 1921. (Courtesy of the National Library of Ireland)

30. Auxiliary on guard duty, Dublin 1921. (Courtesy of the National Library of Ireland)

31. General Sir Neville Macready, General Officer Commanding the British Army in Ireland from April 1920-21. (© National Portrait Gallery)

had hung onto his batman, to deliver the finer comforts of life. Carew told the court that he was still in bed when his batman brought him tea and, on leaving the room, ran back in and called his attention to the events unfolding in the street. Carew drew his automatic from under his pillow and ran over to the front window; from here he saw a civilian with a gun going into Number 38. A little while later a stream of men came out. Many were armed with hand guns. Carew opened the window, fired and some of the men fired back.

Private Lawrence, Carew's batman, told the court he had leaned out of a window and saw the scene unfolding. He noted the time as 8.45 as a church bell clanged nearby – 'I heard a quarter chiming.' The men were emerging from the house across the road. He went down into the street and emptied his revolver in the direction of the running men. He later identified Rochford as one of these men.

Carew and other witnesses were later driven from one prison to another where impromptu and chaotic line ups were held. Some of the witnesses asked that the prisoners be shaved. Most refused, except Moran who told a fellow prisoner he had 'nothing to fear'.[21] He shaved and paraded again before being picked out by Privates Lawrence and Snelling who were together. Carew then joined these two witnesses and was present when Moran was brought in again in circumstances which made plain he had been picked out. Carew, however, showed a careful turn of mind: 'I cannot swear to him positively.'

Moran called a host of witnesses to prove he was at his lodgings and later at mass on the morning of the shootings. As always, timing was a critical part of the alibi. Evidence was called to contradict the batman who had fixed the time by reference to a church bell tolling. The Rector of St Stephen's Church told the court that the church bell had not chimed for years. His sexton told the court there was no other church bell in earshot as far as he knew. This was derided by Travers Humphreys as 'a delightful Irish alibi'. Ridicule is no substitute for analysis but Travers Humphreys had hit upon a point of some truth. The prevalence of false alibis in Ireland at this time was well known.[22] These alibis were constructed with some ingenuity and were usually framed around some real event which was transposed to the day the alibi was needed. For that reason, they were hard to crack in cross-examination.

Rochford had an alibi that he had been at home in bed. It was not the best alibi at first blush but it was a simple one and it was supported by all his family who painted a picture of an idle and difficult young man who was impossible to rouse. At one stage Travers Humphreys suggested to a defence witness that Rochford was 'No 2 in E Company of the Third Battalion of the IRA'. Perhaps realising the case against Rochford was weak Humphreys added a slippery aside, that the suggestion he had put was 'on the basis of documents with which I have been furnished'. In this way, Humphreys had skilfully introduced damning material that could not be called as evidence. He would do the same to Moran.

Moran's case was fraught with difficulty. Moran's workmates Doyle and McCourt had provided police with statements in support of an alibi at an early stage. But the timing of their alibi was entirely out of sync with the rest of his witnesses who had been gathered by Moran's fiancée.

The defence elected not to call Doyle and McCourt and relied on the other alibi witnesses to prove Moran was at early mass and only later caught the train into the centre of the city to chair a trade union meeting. As the trial wore on, Travers Humphreys eagerly awaited the calling of these witnesses which he knew would sink the defence. A plan was hatched by the defence team to catch Humphreys off guard. Defence counsel called all the witnesses he wished and then abruptly closed his case without calling Doyle and McCourt. Realising he had been duped, Humphreys 'went white with rage'.[23]

Humphreys applied for Moran's fiancée to be recalled. Humphreys produced a photo of Moran seized from his lodging. It showed him holding a pistol – it had formed no part of the prosecution case – and put it in front of the witness. Photos like this were as common as brass among the tens of thousands of young men who had been Volunteers in a more innocent age. By the standards of the time, the photo was, in any event, inadmissible to prove identification at the scene. Although the photo was eventually ruled inadmissible, the officers of the court understood what it showed and Humphreys had achieved his purpose.

These trials were redolent with irony. Rochford was acquitted, although he had played a full part. Moran was convicted and it may be that the shooting of Major Carew counted against him: Carew only gave evidence against Moran. While awaiting trial, Moran turned down the chance to escape from Kilmainham with three other prisoners, all of whom got clean away. Why Moran declined to take his chance has never been explained. None of his alibi witnesses had been telling the truth. Evidence later emerged that Moran had played a full part in what took place on Bloody

Sunday but he had never been to Lower Mount Street. He had instead led the group of men who had gone to the Gresham and shot two army officers the same morning.[24] There were no witnesses to that shooting and that perhaps explains why Moran was untroubled by identification parades or his trial, which had gone well and he expected to be acquitted. He was thirty-three. He and his fiancée had a life they might share. Although he had humble origins – a grocer's assistant, he had worked his way up to President of the National Union of Vintners. He could not regain that life as a fugitive in a conflict that might yet be long and drawn out. He needed an acquittal to achieve this.[25] So he stayed and faced his trial and was convicted and hanged.

CHAPTER TWENTY-THREE

The Drumcondra Ambush

The prisoners were tried by General Court Martial at City Hall, on 24 February 1921. Brevet Major Powell of the 2nd Welsh Regiment presided.[1] The prisoners were tried on a charge of levying war against the Crown, contrary to the Treason Act of 1351.[2] All the prisoners were represented by counsel.[3] Sir Richard Muir, perhaps the most famous prosecutor of his generation, led for the Crown.[4] Muir stayed at army HQ at the Royal Hospital and was moved back and forth to the City Hall by armoured car.

The origins of the Drumcondra affair lay in a plan to ambush a lorry load of Auxiliaries on the road out of Dublin to their base in Gormanstown to the north of Dublin. The eight ambushers were armed with handguns and grenades – some homemade. It was a desperate enterprise because the Auxiliaries were probably the most experienced and well-equipped force in Europe.

Binns Bridge was the spot chosen for the ambush. Three events occurred which turned the ambush into a shambles. Firstly, Binns Bridge was busy with pedestrians and the attackers relocated to the Tolka Bridge. They did not reconnoitre a safe line of retreat and this was their undoing.

While the preparations for the ambush were in progress, Dublin Metropolitan Police (DMP) Sergeant Singleton passed by. There was some discussion about holding him until after the ambush. Nineteen-year-old Frank Flood, who led the ambushers, insisted that Singleton be allowed to pass because he had clear orders not to interfere with DMP officers. This, it seems, was because many DMP officers simply turned a blind eye to the insurgency and so some care was taken not to rouse the DMP.

Singleton did report what he saw, though, and F Company of Auxiliaries was despatched from Dublin Castle. This convoy was led by Captain

Lorraine King, a much decorated veteran, a six-foot-four, heavily-muscled, imposing figure.

Back at the bridge the anticipated target had not appeared and the ambushers were getting ready to leave. At this point an army pay van appeared. The attackers decided that this target would do: grenades were thrown and fire opened but the tender raced away and soon passed Captain King with two lorry loads of Auxiliaries coming the other way. A warning was shouted to King's men.

Captain King's heavily armed convoy accelerated to the corner of Drumcondra Road and Richmond Road. Here the ambushers were taken by surprise and began to run. They were called upon to halt but a few made off across the fields.

Captain King fired on the men running through the fields and one, Michael Magee, was wounded and fell and got to his feet and ran again. The other Auxiliaries turned their fire on him and he fell again. Two others escaped through the fields.

The rest of the ambushers made off on foot through the streets followed by the Auxiliaries in Crossley Tenders. Eventually, the fleeing party turned into a cul de sac and found themselves trapped in the porch of a house. Above them, only yards away, the Auxiliaries' carbines were levelled.

Two of the prisoners were holding revolvers and the others had revolvers hanging from 'a lanyard' around their necks. Flood had a hand grenade in his pocket which was identical to the one found at the scene and another found behind the loop-holed wall.

Afterwards an unexploded, homemade hand grenade was found on the roadway. A nearby wall overlooking the road was found to have been loop-holed to allow the ambushers to fire. The prisoners were herded onto a tender. Michael Magee was also put aboard. He was conscious, bleeding profusely and in great pain. He was given a glass of water and taken to hospital where he died later that day.

This was the first time that the charge of levying war had been brought against any insurgent prisoners outside the martial law area. The background was that, in the martial law area, most offences were punishable with death. Outside the martial law area, the death penalty was only available for murder. General Macready wanted to bring capital charges to act as a deterrent and the solution was to revive an ancient offence. The charge was laid after some hesitation. In the corridors of power at Dublin Castle, it was feared that laying this charge would lend credibility to the insurgent movement: 'It goes half way to admitting their contention that they are at war with a tyrant.'[5] The charge was laid and the evidence called in support was overwhelming. None of the prisoners made any statement in their defence or called any witness in support.

Colonel Edgeworth-Johnstone, the Commissioner of the DMP, was called to give evidence that a rebellion had been in progress in Dublin for some time. His evidence was the subject of futile and quite unrealistic objections by the young defence barristers. As the trial wore on, the only issue advanced by the defence was whether there was a rebellion in Dublin at that time and whether it could be proved that these young men had levied war against the Crown.

At this crucial juncture, the High Court delivered its ruling in *R v Allen*, a case arising out of the declaration of martial law and the use of impromptu military courts not sanctioned by law. The essence of the judgment was that a state of war existed in the martial law area and the courts could not intervene in those cases. At this late point in the trial, King's Counsel was instructed on behalf of the prisoners to make submissions on this issue. There was not a great deal to be said and the submissions of Edmund Swayne KC were rambling and a little self-regarding. One of the prisoners recalled seeing an officer who was trying the case doodling on a pad and another dozing.[6]

What happened next was recorded by a Dublin Castle diarist: 'a rattle of shots rang out under the window. The court, I'm told all jumped to the windows and there in the road below were three men – police orderlies – lying dead'.[7]

The officers trying the case had been brought over from England for the trial and, for them, this was probably a key moment in the trial. Sir Richard Muir, who had been prone to wandering round Dublin at night, no longer strayed out of barracks.

All the prisoners were convicted and sentenced to death. The legitimacy of the proceedings was confirmed by the Judge Advocate General, in a terse memo.[8] Macready applied his usual rule of thumb: O'Sullivan was just seventeen and he was spared. The others had fired on the troops and they were ordered to be hanged.

The fallout from the ambush continued. Sergeant Singleton was moved to England and did not return to Ireland. The search for the informant went on in Dublin and suspicion wrongly fell on a local man, an ex-soldier, Robert Pike, who was shot dead. He left a wife and five children.

On 14 March, the executions of the Drumcondra prisoners took place. Also hanged were the two men convicted of involvement in the Bloody Sunday shootings. The justification was deterrence: in the preceding month alone, thirty-three people had been killed as result of the insurgency.[9]

CHAPTER TWENTY-FOUR

Captain William Lorraine King

Williiam King was commander of F Company of the Auxiliaries, stationed at Dublin Castle. King was a huge man. Those that knew him remembered that, off duty, he had a sunny disposition. On duty, he exuded an 'air of command'.[1] He had been twice decorated for bravery on the Western Front. It was the practice of the Auxiliaries to elect their own officers and, since the ranks of the Auxiliaries were packed with decorated veterans of the Western Front, that says much about King.

The other central figure was F Company's intelligence officer, Jocelyn Hardy:

'Slight in build. He walked with a limp. His face was pale, the pupils of his eyes were large and black, around them were a thin rim of blue. He worked his lower lip.'[2]

Hardy had been a captain in the Connaught Rangers. In the autumn of 1914, his unit was surrounded by overwhelming numbers of German troops. Hardy surrendered but in the three years that followed, he made many audacious escape attempts before reaching England in March 1918 where he was received by the King at Buckingham Palace. Hardy went back to the Front within weeks, where he distinguished himself by extraordinary courage and selflessness. He was twice wounded in the closing months of the war, losing a leg. After recovering from wounds, he served with the Intelligence Services until his transfer to the newly formed Auxiliary Division. He was attached to F Company as intelligence officer.[3]

When Bloody Sunday came, Hardy and King were high on the list of officers targeted for assassination but both were out when men came calling.

F Company members all wore the Auxiliary Glengarry but, in the early days, the cadets wore the standard kit from their old units: 'airman's uniforms, highlanders complete with kilt, naval officers and types from every part of the globe. A sprinkling of the crowd wore the blue tunics.'[4] Most Auxiliaries carried a carbine and revolver strapped to each thigh.

Drinking and indiscipline became part of the culture of the Auxiliaries. It is likely that many of these men carried the psychological baggage that comes with war service. There is also no doubt that General Tudor had explicitly given these men the green light to do what they thought necessary.[5]

There is evidence from many sources that Captain King and F Company's intelligence officer, Captain Jocelyn Lee Hardy,[6] were routinely torturing or ill-treating prisoners at Dublin Castle. Here, adjoining the yard, there were half-a-dozen windowless cells holding prisoners awaiting interrogation. 'The intelligence room' was at the heart of the process.[7] If the prisoner could hang on long enough, he might be released, interned or moved to Kilmainham where he might be put on identification parades or held for trial. Some prisoners just broke under questioning.

On 12 April 1921, Captain William Lorraine King, Cadet Harold Hinchcliffe and Frederick Welsh, also of F Company, were tried by court martial at City Hall on a charge that on 9 February they did 'feloniously and wilfully murder James Murphy'.[8] The prisoners were represented by counsel.

The evidence showed that the deceased, James Murphy, and Patrick Kennedy had been arrested at about 9pm on the evening of 9 February. They were taken to Dublin Castle where they were held in the intelligence room and later seen in the yard.

Lieutenant Commander Fryer, who was stationed at Dublin Castle, told the court that he had come into the yard at Dublin Castle and saw one of the prisoners 'being bashed about' by a crowd of men. He told the court that this man 'was smothered in blood from his face and head'. He was taken to a water pump and brought back with his face and head all wet. He told the court that the other prisoner was pushed out into the yard and surrounded by a crowd. At this point, Captain King appeared on the steps of the office and said 'They have got enough.'

At about 11pm, a Ford car was driven into the yard. Captain King and Hinchcliffe got in. Fryer heard Hinchcliffe ask if he would come for a ride: 'We are going out to shoot.' He told the court he did not see the other prisoner get into the car but he later went to the hospital where he identified the deceased as one of the prisoners being maltreated in the yard.

Another officer of General Tudor's staff gave evidence that he had seen the Ford car with its engine running. Close by, there was a man leaning against a wall battered and bleeding. He heard Captain King's voice from the car calling: 'Hurry up.' He conceded, in cross-examination, that he had not known King very long (and, therefore, might have been mistaken in saying it was King's voice).

Later that night, two Dublin Metropolitan Police (DMP) officers were patrolling on foot. They heard sounds like a car backfiring and, soon after, saw a light-coloured car crossing the Tolka Bridge in the direction of Dublin. They heard some moaning from the other side of a wall and soon found the body of Patrick Kennedy. Murphy was close by and was found to be in a very bad way. Murphy was taken to the Mater Hospital where he was found to have a number of injuries and two bullet wounds. He told a Sergeant they had been removed from Dublin Castle by armoured car and three car loads of soldiers and Auxiliaries. They were brought to wasteland and shot. Murphy named Captain King as being present, although he said that the shooting had been done by a man in plain clothes that he could not name.

At the time, a dying declaration was admissible where it was shown that the dying man was under 'a settled expectation of death'.[9] Murphy was seen at the hospital by his brother, a DMP officer and a priest. All recalled that he had been horribly wounded but none could confirm that he believed he was dying. The court was not satisfied the test was met and this statement was ruled inadmissible by the court.

A civilian witness told the court that he had been out that night in Drumcondra when a small car passed him coming from the city. Soon after he heard a volley of shots and a car passed him going back towards Dublin. He told the court the car was full of Auxiliaries in dark blue uniforms.

Frederick Welsh was acquitted for lack of identification evidence at the close of the prosecution case.

Counsel for King applied to hear the defence evidence in camera on the grounds that some of the witnesses were in the Secret Service and might be endangered by coming forward. This request was refused by the court.

In opening the defence, leading counsel for Captain King described him as an officer with 'a brilliant record'. King had worked his way up through the ranks. He won the Military Cross and the Distinguished Conduct Medal on the Western Front. He had previously served as a police officer in South Africa where he had been decorated for saving the lives of a family in a flood.

Leading counsel went on to say that 'F Company had not one black mark against them of any kind and were still on the same duty as when first formed' – an oblique reference to the reputation of the Auxiliary Division.

This was a trial under the Restoration of Order in Ireland Act and the prisoners were not permitted to give evidence on their own behalf. Neither made an unsworn statement to the court, on the advice of their lawyers.

The case for Captain King was that he did have a Ford car but it had broken down that night and was in the garage until the next day. He accepted he had been at Dublin Castle that night and that he and the intelligence officer had questioned Murphy and Kennedy. He had ordered their release because 'there was nothing against them'. He maintained that the prisoners were not maltreated and they left Dublin Castle on foot at 10pm.

Alibi evidence was called from a number of Auxiliaries that Captain King had been part of a patrol that left Dublin Castle at 10.25pm in uniform. The patrol consisted of a lorry and 'a birdcage tender'. King led the raiding party at Leeson Street and Talbot Street and did not return until midnight.

Captain Jocelyn Lee Hardy, the intelligence officer, also gave evidence for the defence. He told the court that Captain King had questioned Murphy and Kennedy and appeared to be 'favourably impressed with their answers'. The prisoners were not maltreated and left the Castle on foot and unharmed.

Hardy was recalled to be cross-examined when the intelligence logs of the raids on Leeson Street and Talbot Street were found. These were not signed by Captain King but by another officer with the obvious inference that the raids were not led by Captain King.

A sergeant from F Company, who was on duty in the intelligence room, gave supporting evidence for the defence. The sergeant explained the fracas in the courtyard as a fight between two constables who had drunk too much.

Both Captain King and Hinchcliffe were acquitted. No evidence was offered in respect of the killing of the other man, Kennedy.

The court martial officers would have been brought over from England. They would have no knowledge of the reputation enjoyed by F Company.

They were also entirely independent of General Macready or any other senior officer. There is also a hint from a Dublin Castle insider that Captain Hardy had tried to intimidate prosecution witnesses.[10] There is no doubt that General Macready[11] and the Auxiliaries' commander, Brigadier Crozier, were both anxious to see justice done. Crozier resigned in disgust over the failure to check reprisals by the Auxiliaries and, about this case, he wrote bitterly: 'the result should have been otherwise'.

According to another prisoner, while King was under arrest awaiting trial, he complained not that he was innocent but that he had been let down by the government who had urged on the Auxiliaries.[12] Once he was cleared, support materialised again and King was reinstated and transferred to command another Auxiliary Company in Galway.[13]

CHAPTER TWENTY-FIVE

Thomas Traynor

Thomas Traynor of McCaffrey Street, Mount Brown, was charged with the murder of Cadet Francis Farrell on the 14 March 1921.[1] He was tried at City Hall in Dublin on 6 April 1921. The President of the court was Brevet Major Montague CB CMG DSO.[2]

This trial arose out of a raid on 144 Great Brunswick Street, in Dublin city centre. Two lorry loads of Auxiliaries and an armoured car appeared at about 8pm and were ambushed from both ends of the street and from the windows of No 144. In the first few moments Cadet Farrell, in the leading tender, was mortally wounded and toppled out of the tender onto the roadway. Four other cadets were wounded. The other cadets jumped out on the roadway and stood over the bodies of the wounded, shooting back at the flashes from the shadows. The shooting lasted nearly ten minutes before the ambushers melted away, carrying their wounded away and leaving three dead and one wounded.[3]

Two cadets were fatally wounded. Three other cadets, Dentieth, Reardon and Dawson, were wounded. Two prisoners were taken. One was wounded and unfit to be tried. The other was Thomas Traynor. He was armed with a loaded automatic and had been captured running from the scene.

The prisoner was prosecuted by R.E. Otter, a London barrister who was a veteran of the Western Front. He was defended by a Dublin barrister, Nolan Whelan, whose conduct of the defence left something to be desired. In the middle of one of his submissions he displayed a casual indifference to the dead officer: 'I forget the name of the deceased Cadet...'

There was a long silence before prosecuting counsel intervened: 'Cadet Farrell', he reminded him quietly.

Cadet Farrell had been a Lieutenant in the Royal Dublin Fusiliers and later in the Tank Corps. The other cadet who died was Cadet Bernard Beard who won the Military Cross and was mentioned in despatches three times during the Great War.[4] Both of the dead men had served on the Western Front with the officers trying the case.

A tank officer, Lieutenant C.B. Webbe told the court that the street was dark and badly lit. Fire had been opened suddenly from different directions. He had seen a man run by. He jumped off the armoured car and 'rugby tackled him'. Once he had the man down, he knelt on him and saw that he had an automatic in his hand.

When Traynor was captured, he shouted 'For God's sake shoot me now'. It was hardly a remark made by an innocent passer-by caught up in a shoot-out. Later he told an officer: 'I am only a soldier like yourself'. He admitted firing the automatic. He was searched and a clip of ammunition was found in his pocket.

The gun seized from Traynor was examined in court. The automatic had one round chambered and four more in the magazine. The gun had the capacity for eight rounds but no evidence was called to show that it had recently been discharged. An impromptu attempt was made by defence counsel to demonstrate that the clip of ammunition found in Traynor's pocket did not fit the gun but this off-the-cuff experiment did not go well for the defence.[5] No ballistics evidence was adduced nor was any attempt made to secure such evidence. The prosecution was unable to prove that Traynor had fired the fatal shot or wounded any officer and simply relied on the inference that he had been party to a joint enterprise to kill.

Under the rules governing these trials, Traynor was not entitled to give sworn evidence or be cross-examined, which was probably a blessing for him because he had little to say and nothing that would withstand scrutiny. Traynor stood to give his account: a small, wiry figure aged about forty, he sported a long, black moustache that gave him a mournful appearance. He told the court he was a boot maker who ran his own business with two of his sons. He had been involved in the Rebellion of 1916[6] but had not been active since, though he was regarded 'as a proper person' to run a message. That day he had been asked to carry a gun to 144 Great Brunswick Street where he would be met. He had agreed to do so and was caught up running from the fighting. The prisoner made no attempt to explain the incriminating remarks attributed to him.

Traynor was convicted. His admission of involvement in the 1916 Rebellion was unnecessary and very damaging. The trial record shows this admission was heavily underscored by General Macready. However, it made no difference. Traynor had been convicted of the murder of a member of the security forces and the policy of deterrence required an execution.

Traynor was hanged at Mountjoy Gaol on 25 April.[7] He left a widow, Elizabeth, and ten children under the age of seventeen.

Some days before, District Inspector Gilbert Potter had been captured in Tipperary and held hostage for the safety of Traynor. It was hardly likely that General Macready would succumb to pressure of this kind. District Inspector Potter was shot dead. He left a widow and four children.

Tipperary was in the martial law area and the Army embarked on a series of official reprisals, blowing up ten farm houses in the area.[8]

CHAPTER TWENTY-SIX

Bryan Kelley

Bryan Kelley was tried at Victoria Barracks on 14 June on a charge of carrying out an act contrary to the Restoration of Order in Ireland Regulations, namely writing a letter to a friend asking him to get witnesses to give false alibi evidence on behalf of John Murphy who was awaiting trial for the murder of Sergeant Gibbs during the Mallow Barracks raid.

Mallow Barracks had been seized in September of 1920. Ernie O'Malley had forced the front door of the Barracks on the pretext of delivering a letter. Once the door was forced, over thirty more men followed and others scaled the walls of the Barracks. Sergeant Gibbs was shot and killed and a quantity of arms was seized. John Murphy was tall, thin and red-headed; he bore a passing resemblance to O'Malley and was wrongly identified by witnesses as the man at the gate. He was sent for trial along with five others. In early March 1921, while still awaiting trial, a letter written by another prisoner (Kelley) at Victoria Barracks was seized.

The evidence in the trial of Bryan Kelley came from a sergeant at the Detention Barracks in Cork. The Sergeant told the court that Kelley had two parcels of dirty laundry to post out. He examined one and found three letters concealed inside. The accused said: 'For God's sake don't take them or I'll get into a terrible row.'

The relevant part of one letter contained a request that the witness be sent to see Barry Sullivan, a local solicitor:

```
'the case of John Murphy is very serious as
four soldiers are swearing against him so it
is absolutely necessary to have plenty of
witnesses to prove an alibi and so save him
from the rope. To do this I would suggest you
see Barry Sullivan, tell him of any person
```

who you think might swear that he, Murphy was
working at Eirie Tarrants on the morning of
the raid and also to look up the people of
barrack street that would say he was not among
the men who made the raid...'[1]

The accused, who was represented by a local solicitor, made an unsworn
statement. He told the court that he believed Murphy was innocent but
others outside the gaol had been slow in coming forward to give evidence
and he was anxious to do what he could for the prisoner. Kelley was
convicted and sentenced to eighteen months' imprisonment.

This small case had serious repercussions. The Kelley letter went to
the Legal Officer for the Sixth Division, Lt Col H.M. Meyler. A few weeks
later Meyler appointed himself to the position of Legal Officer in the trial
of Murphy and five others charged with the murder of Sergeant Gibbs
during the Mallow Barracks raid. Each of the six men would advance
an alibi defence. Meyler's determination to root out false alibis would
become a feature of that trial. Five of the men were convicted and
sentenced to be hanged. Two of these had never been involved in the raid.[2]

The letter had a much wider significance because it was widely circulated
in the press. It was also circulated among the military community in Ireland
at a time when a number of capital trials were getting underway in which
the evidence turned entirely on disputed identifications and alibi defences;
the trial of Maher and Foley for the Knocklong affair was one of these.

The letter was sent to the Judge Advocate General[3] and resulted in
a briefing given to army officers about the prevalence of false alibis in
Ireland.[4] The Army cannot be criticised for briefing officers in this way
but it may have made a dispassionate evaluation of evidence more difficult.

CHAPTER TWENTY-SEVEN

Patrick Maher and Ned Foley

In January 1919 an attack took place on Royal Irish Constabulary (RIC) officers escorting a cargo of gelignite at Soloheadbeg, in which two RIC officers were shot dead before they could put up their carbines. Some months later, the RIC was able to arrest Sean Hogan, one of the men wanted for the Soloheadbeg killings. The others, Breen, Robinson and Treacy resolved to rescue the prisoner before he was moved by train to Cork.

It was the end of a summer evening when the steam train bound for Cork pulled up at Knocklong, a small station with an 'up line' and a 'down line'. The platforms were connected by a footbridge overlooking the fields. Inside a third-class compartment just behind the engine sat four RIC men. The prisoner, Hogan, was manacled and seated beside Sergeant Peter Wallace who was then in his late forties, over six foot and eighteen stone. On the other side of the prisoner was Constable Michael Enright. Constables Ring and Reilly sat opposite holding carbines.

The carriage door that led to the corridor 'slapped open' suddenly and a group of men burst in. 'Hands up!' a man shouted. 'Not likely!' replied Sergeant Wallace who made to raise his revolver.

Another shouted 'Kill them!' as the officers got to their feet. Constable Enright held his gun against Hogan's head and threatened to shoot him. Constable Enright was himself shot and fell back in his seat.

One of the men wrenched the carbine from Constable Reilly's grip. Reilly later recalled a glimpse of Constable Ring being catapulted through the window. He was seen by the train driver running along the side of the train and resurfaced the next day without his boots or tunic in a tearful state. One of the other attackers struck Reilly on the head and he was knocked 'insensible'.

Reilly regained consciousness a little while later. Looking around, he saw Constable Enright lifeless in his seat and the carriage empty. A carbine lay at his side and he got out onto the platform.

Looking up at the train, Reilly saw Sergeant Wallace still aboard but now further down the train framed by the window. Wallace was struggling with two men for control of a gun. One of his assailants was trying to club the Sergeant but Wallace was a huge man and was holding his own. Reilly fired into the train and saw a spatter of blood on one of the attackers. He fired again.

Reilly turned and saw a 'bunch of men running up the platform'. There were now many passengers on the platform, some screaming, others running this way and that. Some jumped off the train and ran off into the fields and others got under the train. Reilly fired on the men running up the platform. He drove off these men wounding two more. He fixed a bayonet to his carbine and walked up the platform, attackers and onlookers scattering ahead of him. All the raiders were gone although four of them had been wounded.[1] The prisoner, Hogan, had been taken off to a local butcher where a meat cleaver was used to cut his manacles off.

Reilly went back to the carriage. Constable Ring had disappeared and he found Constable Enright dead in his seat. Sergeant Wallace was lying on the floor covered in blood – 'you could not see his face for it', Reilly recalled. The post master's daughter from Kilmallock came forward and gave first aid.

Darkness was falling. Wallace was in great pain and Reilly asked 'if I could do anything for him' but there was little that could be done and Reilly held the dying man's hand. There was a hospital at Kilmallock at the next stop and, after an anxious discussion, the train pulled off. Wallace passed away the next morning with his wife at his side.

The same morning a pony and trap rattled up to the National School at Knockea, where Constable Enright's father taught: a stern old man who was a bit too handy with the cane. He was told of his son's death. He sent the children home, walked out onto the porch and stared out over the fields polishing his glasses furiously. He left the school that day and never returned.[2]

From the earliest days, the names of the participants in this raid were known in Knocklong and throughout most of the county. Most of the names were also known to police and reward notices were posted. But none of the men who had burst into the carriage were ever captured or tried. The inquests took place in the boardroom of the old Kilmallock workhouse. Here, events took an odd turn when the presenting officer, District Inspector McLean, ushered Constable Ring out of the witness box while the jurors were still questioning him. This sparked a furious row with some jurors who accused the District Inspector of concealing evidence.[3] The truth was more prosaic: Ring had suffered a breakdown. He left the police force soon after and went into hiding for many months.[4]

In September, a number of arrests were made, including Foley, Michael Murphy (the station porter), Michael and Thomas Shanahan and Michael O'Connell. Maher was also arrested and told the officer: 'You are making a great mistake.' The depositions were taken by George McElroy, a crinkly but formidable old Resident Magistrate in a starched wing collar.[5] During the Great War, McElroy had led the army recruitment drive in Clare and he had no hesitation in sending all the prisoners for trial at the Assizes.

In the ordinary course of events, the case would have been tried at the Limerick Assizes in the spring of 1920.[6] But the prosecution applied to move the trial venue to Belfast on the grounds that no fair trial could be had locally.[7] After a counter application by the defence, the High Court moved the proceedings to Armagh, where the demographics were less unfavourable to the prisoners.

The pool of prisoners began to thin out. O'Connell had played a part in the Knocklong affair and he had joined with many other prisoners in the great hunger strike of 1920. With many others, he was released in error before news came through that the Grand Jury had declined to return a bill against him. The Grand Jury also declined to return a bill of indictment against the Shanahan brothers: neither of these men had been at the station but both had played a minor role in organising the Knocklong rescue.

The only prisoners sent for trial were Foley (who had played a limited role), Michael Murphy, the station porter, and Maher who had played no part in the attack.

The trial at Armagh was set down for the summer of 1920 but the trial was aborted when Constable Reilly disappeared: kidnapped by armed men, according to counsel for the Crown who explained his disappearance in court. This seems unlikely, however, because Reilly's evidence was favourable to the prisoners and undermined other prosecution witnesses. In any event, Reilly turned up soon after safe and well. Reilly was from Antrim and it was rumoured that he had met his brothers in a tavern the night before the trial and had gone out on a drinking spree. Afterwards, the kidnap story was invented to avoid difficulties with his senior officers.

At this point, the Restoration of Order in Ireland Act (ROIA) was passed and the Army asserted court martial jurisdiction on 'all untried indictments'.[8] The prisoners challenged the right of the Army to try them in the High Court on the grounds that the provisions of the ROIA did not apply because the High Court had made an order sending them for trial by jury at the next Assize. The application was refused and the case went for court martial.

Murphy secured a separate trial and an adjournment of his case.[9] Maher and Foley were tried by court martial in mid-March 1921 in the council chamber at City Hall[10] and were represented by King's Counsel.[11]

On the second day, the President of the Court interrupted the proceedings and announced the court would not sit on Saint Patrick's Day. This announcement was met with some bleating from counsel about how 'frightfully inconvenient' it all was. But Colonel Powell, the President of the Court, related that it was a direct order from General Macready: as a mark of respect to national sentiment. This decision caused some surprise: six young men had been executed at Mountjoy the day before. There were many diverse views about the insurgency but few had approved of the executions. On the morning of the executions, the commercial life of Dublin had ground to a halt: the trams did not run; post offices did not open; shops remained shuttered; hotel staff stayed away and there was barely any traffic apart from military vehicles. Outside Mountjoy, a crowd of 20,000 gathered, some hanging off the railings around the prison or sitting or standing in the branches of the trees that flanked the avenue to the prison. Hymns were sung and prayers were said as the prisoners were hanged in pairs.[12] The executions had been publicly condemned by the Lord Mayor of Dublin. The newspapers, for the most part, came out against the executions. However, General Macready reckoned a day off to remember Ireland's most famous saint might sweeten the pill.

The trial resumed after Saint Patrick's day. The evidence against Maher and Foley rested on identifications carried out at parades conducted nearly a year and a half previously at the yard at William Street Barracks in Limerick. Prosecuting counsel Henry Delacombe Roome told the court that each of the witnesses had a good opportunity to view the raiders and had seen the prisoners 'distinctly'.

The key to the case against Maher lies in understanding how he came to be in police custody. All of those involved in the Knocklong affair had gone on the run or taken ship to America. Maher continued to live with his parents and went each day to his job as an 'egg checker'. When he had time off he went horse racing or to the pub. He was a single man with no political affiliations. Police files suggest that Maher's name came up because of 'private information' – an informant: this, in itself, is enough to raise eyebrows because the supply of information to the police was drying up at this time.

There had been a strike at Cleeves Creamery where Maher worked. All except Maher had taken part and he had been placed under considerable pressure to join the strikers. He had been boycotted, threatened and sought police protection and it is probable that his name was put forward to the police out of spite.

Maher also bore a passing resemblance to Dan Breen who had been on the platform in the Knocklong rescue.[13] Breen had gone on the run and escaped capture and was never viewed by the witnesses on a parade. It was in these circumstances that Maher was put on a line up and picked out by two-off duty police officers and a soldier.[14] Constable Reilly was unable to identify anyone nor was Constable Ring who gave evidence for the defence.

An additional factor was that the line ups were not well conducted even by the standards of the time. At the time the identifications took place, the prisoners had been in custody for some time and there was a marked difference between them and some of the others who made up the numbers on the parade. Both prisoners suggested that the witnesses had been allowed to view them covertly before the parades, although this was denied by the witnesses.

Foley made a short statement setting out his alibi and pleading ill health. Maher's statement was long, extempore and quite compelling in its detail. Both prisoners called a number of alibi witnesses however, it is now acknowledged that Foley's witnesses were lying but Maher's were not.

Edmund Foley and Patrick Maher were convicted and subsequently hanged on 7 June 1921. They were the last men to be executed during the insurgency. Their executions took place even while peace talks were ongoing. At GHQ Parkgate there was some satisfaction that the executions had been signed off before the Truce came into effect. As far as the authorities were concerned, the right men had been executed.

Foley had been present on the platform at Knocklong.[15] He had been part of the attacking group even though he had never boarded the train. Although he had been unarmed, he must have known that his associates would use deadly force if necessary. His alibi was false and it may have undermined the case for Maher.

Maher's trial was conducted according to law; he was represented by senior counsel; he had time and facilities to prepare and to call witnesses in his defence. But there is now a consensus that Maher had no part in the events at Knocklong.[16] His alibi was a true one.

CHAPTER TWENTY-EIGHT

Edward Carmody, John 'Jaco' Lenehan, Thomas Devereux and Daniel O'Carroll

On 30 May 1921, at Victoria Barracks, Cork, four men were tried by Field General Court Martial for the murder of District Inspector Tobias O'Sullivan.[1] These young men were Jaco Lenehan, Edward Carmody, Thomas Devereux and Daniel O'Carroll, all from Listowel. The prisoners were represented by counsel.[2]

Listowel is a pretty market town on the road from Limerick to Tralee. Visitors remember the five-arch bridge over the river Feale and the remains of the castle which fell after a siege in the Elizabethan wars: the surrendering garrison were all executed.

District Inspector Tobias O' Sullivan was killed here in the winter of 1921. Tobias O'Sullivan came to prominence during the siege of Kilmallock Royal Irish Constabulary (RIC) Barracks in 1920. Kilmallock had long been a strong point for the RIC; during the Rebellion of 1867 the Barracks had been attacked by a huge crowd of rebels. They lacked arms and tried to burn out the Barracks, while inside the policemen fired through loopholes. Their wives loaded and reloaded the guns and contained the fires that threatened the roof. A relief force arrived in the morning and the attackers were dispersed by a few volleys of musket fire. The Barracks were again attacked in May 1920. This time the attackers were better prepared: the telephone lines had been cut and, for miles around, the roads were blocked by fallen trees. The Barracks was set ablaze and burned all night. Two officers died under falling masonry and a third was seriously wounded but O'Sullivan and his men held on, retreating from room to room until nothing was left except the cellar.[3] A little after dawn they emerged from the charred wreckage with fixed bayonets.[4] The defence of Kilmallock Barracks became synonymous with duty and courage.

O'Sullivan was forty-three years old, a slim, intense, bespectacled figure. He was promoted District Inspector. In the summer of 1920 he was posted to Listowel where the police garrison had mutinied and most of the officers had been sacked or transferred. His task was to restore discipline, which he did in short order.[5]

O'Sullivan was an uncompromising and robust officer who was 'on top of the wave' according to one of his colleagues. It was feared that he would be sent to Spike Island to identify suspects held there who had taken part in the Kilmallock Barracks siege. He was killed for that reason. His death was also part of a pattern as senior police officers were targeted for assassination in Listowel, Tralee[6] and Castle Island.[7]

O'Sullivan lived in the RIC barracks on Church Street, for his own protection. But his family had a house a few doors away and the bond with his wife, Mary, was a strong one. O'Sullivan liked to walk home for dinner each day. Whenever he was out in the street, he was watched by his officers. But when the Winter Assizes came on, most of his officers were needed at court and he was shot down while he was walking home.[8]

The main prosecution witness was Kathleen Burke, then aged twenty-two; she was a 'domestic' in O'Sullivan's home which was only twenty yards from the Barracks. She told the court that she was waiting by the front door of the house watching the children coming home from school and that she saw the inspector close by. Then she saw Carmody and Lenehan come out of Walsh's pub. She had known them both 'some time'. Carmody wore a cap, a short coat belt, knickers and black leggings. Lenehan wore a suit and a cap. She saw Carmody fire at the inspector who was walking towards her. She 'saw smoke and a pistol in Carmody's hand'. The inspector continued walking and then she saw Lenehan fire and the inspector fell into the gutter by a donkey cart. The two men made off. Then Devereux appeared with another man and they too fired on the inspector.

She told the court she went to an identification parade at Tralee gaol and picked out Carmody and Lenehan as she peered through a gap in the window blind into the yard. She did not pick out Devereux but recognised him now. She added that, when she saw him in the laneway, his back was turned to her.

When she was cross-examined, she told the court that she went home later that day and told her mother she had not seen the shooting. She said she told this lie because she was afraid others would learn she was a witness. She saw a policeman the same day but did not reveal she had seen the shooting.

Question: 'Why?'

Answer: 'Well I was afraid.'

Question: 'Why?'

Answer: 'Well I was afraid I might be shot myself.'

It was not a good line of cross-examination and it went from bad to worse when defence counsel Fitzgerald elicited the fact that the witness had served in the Woman's Auxiliary Corps during the war which must have bolstered her standing with the Court. He pressed on:

'When you returned from service you had the misfortune to have an illegitimate child?' The prosecutor objected but the question was allowed.

Answer: 'Yes.'

Some days later she was seen by the Head Constable and told him what she saw and she had been placed under guard since then.

The next witness was John Nolan, a tailor who lived on Church Street with his wife and children. He told the court that he had heard shots and seen the District Inspector with his hands raised. Two men stood close by. One wore 'a light grey suit' but he could not describe the other. He told the court he was frightened and left the scene and went home. When cross-examined, he agreed he knew Carmody and Lenehan well and they were not the men involved in the killing.

Two RIC officers gave some evidence identifying O'Carroll and Devereux behaving furtively as Tobias Sullivan walked down the street just before the shooting. But this evidence fell short of incriminating them in the killing.

This concluded the prosecution case and O'Carroll and Devereux were acquitted by the court for lack of evidence.

The remaining two accused were Edward Carmody, a farmer's son from Ballyhogan and Jaco Lenehan, a twenty-seven-year-old carpenter. He had a workshop at the back of the RIC barracks. These two prisoners were not free to give sworn evidence according to the law then in place but both called alibi witnesses. Ultimately, it all hinged on the evidence of Kathleen Burke. She had viewed the incident in good light from a close distance. Neither defendant disputed that she knew them well: Listowel was a small town and they could advance no credible reason why she should lie.

There followed a very short summing up by the Judge Advocate which, by the standards of the time, was fair. After retiring, the officers in the court returned and asked to hear character evidence. This meant conviction for both men.

Carmody reiterated he was innocent. Lenehan also protested his innocence and said he 'would take the book and swear that'.

'We cannot take a sworn statement' replied the President of the Court. It was, in any event, too late. Lenehan and Carmody had been convicted and sentenced to hang.

Kathleen Burke was moved out of the country.[9] It is likely that she received a resettlement grant as witnesses often did. She remains an enigmatic figure.

The two men were sentenced to death and the Judge Advocate General (JAG) reviewed the case and directed that the sentence could go ahead. Only a few days later, there was further correspondence on the case. There is another note in the JAG's file asking whether the main witness had been paid a reward.[10] The Truce intervened and the prisoners were released by Christmas.

In the years that followed, few people remembered why Lenehen had been convicted, only that he had narrowly escaped execution. He became a minor celebrity, playing a mournful tune on his bugle at commemorations. Occasionally, he talked in a puzzled way about the great event in his life: his trial for murder and his escape from the hangman's noose. He did not shoot the District Inspector and was unable to name the killers.[11]

Who did kill Tobias O'Sullivan? The truth only emerged at the turn of the century when the records of the Bureau of Military History were published. Devereux and O'Carroll had played no part in the killing and Edward Carmody and Jaco Lenehan had come within an ace of being hanged for a killing in which they took no part.

Cornelius Brosnan and Jack Ahern revealed that they had killed O'Sullivan.[12] In later life, Brosnan became a legendary GAA footballer who was credited with doing much to overcome the bitterness of the Civil War. In 1921, he was barely out of his teens and took the lead role in this affair. Lying in wait in Walsh's pub and getting the signal, he rushed out into the street and fired.[13]

CHAPTER TWENTY-NINE

J.J. Mac Eoin

Mac Eoin was a Blacksmith from Kilshruley in County Longford. He came to prominence in 1920 after an ambush at Ballinalee.[1] In February 1921, Mac Eoin led and organised an attack on a convoy of Auxiliaries on 'a graceful sweep of road' near Clonfin.[2] A mine immobilised the first tender and injured many of the Auxiliaries. The second tender came to a halt immediately behind and the Auxiliaries jumped out and took cover. Colonel Wilford MC and his men were trapped in the river under a small bridge. He and his men fought a brave action until their ammunition ran out. Most of the seventeen-strong company were wounded and two died of their wounds that day.[3]

The following month, Mac Eoin was captured at Mullingar railway station. He was handcuffed and was being escorted by eighteen Royal Irish Constabulary (RIC) men to barracks but broke free and ran. He was shot once in the chest and came close to death but made a recovery.

Mac Eoin was tried by court martial on 14 June 1921 at City Hall, for the murder of District Inspector T.J. McGrath in January of that year. He was represented by Charles Bewley.[4]

The evidence showed that the Inspector and six RIC men had gone to an old lady's house near Ballinalee looking for the prisoner. The door opened and Mac Eoin appeared and fired. The inspector span round and fell to the ground. He threw a hand grenade wounding a constable and ran out of a side door conducting a running battle with his pursuers.

Part of the evidence against him was a confession he made when wounded during his escape attempt a few weeks later at Mullingar. A constable recalled the wounded prisoner 'half standing, half sitting' and obviously in great pain as he waited for a priest and a Doctor to arrive:

```
'I shot DI McGrath. I was in a cottage near my
mother's house when I saw the police coming on
the street. I had a revolver in my right hand
```

and a bomb in my left. When the DI knocked at
the door I opened it slightly and, with the
revolver I had in my right hand, I shot the
DI. and then threw the bomb at the police who
were in the street and then they ran away.'

At his trial, Mac Eoin did not deny firing at the inspector. His defence was that he had fired at his attackers and they had fired at him. The inspector 'fell in the fight'. He had no idea who had fired the fatal shot. He maintained the other officers had seen little of what had happened and run off. Contrary to their evidence he had quickly gone back to the scene of the shooting. The other officers had gone but the inspector lay mortally wounded. He, Mac Eoin, whispered an act of contrition to the dying man.

As to the confession, he maintained he had no recollection of that. His defence on the facts was unlikely to find favour with the court and it was barely tenable.

Three of the Auxiliaries wounded at Clonfin gave character evidence for Mac Eoin. Colonel Thomas Jocelyn Wilford MC told the court that his men were well treated and Mac Eoin had provided medical treatment for the wounded and transport to hospital. Not surprisingly, Mac Eoin was convicted and sentenced to hang.

The Truce intervened and those TDs in custody were released to take part in the Treaty debates. The exception was Mac Eoin who remained under sentence of death. Collins threatened to break off the Treaty talks with Westminster unless Mac Eoin was released to take part. General Macready studiously refused to release the prisoner or express an opinion on what he regarded as a political matter. Westminster finally took the initiative and released the prisoner and Macready later hinted at a grudging relief.[5]

Mac Eoin fought in the Civil War on the pro-Treaty side. He later enjoyed a long career in the Dáil. He served as Minister for Justice and Minister of Defence. Much of his career after 1921 was devoted to suppressing IRA violence. He did so with no lack of vigour.

Notes

DRAMATIS PERSONAE

1. *Hansard* 4 March 1920 Vol. 126, Col. 615.
2. Ferguson, K. *Kings Inn Barristers 1868–2004* (Dublin: The Honourable Society of Kings Inns, 2005).

INTRODUCTION

1. *The Record of the Rebellion, Operations*, Vol. I, p.51. The Record provides the most reliable source for army casualties between 1918 and 1921. Casualties during the Easter Rising included 106 soldiers killed and 334 wounded. See Kiberd, D. (ed.) *1916 Rebellion Handbook* (Dublin: Mourne River Press,1998).
2. Abbott, R. *Police Casualties in Ireland 1919–22* (Dublin: Mercier, 2001), p.9. Including fifteen police officers killed during the Easter Rebellion and at least twenty-two wounded. Additionally from 1917–18, one officer died of injuries during a demonstration and a significant number sustained serious injuries during public order incidents. In this period at least six officers were wounded by gunfire.
3. And later courts martial under ROIA.
4. See for instance *R v Allen* [1921] 2 IR 241.

CHAPTER ONE

1. O'Faolain, S. *De Valera* (London: Penguin, 1939), p. 40.
2. Warwick-Haller, A. & S. (eds) *Letters from Dublin, Easter 1916: Alfred Fannin's Diary of the Rising* (Dublin: Irish Academic Press, 1995), p.51.
3. Gibbon, M. *Inglorious Soldier* (London: Hutchinson, 1968), p.64.
4. BMH WS No. 699, Clarke.
5. BMH WS No. 327, Egan.
6. Bonsall, P. *The Irish RMs* (Dublin: Four Courts Press, 1997), p.142. The late Dr Bonsall suggests that the RM's, working in conjunction with the RIC, used their local knowledge to identify nationalist leaders. A recommendation for internment by an RM would have carried a good deal of weight.
7. See for Instance Toomey, T. *The War of Independence in Limerick* (Privately Published, 2010), p.157. See BMH WS No. 39, Ahern, p.4. See also *Killarney Echo and South Kerry Chronicle*, 13 May 1916 and BMH WS No. 1598, Murphy.
8. Ó Ruairc, Padraig. *Blood on the Banner* (Dublin: Mercier, 2011), p.54.
9. BMH WS No. 138, Riordan, p.4.

10. With Mellows were two other fugitives, Alfie Monaghan and Hynes.
11. BMH WS No. 1047, McNamara.
12. BMH WS No.277, McCabe: 'mobilise as many men as you can, destroy communications and await our arrival.' See also BMH WS No. 917, O'Grady.
13. BMH WS No. 20, Hales, T. Seán Hales was later TD on the side of the anti-Treaty faction. He was shot dead outside the Dáil in December 1922. Shot and wounded with him was another TD, Padraic O Maille. This shooting triggered the killing of four anti-Treaty prisoners without trial. It marked an escalation of the Civil War.
14. Dwyer, T. Ryle. *Tans, Terror and Troubles* (Cork: Mercier Press, 2001), p.101.
15. BMH WS No. 376, O'Kelly, p.4.
16. BMH WS No. 132, Spillane (released after a few weeks) and McNamara from Crusheen, County Clare, BMH WS No. 1,047, p.9 (released after some hours after a character reference from a local RIC man).
17. See Gibbon, *Inglorious, Soldier*, p.54.
18. Chief Secretary's List, PRO. CO 903/19. This was a contemporaneous list provided by the Military to the office of the Chief Secretary for Ireland. The list records the details of 171 prisoners whom it asserts were tried by FGCM. In fact, there is an error in that record. There is no doubt that 160 prisoners were tried by FGCM which was a rudimentary form of trial used for soldiers on active service. But, in fact, a few of the prisoners named were tried by General Court Martial in late May 1916. These included Eoin MacNeill, as well as Seán MacEntee, Martin, Leahy and Sally for the murder of Constable Magee and the attempted murder of Lieutenant Robert Dunville. Also, James Quigley was tried for his alleged part in the Ashbourne ambush. Finally, Austin Stack and Con Collins were tried for their part in the Kerry arms landing. The Chief Secretary's List does provide useful background information about the prisoners tried.
19. BMH WS No. 1511, Doyle.
20. Ibid., p.36.
21. BMH WS No. 510, Thornton, p.26.
22. BMH WS No. 679, Shouldice.
23. Ibid., p.8.
24. BMH WS No. 1511, Doyle.
25. See for instance Howard, P. & Nichols G. *Past Nichols the Undertakers* (Dublin: Privately published, 2014).
26. Kennerk, B. *Temple Street Children's Hospital* (Privately Published, 2014).
27. BMH WS No. 196, Mitchell, p.3.
28. *Sinn Féin Rebellion Handbook* (Dublin: Mourne River Press, 1998), p.17.
29. BMH WS No. 333, O'Rahilly, p.8.
30. O'Sullivan, M. and O'Neill B. *The Shelbourne and its People* (Dublin: Blackwater Press, 1999).
31. Duffy, J. *Children of the Rising* (Dublin: Hatchette Books, 2015).The boy was William Lionel Sweny who is believed to have died on Wednesday 26 April at Mount Street.

32. A government committee was eventually formed and paid out compensation to bereaved and wounded. No payments appear to have been made until February 1917 and the immediate need had to be filled by voluntary subscription.

33. The National Aid Society. It appears that, despite the opprobrium attaching to the rebels, the Fund achieved significant success. A gift sale at the Mansion House attracted wide support from the public. There were many instances of members of the public putting up jewellery and valuables for auction. The artists, Lavery and William Orpen supplied blank canvases for a sale, setting £600 as the price of a picture, See for instance, O'Malley, E. *On Another Man's Wound* (Dublin: Anvil Books, 2002), p.50. There were significant donations from Australia and America. Another organisation active in relief work was The Volunteer Dependents' Fund. These two organisations merged in August 1916.

34. See *Sinn Féin Rebellion Handbook* p.272.

35. Laffan, M. *The Resurrection of Ireland* (London: Cambridge University Press, 1999).

36. Cd 8279.

CHAPTER TWO

1. Mr Justice Montague Shearman, 1857–1925. As a young man he had been a gifted amateur footballer, a sprinter and Oxford Rugby Blue (*The Burlington Magazine*, Vol. 76, May 1940). Shearman was a founder member of the Amateur Athletic Association. His first love was football about which he wrote a notable history: *Football: It's History for Five Centuries* (1885) with J. E. Vincent. He later tried the two men convicted and executed for the murder of Sir Henry Wilson.

2. *The Royal Commission on the causes of the Rebellion in Ireland* 1916 Cmnd 8279. For minutes of evidence to the Royal Commission HO/10810/312350. For documents and correspondence submitted to the Commission, see PRO 30/67/31. It has not been possible to trace any record of the private deliberations of the Commission and the likelihood is that no record was kept or it was destroyed. All the sensitive or interesting documents that are referred to in the minutes of evidence of the Royal Commission are not in the file at the PRO.

3. Evidence of the Viceroy to the Royal Commission, para 851: 'The military explained that there was not sufficient time to ensure it was a success...' It is fair to add that Wimborne did not suggest the Military were being deliberately obstructive. Apart from Cowan, the officers gave no public account of these meetings and there is no minute of the crucial meetings. The only accounts that we have are those which were given in evidence to the Royal Commission by Nathan, Wimborne, Cowan, Price and Edgeworth-Johnstone. All of these witnesses were fighting for their reputations and their accounts cannot be regarded as impartial.

4. The in-lying piquets were mobilised early on Sunday evening and stood down just after 10pm. Augusteijn, J. (ed.) *The Memoirs of John M. Regan* (Dublin: Four Courts, 2007), p.91. Regan was a junior officer with the Royal Irish Rifles stationed in Dublin during Easter 1916. He later related that his men were kept

in readiness for rebellion. They were ordered to 'stand to' early on the Sunday evening and stood down some hours later. He was unable to say why the order was given but remembered it as a moment of some significance. He has proved a reliable witness in all other respects.

5. Evidence of Sir Matthew Nathan to the Royal Commission.
6. Letter, 2 May, Lady Wimborne to her mother.
7. Wimborne, Evidence to the Royal Commission.
8. BMH No. 531, Young.
9. BMH WS No. 348, Gerrard.
10. Asquith, C. *The Diaries of Lady Cynthia Asquith,* 1915–18 (London: Century, 1987), p.163.
11. See Asquith, *The Diaries of Lady Cynthia Asquith.* Drawn to my attention by Townshend, C. *Easter Rising* (London: Penguin, 2005), p.187.
12. See Asquith, *The Diaries of Lady Cynthia Asquith.*
13. Evidence of Sir Matthew Nathan to the Royal Commission, para. 17.
14. By S1(7) of the Defence of the Realm Act 1915, in the event of invasion or other military emergency, the executive was permitted to suspend jury trial and permit trial of civilians by courts martial.
15. Evidence of Major General Friend to the Royal Commission, para. 1480.
16. A crucial piece of information provided by a trusted Castle informant related to a speech made by MacDonagh to his unit earlier that week: 'We are not going out on Friday, we are going on Sunday. Boys, some of us may never come back.' Evidence of Sir Matthew Nathan to the Royal Commission, para. 22.
17. Diary of Colonel Bertram Portal, officer commanding 3rd Reserve Cavalry Brigade. The Portal Diary emerged in 2013, when it was sold by reputable auctioneers. But it has yet to receive any public scrutiny.
18. Nathan Papers MS 476 Bodleian Library. Drawn to my attention by Sloan, G. 'The British State and the Irish Rebellion of 1916: An Intelligence Failure Or a Failure of Response'. *Journal of Strategic Studies* Vol. 6, No. 5, 2013.
19. Major General Friend acknowledged in evidence to the Royal Commission that he had seen this intelligence before going to London.
20. As late as 20 April, the forces at the Curragh were reinforced by the 5th Battalion of the 2nd Leinster Regiment for the purpose of suppressing a rebellion. See Whitton, F.E. *The History of the Prince of Wales's Leinster Regiment* Vol. 2, p.270.
21. See Sir Reginald Brade, Secretary of the War Council to Lord French, 28 April 1916. Quoted by O Broin, L. *Dublin Castle and the 1916 Rising* (London: Sidgwick and Jackson, 1970), p.136. In evidence to the Royal Commission, Major General Friend acknowledged this warning but for security reasons and perhaps to save himself, he framed his reply in a guarded manner: 'During March and April of this year we received further warnings of a possible landing of arms and a simultaneous rising of disaffected persons.' See para. 1445, Evidence 26 May.
22. Major General Sir Lovrick Friend 1866–1944. As a young man he kept wicket for MCC and Kent and played in the first FA Cup Final. Major General Friend

After The Rising

had seen action at the battle of Omdurman in 1998. In 1912 he was appointed General in charge of Administration in Ireland and appointed C in C in Ireland in 1914. He was in post at the time of the Curragh Mutiny. After the Rebellion he lost his command in Ireland and was transferred to administrative duties until his retirement in 1920. He died in 1944 aged 78.

23. De Valera Papers P150/512.

24. It was found as a fact by the Commission that Casement's identity was not known until late on Saturday; Commission Report p.8. Casement had been arrested by the police and held in custody overnight until the Saturday when he was sent up to Dublin by train. RIC Inspector Brittan's report noted that the prisoner looked like Casement but had not given a name. HO 144/1636/311643/3A.

25. *R v Casement*. Evidence of Sidney Waghorn, leading signalman. His evidence is consistent with the log for *HMS Bluebell*, see PRO ADM 53/35653 and also the account given by Karl Spindler, Captain of the *Aud*.

26. See PRO ADM 53/35653.

27. According to evidence given by Wimborne to the Royal Commission, Major General Friend left Ireland on the Thursday! Evidence of the Royal Commission, p.38.

28. It was not business because it was the Easter weekend. It was unlikely to be a family matter because his parents were long dead and he was a confirmed bachelor.

29. In evidence to the Royal Commission, Major General Friend dismissed the Castle Document as 'a pure invention'. Professor Townshend rightly acknowledges that all those involved in getting the Castle Document out of Dublin Castle believed completely in its authenticity. Even on the night of his execution MacDiarmada was still maintaining that the Castle Document was real. BMH WS No. 729, Browne.

30. Summed up by Townshend, C. *Easter 1916* (London: Penguin, 2005), p.131. It is submitted that the likely suspect is Plunkett who had the document at Kimmage (where he had a press) before it went to P.J. Little for publication in New Ireland.

31. BMH WS No. 344, Smith. See also BMH WS No. 1769, Little.

32. Henry Vivian Cowan, 1854–1918, Royal Artillery, fought in the Afghan War of 1878–1880 and later wounded in Egypt at the battle of Tel-el-Kebir. He was an aide de campe to Lord Roberts in the Boer War. He was briefly commandant of the Royal Military Academy and then from 1904–1911, he was aide de campe to the King. From 1914–1917 he was Assistant Adjutant General in Dublin. He died the following year.

33. The Cavalry at Marlborough Barracks, the Third Royal Irish Regiment at Richmond Barracks, the Royal Irish Rifles at Portobello and the 10th Dublin Fusiliers at Kingsbridge.

34. Royal Commission, Conclusions, p.13 and pp. 60–61.

35. Major Price in evidence to the Royal Commission, para. 345.

36. Major Ivon Henry Price, a law graduate of Trinity Dublin. He joined the RIC in 1891 and was an RIC officer of wide experience who served with the Army

during the Great War. Appointed DSO in 1917, he was promoted Brevet –Colonel in 1919 and, once demobbed, returned to the RIC with the rank of County Inspector. He was soon promoted to Assistant Inspector General of the RIC.

37. Royal Commission, Evidence of Major General Friend para. 1,467 et seq. Also evidence of Sir Matthew Nathan.

38. Royal Commission, Evidence of Major General Friend, para. 1,499 et seq.

39. The Royal Commission identified the seminal moment as the Howth arms landing in 1914, when a decision was made by Dublin Castle not to prosecute the gun runners although their identities were well known, in order to avoid conflict with separatists.

40. Royal Commission, Evidence of Major Price.

41. Alex McCabe was a National School teacher and a Volunteer organiser in Sligo. He was tried and acquitted in February 1916. See *Record of the Rebellion, Vol. III Law,* and p.7.

42. Royal Commission, Evidence of Major Price, para. 1347.

43. BMH WS No. 217, Keegan, J. J.

44. It should be remembered that, in this period, there was a real prospect of civil war in Ireland over the Home Rule crisis: Carson's Volunteers were formed in 1912 and drilled unlawfully with the connivance of the magistracy. Bonar Law urged Carson's Volunteers to resist Home Rule 'by any means' and it seems clear Carson's men were ready to resist the will of Parliament by force of arms. The Volunteers were formed in 1913 as a counter threat. The Curragh Mutiny followed in March 1914 and was followed, in turn, by the Ulster Volunteer Force (UVF) arms landing the following month. The Volunteer arms landing took place a few months later at Howth.

45. Drawn from the 5th and 16th Lancers and 4th Hussars at the Curragh.

46. The Third Cavalry Brigade served with distinction at Mons, Le Cateau, Neuve Chapelle and the first and second battles of Ypres.

47. The Third Reserve Brigade included 16th and 17th Lancers and 4/8th Hussars.

48. Lowe was inspector of Cavalry in 1916. He had formerly been keeper of the Cavalry Records and, during the Boer War, he had been colonel of the 7th Dragoon Guards. Colonel Portal's regiment was 17th Lancers. Kennard's regiment had been 5th Dragoon Guards.

49. By General Maxwell to Lord French, De Valera Papers UCDA. Also echoed in despatches, Lord French, *London Gazette Supplement* 21 July 1916.

50. Andrew, C and Dilks, D. *The Missing Dimension – Governments and Intelligence Communities in the Twentieth Century* (London: MacMillan, 1984) in which it was argued that Captain Hall wanted a policy of repression in Ireland. It is submitted that the evidence indicates a more nuanced desire: namely that the nationalist element obstructing recruitment to the British army be flushed out and dealt with. Throughout the war Hall was in contact with Major Price, the intelligence officer at the Irish Command in Dublin. Price believed that rebellion was a real prospect from early 1916. But the damage to recruitment was his primary concern which he had voiced to anyone who would listen. See evidence of Major Price to the Royal Commission.

51. In 1914, a German Cruiser, the Magdeburg, was sunk by Russian cruisers. The code books had been saved and passed on to the Naval Intelligence Department. Even after the codes were changed, the shooting down of a Zeppelin in September 1916, yielded the new German naval code book. In 1915 the luggage of a German agent was stolen in Turkey and despatched to London. It contained a German diplomatic code book and permitted access to all diplomatic telegram traffic and the interception of coded telegrams between the German Foreign Ministry and the Germany Embassy in Washington. See *Documents Relative to the Sinn Fein Movement*, 1921 Cmd 1108. One telegram reads 'Between two or three steam trawlers could land 20,000 rifles and 10 machine guns, with ammunition and explosives at Fenit Pier in Tralee Bay. Irish pilot boat to await the trawlers at dusk, north of the island of Inishtooskert at the entrance to Tralee Bay, and show two green lights close to each other at short intervals...' It is, therefore, abundantly clear that the Royal Navy had the most detailed information to hand. In the final analysis all that was lacking was the name of the arms ship: the *Aud*.

    Reference should be made to Admiral Bayly's memoir *Pull Together!* (London: George G. Harrap, 1939). Admiral Bayly does not refer to the fact that the German codes had been broken. A close reading of his memoir suggests that he goes to some lengths to disguise that fact even though the war was long since won. Admiral Bayly even suggests that the Royal Navy interest in Tralee Bay as a contender for an arms landing was generated by local information that '240 cars' had assembled at Fenit. In fact, those who planned the Rebellion had made arrangements for the guns to be moved up to Dublin by rail, dropping off consignments at Cork and Limerick. The responsibility for this lay with William Partridge who had the necessary trade union connections in the area. Fenit was ideal for this purpose because the jetty had a light rail link to Tralee which had a mainline connection to Limerick, Cork and Dublin. It can be seen that there was no need for a convoy of cars.

    Additionally, none of the hundreds of witnesses to these momentous events has ever referred to arrangements for a huge convoy of cars to distribute guns. Nor does any other contemporary source refer to such a convoy. For all these reasons, Admiral Bayly's reference to 240 cars at Fenit can be seen as a piece of subterfuge. His memoir was published on the eve of the Second World War and it may be that he thought it prudent to avoid reference to trade secrets and working practices.

52. Brock, M. and E. (eds) *Margot Asquith's Great War Diary 1914–16 The View from Downing Street* (Oxford: Oxford University Press, 2014), p.255.

53. De Courcy Ireland, J. *The Sea and the Easter Rising 1916* (Dublin, 1996) suggests that Spindler's account is unreliable in some respects and should be treated with caution. By way of example, he notes that Spindler claimed to have scuttled the *Aud* in such a way as to block Queenstown Harbour but it is clear that the *Aud* was scuttled some miles from the Harbour. This is an unkind interpretation of Spindler's account; he certainly intended to block the channel and hoped that he had obstructed the passage of ships. He certainly delayed scuttling the *Aud* as long as he could. What is clear is that, *Setter II* was in service in 1916: see Dittmar and

Colledge, *British Warships 1914–1919*. In Spindler's account he describes *Setter II* (although he recalls the name *as Shatter II*); he correctly describes a single gun mounted between dummy lifeboats. The name *Setter* had been changed to *Setter II* only a few months previously to accommodate a new destroyer assigned that name and due to be launched in August. On balance it is highly probable that the crew of *Setter II* boarded the *Aud*. The log book for *Setter II* has not been preserved at the Public Record Office.

54. Spindler's account was first published under the name *Das Geheimnisvolle Schiff* in 1920 and again under Spindler, K. *The Mystery of the Casement Ship* (Berlin: Kribe-Verlag, 1931). The relevant passage is at p.133 et seq. See also the log for *HMS Bluebell* ADM 53/ 35653 which is a document compiled contemporaneously: the log for *HMS Bluebell* for Good Friday shows an entry timed at 6.15pm: 'Stopped to examine steamer S/S "Aud"'.

55. See for instance *The Royal Commission on the Arrest and Subsequent Treatment of Mr Francis Sheehy Skeffington, Mr Thomas Dickson, and Mr Patrick James Macintyre upon and after their arrest on the Twenty-fifth day of April last*. Cd 8376. In that Royal Commission, the Army and all other parties were represented by counsel.

56. Considerable hesitation attaches to forming conclusions without the fullest information but there is no record of the evidence given to the Commission in private. However, the Commission's report accords entirely with the evidence given in public session and there is no hint that the Commission was influenced by other considerations. It is likely that the evidence given in private related to informants and the fact that German naval and diplomatic codes had been compromised. If this is so, then the conclusions set out in this chapter are well founded.

57. Although, the Volunteers were modelled on the British Army, it had no intelligence unit. But the men organising the rebellion were so intransigent and so busy with their own intrigues that nothing would cause them to draw back.

58. Major General Friend did not regain his command in Ireland but he was not censured or criticised, at least in public.

CHAPTER THREE

1. Junior counsel for the defence was Charles Wyse-Power who later recounted the submission made by Healy: see BMH WS No. 420, p.4. See also WO 32/4307 'I have referred the Tullamore case to the Judge Advocate General. And will not confirm the proceedings as long as there is any doubt as to their legality.' In a later case, the High Court ruled that, in such circumstances, trial by court martial was lawful because the Proclamation was procedural: it simply prescribed the method of trial after that date – *R v Governor of Lewes Prison ex parte Doyle* [1917] 2 KB 254.

2. WO 32/4307. The prisoners are named in the Chief Secretary's List PRO CO 903/19 as: James Brennan, Francis Brennan, Peter Bracken, Thomas Byrne, James

Clark, John Delaney, Thomas Duggan, Joseph Graham, Thomas Hogan Joseph Morris, Henry McNally and Joseph Rafter. Three unnamed juveniles were released on bail and appear to have escaped trial. All the prisoners were from Tullamore.

3. WO 32/4307.
4. See PRO WO 35/94.
5. *Record of the Rebellion in Ireland 1920–21 and the Part Played by the Army in Dealing with it*, Vol. 3, Law, p.8.
6. RDFA Archive/Dublin City Library and Archive.
7. *Irish Law Times*, 2 September 1916.
8. For an account of the inquests, see *The Sinn Féin Rebellion Handbook* (Dublin: Mourne River Press, 2005). And see also *Revolutionary Lawyers*, Foxton, D. (Dublin: Four Courts, 2007).
9. Dublin Diocesan Archives. Reported by Ronan McGreevy, *Irish Times*, 15 September 2015.
10. Asquith Papers, 42. Maxwell to Lord French 16 June 1916. Maxwell submitted weekly handwritten reports to Asquith. This report is broadly typical of those submitted in the summer of 1916. See W0 32/4307.
11. See court martial of John Bowen-Colthurst, this Volume. And see *The Royal Commission on the Arrest and Subsequent treatment of Mr Francis Sheehy Skeffington, Mr Thomas Dickson, Mr Patrick James MacIntyre upon and after their arrest on the twenty fifth day of April last*. Cd 8376.
12. Sergeant Samuel Lomas, who took part in the executions of Pearse, MacDonagh and Clarke, wrote a revealing diary entry which showed that the first two executions had gone according to plan but the third, Tom Clarke, did not:'an old man was not quite so fortunate, requiring a bullet from the officer to complete the ghastly business.' Diary of Samuel Henry Lomas of the Sherwood Foresters. National Army Museum. Accession No. 1990-12-107. For a full analysis see Enright S., *Easter Rising The Trials* (Dublin: Merrion Press, 2014) Chapter 7.
13. Dunn, H. *The Minstrel Boy* (Dublin: Book Link, 2006).
14. One notable recruit was Company Sergeant Major Martin Doyle V.C. from New Ross who would later take up arms against the Empire. Hundreds of other ex-servicemen joined the Irish Republican Army (IRA).
15. *The Time (Ireland) Act 1916* 6 & 7 Geo V c.45. For this fine turn of phrase I am indebted to Parsons, M. *Irish Times*, 26 October 2014.
16. Macardle suggests that only a few prisoners engaged with the process. Macardle, D. *The Irish Republic* (London: Corgi, 1967), p.190. That assertion is based on anecdotal evidence and is hard to evaluate.
17. BMH WS 889, Seamus Ua Caomhanaigh.
18. The other members of the Sankey Committee were Mr Justice Pim, Mr Justice Younger and three backbench MPs.
19. See for instance BMH WS, McCarthy No. 1497; Robbins No. 585 and Lawless No. 1,043. The accounts of some prisoners smack a little of what they wished they had said.

20. Foxton, D. *Revolutionary Lawyers* (Dublin: Four Courts Press, 2007), p.99.

21. Brennan-Whitmore, W.J. *With the Irish in Frongoch* (Cork: Mercier Press, 2013), p.186. Brennan Whitmore's account first appeared in 1917. Twelve of the fifteen hut leaders were convicted and sentenced.

22. Hugh Thornton was one. He was sentenced to two years' imprisonment. Patrick, George and John King were also court martialled for declining to serve.

23. BMH WS No. 1744, Nunan.

24. Nunan was released from army service after serving the twelve-month sentence.

25. DORR Reg. 27 Conduct likely to cause disaffection, DORR Reg. 9A Power to ban processions.

26. Macardle, D. *The Irish Republic* (London: Corgi, 1967), p.197.

27. *R v Governor of Lewes Prison ex parte Doyle* [1917] 2 All E R 254.

28. Tadhg Barry, later Alderman Barry, a writer and poet. Barry was in and out of custody until 1922. He was shot dead by a sentry at Ballykinlar Internment Camp in November 1922 in circumstances which were never fully explained.

29. *Sixth Division Record of the Rebellion*, p.9.

30. Prosecutions were brought before a District Court Martial. The legislative provision used was Reg. 9E of DORR and *The Military Exercises and Drill (Ireland) Order 1916*. The standard wording of the charge alleged being concerned in movements of a military nature in an area in which Reg. 9E was in force.

31. *Killarney Echo*, 24 November 1917.

32. These powers were invoked under *The Criminal Law and Procedure Act 1887* which permitted such trials to take place where an area had been 'proclaimed' Under the Act.

33. *Criminal and Judicial Statistics, Ireland 1917. Appendix 31*. Cmd 43, 1917. Of the 261 prosecuted for unlawful assembly, 166 were convicted and 157 went to prison. Seventy-four received sentences of fourteen days or less and twenty-three received sentences in excess of one month's imprisonment.

34. BMH WS No. 907, Nugent, p.81.

35. *Mayo News* 17 February and 19 May 1917. For these two examples I am indebted to Dr Penny Bonsall. See *The Irish RMs* (Dublin: Four Courts, 1997), p.143–4. See BMH WS No. 896, Moane.

36. *Hansard* 25 June 1920, Vol. 130, cols 2257 et seq. Sir Denis Henry, A.G.

37. Bonsall, P. *The Irish RMs* (Dublin: Four Courts Press, 1997).

38. The attempt failed and one man, Edward Punch, was captured and court martialled and sentenced to five years' penal servitude in October 1917. PRO CO 904/201.

39. Ashe was tried in Dublin for an alleged contravention of Regulation 27 of DORR. Prosecuting counsel was Captain McCaw, 3rd Royal Hussars. Ashe declined legal representation.

40. Letter from Collins to Nora Ashe. Brought to my attention by Dwyer, R. T. *Tans, Terror and Troubles* (Dublin: Mercier, 2001), p.121.

41. *Prisoners (Temporary Discharge for Ill Health) Act* 1913. 3 Geo V c.4.

CHAPTER FOUR

1. Regulation 10B.
2. See for instance *DORR Bacon, Ham and Lard (Provisional Order, 1917, No. 1180); DORR Bread Order (1917, No. 189) Butter (Maximum Prices (Amendment) Order) (1917, No. 913).*
3. For a comprehensive account of the Regulatory framework: Campbell, C. *Emergency Law in Ireland 1918–25* (Oxford: Oxford University Press, 1994).
4. *Record of the Rebellion*, Vol. III, p.8.
5. Comyn, J. *Their Friends at Court* (London: Barry Rose, 1973), p.49.
6. Augusteijn, J. *The Memoirs of John M. Regan. A Catholic Officer in the RIC and RUC 1909–48* (Dublin: Four Courts Press, 2007), p.142.
7. The Royal Commission, Cmd 8,279, pp. 5–7.
8. See Silvermines Trial, this volume.
9. See for instance McEldowney, J. 'The Queen v McKenna (1869) and Jury Packing In Ireland' *Irish Jurist* Vol. 12 (1977).
10. The following year a special jury drawn from County Dublin acquitted the prisoners.
11. See the trial of J.J. Madden, 1920, this volume, chapter 16.
12. This was done in the Silvermines Trial.
13. Criminal and Judicial statistics of the period are not susceptible to an analysis of offences linked to the insurgency. The provisions of the *Criminal Law and Procedure Act* were invoked at times of crisis and the special courts of summary jurisdiction provide the most reliable barometer of the level of unrest.
14. *Criminal and Judicial Statistics 1918*. Cmd 438, Appendix 31.
15. The evidence is anecdotal on this point. But see Bonsall, P. *The Irish RMs* (Dublin: Four Courts Press, 1997), p.147.
16. *Killarney Echo* 19 November 1917.
17. The prisoners were Joe Ring, William O'Malley, William Malone, Charles Garvin and Thomas McKittrick. The scenes in court resulted in widespread disorder in the town. The case was reported in the *Mayo News,* 23 March 1918. See Bonsall, *The Irish RMs.*
18. See Augusteijn, *The Memoirs of John M. Regan,* p.115.
19. Oldham C. H. 'The development of tillage in Ireland during the World War', *Journal of the Statistical and Social Inquiry Society of Ireland.* Vol. XIV, No. 2.
20. See for instance BMH WS No. 1013, McGelligott, No.1313, Gildea and No. 1287, Noonan.
21. See for instance Gildea, BMH WS No. 1313. Charles Gildea was sentenced to one month.
22. The Lawns had been to a pair of local men for grazing for eleven months. Where land was let for less than a year for grazing only, then the provisions protecting tenants under s58 of the Land Act 1881 were avoided. This was another bone of contention in the Tillage War and a reason why this land was selected for a confrontation.

23. See Dwyer, T. *Tans, Terror and Troubles* (Dublin: Mercier, 2001), p.136 and BMH WS No. 1013, McElligott.

24. See BMH WS No. 1770, Shiels who suggests that the Dáil Arbitration Courts were brought into being the following year at the request of Unionist landowners in an attempt to restore order.

25. *The Potatoes (Growers Return) Order 1918.*

26. See BMH WS No. 1680, p.10, Golden. See also the trial of Denis McCullough and Herbert Pim at Belfast, BMH WS No. 1765, O'Kelly, Part II.

27. *The Military Service Act 1918.*

28. *Hansard* HC Debates 9 April 1918, Vol. 104 cols 1357-1364.

29. For a vivid, if partisan account of this period, see Macardle, D. *The Irish Republic* (London: Corgi, 1967), p,195 et seq.

30. A point well made by Dwyer, Ryle. T. *Tans, Terror and Troubles* (Cork: Mercier, 2001), p.127. Dwyer's view was shared by the Army. See *Sixth Division Record of the Rebellion*, p.9. Although in his BMH WS McEllistrim does not speak of conscription as a driving force. BMH WS No. 882, McEllistrim. It is probable the conflict was by now simply inevitable.

31. Sir Frederick Shaw.

32. The new Lord Chancellor was Sir James Campbell. Appointed Lord Chief Justice was Thomas Molony and the new Chief Secretary was Edward Shortt, an ally of Lloyd George.

33. Callwell, C. *Diaries of Sir Henry Wilson* (London: Cassell, 1927).

34. The narrative verdict delivered by the jury was that: 'Browne and Laide died as a result of wounds inflicted by Constable Fallon and Sergeant Boyle but there was not sufficient evidence to say if the police were justified in firing on the men in the police hut.' *Freeman's Journal* April 1918.

35. McEllistrim BMH WS No. 882. McEllistrim was captured in 1920 after an ambush on an RIC patrol. He was tried, convicted by an ROIA Court Martial and imprisoned. He was later a TD for Kerry.

36. The only man arrested was Moss Carmody who had taken no part in the attack. See Ryle, *Tans, Terror and Troubles*, p140. McEllistrim and Cronin laid low and became organisers and leaders in the guerrilla war in Kerry.

37. Brought to my attention by Macardle, *The Irish Republic*, p.235.

38. *Sixth Division Record of the Rebellion*, p.10.

39. BMH WS No. 1131, Burke, p.8.

40. BMH WS No. 907, Nugent, p.151.

41. See for instance BMH WS No. 666, Hales.

42. BMH WS No. 1,570, Molloy, p.2.

43. BMH WS No. 741, Kehoe, p.57.

44. At first, all inquiries in the House of Commons were blocked: see HC Deb 30 May 1918 Vol. 106 c994. But a few weeks later, as the situation in Ireland worsened, it appears the government felt obliged to put as much as they could before the public. See: HC Debates 25 June 1918, vol. 107, Col. 994.

45. BMH WS No. 1770, O'Shiel, p.19.
46. See WO 141/72. He was tried by General Court Martial on 8 July 1918 at the Middlesex Guildhall. Lord Cheylesmore presided. An account of the trial can be found in *Freeman's Journal*, 9 & 10, July 1918. Dowling was released in 1924. He was probably the last prisoner to be released, soon after the Connaught Mutineers.
47. BMH WS 1232, p.7, Fraher.
48. In many courts, order was barely maintained and then only by a substantial police presence or military. See, for instance, the trial of Gearoid O'Sullivan at Skibbereen in 1918: BMH WS No. 807, p.10. Fr Patrick Doyle
49. See BMH WS No. 1042, Neylon p.7 suggests this was March 1917. An entry in *Hansard* suggests March 1918 may be more accurate.
50. *Hansard*, House of Lords Debates 14 April 1919, vol. 34, cols. 307-315. See Dwyer, *Tans, Terror and Troubles,* p.119 for the death of Daniel Scanlon killed during a disturbance outside the RIC Barracks. The jury returned a verdict of wilful murder against a named RIC officer.
51. Permitted by the *Criminal Law and Procedure Act 1887* where a district was proclaimed under the Act.
52. See Macardle, *The Irish Republic*, p.238.
53. *Freeman's Journal* 8 July 1918.
54. *Hansard* 25 June 1918 col. 908, Statement of Chief Secretary Andrew Shortt.

CHAPTER FIVE

1. The other two escapees were Sean Milroy and Sean McGarry.
2. The Coroner was Dr P. Morrissey. The foreman, Mathew O'Dwyer, related a formal narrative verdict that the two constables had been killed by unknown attackers. He offered the commiseration of the jury to the families of the dead men.
3. From Bonsall, P. *The Irish RMs* (Dublin: Four Courts Press, 1997), p.149.
4. William Wylie appeared for the Crown in most of these cases. It was usual for the crown advocate to ask the jury for a rider condemning killings but these were no longer forthcoming. In Wylie's opinion jurors were afraid of the consequences, although it is also evident that many jurors were hostile to the administration.
5. County Inspector's Report, May 1919. Jane Gallagher was the young woman who came to the aid of Sergeant Wallace. Her father was postmaster at Kilmallock. She moved to England. The inquest heard evidence that Mrs Wallace was heckled on her way to church. Mrs Wallace appeared at the Limerick Quarter sessions the following year and was awarded compensation to the sum of £1,600.
6. The inquests were both held in the boardroom of the Kilmallock Workhouse. Coroner, Dr P.J. Cleary presided. See *Freeman's Journal* 22 May 1919.
7. Inquest evidence. See *Freeman's Journal* 25 June 1919.
8. Joseph Ring and a number of other young men appeared before RM Milling in the Spring of 1918. They were charged with unlawful assembly. Ring refused to

recognise the court and added, as his parting shot to the RM, 'You already said at the hotel below that you were going to give Ring 18 months.' RM Milling did not answer this sally and it was, in fact, true. In a moment of indiscretion RM Milling had said just that in the hotel bar and he had been overheard. Milling was shot dead soon after Joe Ring was released and there is little doubt as to who fired the shots. This exchange was drawn to the author's attention by Dr Penny Bonsall, *The Irish RMs* (Dublin: Four Courts, 1997),p.144–5.The accuracy of her suspicions has been borne out by the release of statements made to the BMH. See BMH WS No. 1668, Hevey, p.16.

9. Two sisters of the Hogan family from Clash, near Toomevarra, gave evidence against men who had stolen arms from their home. A boycott was initiated and the family remained under police protection until the two sisters moved away. See Hogan, S. *The Tans in North Tipperary* (Privately Published, 2013), Chapter 6.

10. *Freeman's Journal,* 22 May 1919.

11. BMH WS No. 1284 Broy.

12. BMH WS No.1131, Burke.

13. BMH WS No. 872, Ketterick.

14. In Dan Breen's account he insists the purpose of the raid was to start the conflict not seize gelignite. If that was so why go to such efforts to seize a sizeable amount of gelignite? See BMH WS No. 1763, Breen. His account, though lucid and detailed, is unreliable in certain obvious respects and should be treated with considerable caution. His memoir *My Fight for Irish Freedom* was also persuasively contradicted by Seamus Robinson on many significant issues: BMH WS No. 1721.

15. *Freeman's Journal,* 20 June 1919.

16. *Freeman's Journal,* 26 June 1919.

17. *Freeman's Journal,* 6 August 1919.

18. The Fermoy Chapel Raid, 7 September 1919. Four soldiers were injured, one Private Jones, died of his injuries.

19. BMH WS No. 1706, O'Connell.

20. Diaries of Sir Henry Wilson, Imperial War Museum. For a more accessible account, see Callwell, C. E. (ed.) *Field Marshall Sir Henry Wilson: His Life and Diaries* (London: Cassel and Co, 1927).

21. *The Criminal Injuries (Ireland) Act 1919,* 9 Geo 5 c 14.

22. This Act extended an old scheme and allowed claims for deaths or injuries including those already sustained before the passing of the Act. See *Irish Law Times and Solicitors Journal,* 10 May 1919.

23. *Irish Law Times,* August 1920.

24. Prosecuting the proprietors of newspapers for sedition was another option but this took place only once during the conflict. The editors and owners of the *Freeman's Journal* were court martialled for sedition in the Autumn of 1920. They were convicted and released after adverse publicity caused what can only be described as a failure of nerve at Dublin Castle.

25. PRO CO 904/118.

26. Evans G. has persuasively argued that the suppression of the Dáil Loan was counterproductive in that it alienated people from the government: see, *The Raising of the First Internal Dáil Loan and the British Responses to it, 1919–1921* (NUI, 2012). On the other hand, the British government could hardly ignore the emergence of an alternative state.

27. See Evans, G. *The Raising of the First Internal Dáil Loan and the British Responses to it, 1919–1921* 11th Irish-Australian Conference, 2000. Murdoch University (NUI, 2012).The steps taken to suppress the Dáil loan generated more advertising than Michael Collins could ever hope to buy and the loan was heavily oversubscribed.

28. See Ainsworth, J. *British Security Policy in Ireland, from The Australian Journal of Irish Studies.*

29. A point drawn to my attention by Abbott, R. *Police Casualties in Ireland* (Dublin and Cork: Mercier, 2001), p.48. See also *The Record of the Rebellion, Intelligence,* p.1 where the Army complains that the Secret Service in Ireland had been dismantled while Augustine Birrell was Chief Secretary and never restored. After the Great War, Major Price, Dublin Castle's intelligence officer had been demobbed and sent back to the RIC. The officers involved in following suspects and observation duties at the ferry ports found their pay uplifts were stopped as a result of *The Vice- Regal Commission on the Reorganisation and pay of the Irish Police Forces,* 1919.

30. Andrew, C. *The Defence of the Realm* (London: Allen Lane, 2009), p.117. Memo from MI5 2nd in C: 'Despite statements to the contrary in the press and elsewhere, Sir Basil Thomson's organisation has never actually detected a case of espionage, but has merely arrested and questioned spies at the request of MI5...' This memo, written by Major Eric Holt-Wilson, is one of a number of strands of evidence which suggest that Sir Basil was an excellent self-publicist but not a spy chief worthy of the name.

31. The standard work on MI5, which is very full, makes no reference to any covert operations in Ireland in this period: See Andrew, *The Defence of the Realm.* This reinforces the view that Irish operations, when they began in early 1920, were run by Winter answering to Sir Basil Thomson, although Winter's autobiography does not acknowledge that any of the officers killed on Bloody Sunday were his men. Nor does General Macready's very full autobiography acknowledge these men were involved in intelligence or any covert operations. See Macready, N. *Annals of an Active Life* (London: Hutchinson, 1926) Vol. II, p.487 in which the killings are portrayed as a revenge attack for the execution of Kevin Barry. *The Record of the Rebellion Vol II (Intelligence)* does acknowledge most of the dead as Special Branch men. This analysis, which is not free from error, does show a notable dispassionate tone and clarity of thought.

32. The final trial of the O'Brien brothers for the Silvermines murder ended in acquittal in July 1919. For an account of the trial see this volume, Part II.

33. *Criminal and Judicial Statistics* 1919 Cmd 1431.

34. O'Malley, E. *On Another Man's Wound* (Dublin: Anvil, 2002), p.90.

35. The sentences ranged from fourteen days to nine months. In all, 132 were ordered to find sureties for good behaviour or face imprisonment and, for many, this meant a consecutive term of imprisonment. A small number of prisoners were tried for stealing arms.
36. *Criminal and Judicial Statistics Ireland 1919,* Cmd 1431, Appendix 31.
37. Alex McCabe (Sligo) James Dolan (Leitrim) and Joseph O'Doherty (Donegal). For this information I am indebted to Evans, *The Raising of the First Internal Dáil Loan and the British Responses to it, 1919–1921.*
38. In total, 140 were convicted. *Record of the Rebellion,* Vol. III, p.8. Professor Campbell suggests that the records kept by the *Irish Bulletin* may form an alternative source for the number of trials under DORA. It is submitted that those records are, at least in part, anecdotal and are not to be regarded as more reliable than those compiled by the British army. It is a feature of this period that some prisoners described an interview with an army officer as a court martial.
39. Including two members of the Dáil. Beaslai and J.J. Walsh. See *Irish Times,* 29 March and 15 May 1919.
40. *Sixth Division Record of the Rebellion,* p.18. The Record suggests that shots were fired on the Army but *The Memoirs of John M. Regan* (Dublin: Four Courts, 2007), p.123 – written by an RIC officer who was present – suggests that the only shot was fired by an army sergeant accidentally discharging his firearm.
41. *Hansard Debates* 2 December 1919 vol. 122, col. 241.
42. Sir James Macpherson, Liberal M.P. Vice-President of the Army Council 1918 and Chief Secretary to Ireland 1919. Minister for Pensions, 1919–22. Later accorded the title of Baron Strathcarron.
43. Middlemas, K. *Thomas Jones Whitehall Diaries 1918–25* Vol. III, (London: Oxford University Press, 1969), p.12.
44. Under Secretary McMahon was another notable casualty. See Ó Broin, L. *W.E. Wylie and the Irish Revolution* (Dublin: Gill & Macmillan, 1989).
45. *Freeman's Journal* 16 December 1919.
46. Leeson, D. *The Black and Tans* (Oxford: Oxford University Press, 2011). Leeson suggests that there was a question mark about Byrne's commitment. Byrne was said to favour negotiating with the rebels. Byrne was, of course, a Catholic from Derry and T.J. Smith was a unionist from Belfast. It should be said that Byrne had been Maxwell's DAG in 1916. Byrne signed the orders for executions in the aftermath of the Rising, so the suggestion that he was anything less than completely loyal was probably unfair. The reality was that he had the foresight to recognise the likely consequences of recruiting a quasi-military force of this kind.
47. *Blackwood's Magazine,* August 1922. 'The Last Days of Dublin Castle'.

CHAPTER SIX

1. Walter Edgeworth-Johnstone 1863–1936. Formerly of the Royal Irish Rifles. DMP Commissioner from 1915–23. Appointed KBE in 1924.

2. Abbott, R. *Police Casualties in Ireland 1919–22* (Dublin: Mercier 2001), p.52.

3. For material relating to this inquiry see PRO CO 904/227. The inquiry was carried out under S.1 of the Criminal Law and Procedure (Ireland) Act 1887, pursuant to a direction by the Attorney General. This procedure entitled a Resident Magistrate to examine on oath any person who he believed was capable of giving material evidence about the offence being investigated.

4. A lawyer instructed by Collins attempted to gain access to the hearings but was turned away. See BMH WS No, 707, Noyk. Michael Noyk was a solicitor who appeared for many prisoners in this period.

5. RM Alan Bell, 1857–1920 had been an RIC Inspector for nearly twenty years. He was appointed Resident Magistrate, Third Class in 1898. He was shot dead on 26 March 1920. The account of his death is taken from contemporary press interviews with witnesses which were published the following day.

6. Dwyer, R.T. *Tans, Terror and Troubles* (Dublin: Mercier, 2001), p.169; Hopkinson, M. (ed.) *The Irish War of Independence* (Dublin: Gill & Macmillan, 2004), p.55. And see also Hittle, J. *Michael Collins and the Anglo Irish War* (Virginia: Potomac Books, 2011), p.95 where it is suggested that Bell had recommended T.J. Smith and Forbes Redmond for the posts of Inspector General and Deputy Inspector General. It is also suggested that he was liaising with Sir Basil Thomson on operations and shaping policy at Dublin Castle including shooting down insurgent suspects. These assertions have been made in varying forms by many historians but there is very little evidence. But see Andrew and Dilks (eds) *The Missing Dimension* (London: Macmillan 1984) in which O'Halpin's research points to a document at the Public Record Office CO 904/118 which tends to indicate that Bell had passed on information to Sir Basil Thomson at New Scotland Yard. It would be surprising if he did not pass on information that came his way in the course of his duties. These matters, whatever they amount to, came to light much later. It is submitted that the actual reason he was killed was that he was exercising a legal jurisdiction under the Crimes Act which was not well known, then or now.

7. The external bond in America raised over $5m.

8. See the trial of Fr Delahunty, this volume. Fr Delahunty was sentenced to two years' imprisonment for his role as a local organiser of the Dáil loan.

9. The account of this inquest is taken from PRO CO 904/47 and the Wylie Memoir.

10. James J.McCabe was a part-time deputy coroner. He ran a solicitor's practice in Cork.

11. *Cork Examiner* and *Freeman's Journal,* 21 March 1920.

12. Jasper Wolfe, 1872–1952. Crown Prosecutor in Cork. Also a newspaper proprietor and later President of the Law Society of Ireland. He sat in the Dáil as an Independent TD 1927–32.

13. Wylie relates that Sergeant Sullivan belatedly offered to act but was refused 'without thanks'. Sullivan had been a prosecution witness at Cork Assizes in an attempted murder case but had lost his nerve when called upon to give evidence.

14. *Blackwood's Magazine, The Last Days of Dublin Castle*, August 1922.
15. Jury Note signed by William J. Barry, Foreman, 12 April 1920: 'To enable the jury to arrive at a just conclusion touching the circumstances into which we are enquiring, we are of the opinion that His Excellency Lord French and Sir John Taylor, Under Secretary should be summoned...'
16. 'We find that the late Alderman Tomás Mac Curtain, Lord Mayor of Cork, died from shock and haemorrhage caused by bullet wounds and that he was wilfully murdered under the circumstances of the most callous brutality and that murder was organised and carried out by the Royal Irish Constabulary, officially directed by the British government and we return a verdict of wilful murder against David Lloyd George, Prime Minister of England, Ian MacPherson, late Chief Secretary of Ireland, Acting Inspector General Smith of the Royal Irish Constabulary, Divisional Inspector Clayton of the Royal Irish Constabulary, District Inspector Swanzy and some unknown members of the Royal Irish Constabulary.'

    The RIC transferred a number of officers out of Cork for their own safety. Swanzy, most of all, was a marked man. In a breach of the usual practice, he was posted to his home town, Lisburn, where it was thought he would be safe. But Michael Collins sent a group of men after him. He gave one man Mac Curtain's revolver to carry out the killing. By this act, Collins sought to confer legitimacy on a murder that Mac Curtain would never have sanctioned. A few weeks later Swanzy was shot and killed. Hundreds of Catholic men left Lisburn that day hoping this would satisfy the gathering loyalist mob. It did not. That night hundreds of Catholic women and children were trudging out of Lisburn on the back road over the mountain. Looking back, the flames from their burning homes lit up the night sky.

    Evidence has since emerged that the day before the killing, Swanzy and other senior RIC officers had met with an army unit sent to arrest Mac Curtain on suspicion of an attempt to ambush the Viceroy. Swanzy and the other RIC officers disbelieved the report and opposed the plan to arrest Mac Curtain. They sent for two RIC sergeants who confirmed that Mac Curtain had not left Cork on the day of the alleged ambush. Swanzy's view was that Mac Curtain was a moderate and had the influence to stop Cork sliding into anarchy. If that evidence is reliable it strongly suggests that Swanzy was not involved in what took place. BMH WS No. 68, Feeley, p.5.
17. See for instance *Daily Chronicle,* January 1920.
18. Lloyd George's approval 'gunning' was contemporaneously documented in the diary of the Chief of the Imperial General Staff, Sir Henry Wilson. The diaries are now held at the IWM. See Jeffery, K. *Field Marshall Sir Henry Wilson* (Oxford: University Press, 2006), p.265–6.
19. Macardle, D. *The Irish Republic* (London: Corgi, 1967), p.305. Macardle's work is self-evidently partisan and she quotes no source for these figures although her work has proved factually accurate in most respects. Her figures derive support from the Chief of the Combined Intelligence Services, Winter, who later wrote

that, in the Dublin District Area alone, between October 1920 and July 1921, 6,311 raids and searches took place. See Winter, O. *Winter's Tale* (London: The Richards Press, 1951), p.304.

20. Replacing General Shaw who had first seen action against the Fenians at Tallaght in 1867. In private correspondence with Sir Ian MacPherson, Macready wrote that he loathed the country and its people 'with a depth deeper than the sea and more violent than that I feel about the Boche'. Curiously Macready was married to an Irish woman.

21. *Blackwood's Magazine* August 1922, 'The Last Days of Dublin Castle'.

22. A raft of new civil servants was brought into Dublin Castle. Curiously, these men were very different to Hamar Greenwood. They were headed by Sir James Anderson *'The ablest man I ever met'* wrote Wylie. His new subordinates were *'a damn good team'*.

23. *Record of the Rebellion*, Vol. III Law. PRO WO 141/94.

24. Wylie Memoir PRO 30/89/2. In fact the error lay with a civil servant not with Lord French. As a face saver, Lord French put it about that the released internees had given their 'parole' and he expected them to 'keep their word'. French Papers 75/46/12. Quoted by Peter Hart *The IRA and its Enemies* (Oxford: Oxford University Press, 1999), p.75. There were some attempts to get the prisoners to sign a written parole but these foundered. The Cabinet at Westminster backed the judgement of Lord French over what they regarded as a grave crisis. See *Thomas Jones Whitehall Diaries 1918-25*, Vol. III, p.20 et seq. Middlemas, K. (ed.) (London: Oxford University Press, 1969).

25. Wylie Memoir PRO 89/2. James Madden was tried in the spring of 1920 for the murder of Sergeant Brady and the wounding of another officer. There had been a night time ambush of an RIC patrol. Sergeant Brady had been killed outright. Another constable was gravely wounded. The third constable fired on the attackers and drove them off. John Gilligan went to the police and made a statement implicating others. A second statement was taken from him which corroborated the accounts of the surviving officers in all respects. This statement was disclosed to the defence. The first statement was withheld. Like many people who gave information, he proved to be unreliable and self-serving and was probably motivated by the prospect of a resettlement grant which was sometimes paid to witnesses. My attention was drawn to this case by Seán Hogan and I am grateful for his help.

26. In fact Madden had nothing to do with the ambush. See the trial of J.J. Madden, this volume.

27. Replacing the very able General Sir Joseph Byrne who was dismissed for reasons which were kept secret at the time: *Hansard* 4 March 1920 Vol. 126, col. 605.

28. 1871–1965, KCB, CMG. He served with the Artillery in the Boer Campaign and was wounded at Magersfontain. He later served in India, Egypt and on the Western Front where he rose from Captain to Major General which suggests he was a man of some ability.

29. *Hansard* Debates 6 May 1920 Vol. 128, col. 2206.

30. Baltinglass, Ballytrain, Carrigtwohill, Castlemartyr, Cloyne, Allihies, Camp, Ballybunion, Mount Pleaseant, Hollyford, Feakle, Cappawhite, Drumban, Ballyheigue, Castlegrove, Shevry, Newtownhamilton, Carrigadrohid, Geashill, Gortatlea (for the second time) and Kilmallock.

31. *Thomas Jones Whitehall Diaries 1918*–25 Vol. III, Middlemas, K. (ed.) (London: Oxford University Press, 1969), p.17 & p.27.

32. *Hansard* Debates 18 March 1920 Vol. 126, col. 2351.

33. For instance Divisional Commissioner for Munster was Lieutenant Colonel Gerald Ferguson Smyth DSO of the Royal Scottish Borderers. His successor was Major Holmes (formerly of the Royal Irish Rifles).

34. For an example of orders issued by Divisional Commissioner Smyth see Abbott, R. *Police Casualties in Ireland 1918–22* (Cork: Mercier, 2001), p.101–3.

35. What Macready asked for at this time was a substantial reinforcement of the army by men who would be under his command. What he eventually got were 1,500 ex-officers who would be under an independent command. Macready had conducted a review of his new command and asked the Cabinet for eight battalions and 600 signallers. This was resisted by Sir Henry Wilson, Chief of the Imperial General Staff. As he put it, the movement of eight battalions to Ireland meant 'we should have very little for our own internal troubles & nothing for India, Egypt, Constantinople etc.' (See Diary of Sir Henry Wilson). 'Internal troubles' referred to industrial unrest in Britain on a massive scale. The term General Strike had not yet been invented but it was this eventuality that the military planners were getting ready to meet. Additionally, war in the Middle East was reckoned not just possible but highly probable.

    Reinforcements to Ireland were deferred on account of these difficulties. There was no additional money from the Treasury for the Army but funding could be found in the police budget and Churchill suggested that 8,000 ex-soldiers be recruited to bolster the RIC and this found favour with the Cabinet. These new troops would be known as the Auxiliary Division.

    The evidence suggests they were selected with some care from the ranks of ex-officers – 'we do not want the scallywag' but goaded on by General Tudor and undermined by lack of training, isolation and hard drinking, some Auxiliaries would soon take the law into their own hands.

36. For an account of the Listowel Mutiny see O'Donoghue, F. *No Other Law* (Dublin: Irish Press Limited, 1954), pp.68–9. For an account by one of the participants, Jeremiah Mee BMH WS No. 379. It does appear that the constables were also motivated by the threat of being transferred to remote stations where they would be more vulnerable.

37. Not all of his efforts were successful. Tudor was present at the tail end of the Listowel Mutiny when fourteen officers refused to accept redeployment and declined an invitation to shoot down unarmed suspects. Twelve of the fourteen resigned.

38. The Hefferans from Nenagh are an example of a family who gave evidence against Volunteers who had stolen guns from their homes. The family was boycotted and

forced to leave the area and emigrated soon after. See Hogan, S. *The Tans in North Tipperary,* Chapter 6 (Privately published, 2013), p.144.

39. PRO CAB/27/108. Cabinet Weekly Survey.
40. *Irish Law Times,* 10 July 1920.
41. *Irish Law Times and Solicitors Journal,* July 1920.
42. Affidavit of Jasper Wolfe, Crown Solicitor. See *The King v Fitzgerald and Others* IR [1920] 429.
43. *Irish Law Times and Solicitors Journal* July 1920.
44. *Hansard* 16 August 1920 Vol. 133, col. 576.
45. *Sixth Division Record of the Rebellion,* p.20.
46. A pay award was made: see the Resident Magistrates (Ireland) Act 1920. It was the first pay award for forty-six years and it was a very modest one. It was an insult to the loyalty and dedication shown by these men.
47. On the long narrow road that runs from Causeway to the sea, Resident Magistrate Wynne was driving his jaunting car to the petty sessions when a group of men jumped out of the hedgerows. The RM drew a pistol and fired five shots and one of his attackers fell dead and the others ran. RM Wynne packed up his belongings a few days later. He sent his furniture and possessions to the railway station but they were intercepted and burned. His house at Tralee was torched and he left the country in a hurry. See Dwyer, R.T. *Tans, Terror and Troubles* (Dublin: Mercier, 2001), p.195.
48. RM Milling and RM Lendrum.
49. Toomey, T. *The War of Independence in Limerick* (Privately Published, 2010), p.259. Lt Colonel Michael Williamson was a former Munster Fusilier.
50. He received no medical attention and died that evening. His body was weighted down and dropped into the sea. All that the raiders had wanted was his car. See BMH WS No.474, Haugh. Little is known about Captain Alan Lendrum 1887–1920. He was from Tyrone. He served as an officer in the British Army during the Great War. He was wounded and awarded the Military Cross. He was appointed Resident Magistrate in Kilkee in 1920.
51. See Dwyer, *Tans, Terror and Troubles,* p.177.
52. The Firearms Act 10 & 11 Geo. 5 Ch. 43.
53. Middlemas, K. *Thomas Jones Whitehall Diaries 1918–25* Vol. III (London: Oxford University Press, 1969), p.19.
54. Decree issued 29 June 1920. The Minister responsible for implementation was Austin Stack, Minister for Home Affairs.
55. *Irish Law Times,* 6 November 1920, p.273. It appears the Bar Library decided it was an issue that they need not fall out over. A motion criticising the Bar Council was adjourned indefinitely and counsel continued to attend the new courts without objection.
56. On the advice of Wylie, Dublin Castle took the view that courts which asserted jurisdiction to hear criminal and or civil cases were illegal. The Land Arbitration Courts where the parties agreed to submit to a decision were not.
57. See for instance BMH WS No. 708, Maguire.

CHAPTER SEVEN

1. For the detail of the courts martial scheme see Campbell, C. *Emergency Law in Ireland 1918–1925*, p.598 et seq. (Oxford: Clarendon, 1994). For the political background in which the legislation was passed see Foxton, D. *Revolutionary Lawyers, Sinn Féin and Crown Courts* (Dublin: Four Courts, 2007).

2. The power was used against local government bodies that had declared their allegiance to the Dáil. The power was used extensively.

3. Such a power was created pursuant to the ROIA by Clause 13, Order in Council, 13 August 1920. See *Irish Law Times and Solicitors Journal*, 2 July 1921.

4. Hittle, J. *Michael Collins and the Anglo Irish War* (Virginia: Potomac Books, 2011), p.140.

5. *R v Governor of Lewes Prison ex parte Doyle* [1917] 2 KB 254.

6. PRO WO 35 173/1.

7. See for instance O'Malley *On Another Man's Wound;* BMH WS No. 968, Lenihan and No. 845, Malone; Kevin Barry, affidavit sworn before execution.

8. *Record of the Rebellion*, Vol. II (*Intelligence*), p.27. Brought to my attention by Campbell, *Emergency Law in Ireland 1918–25.*

9. James Pierce of Clarecastle and John Murphy of Cork Alley Lane, Ennis were tried for larceny of six geese at New Barracks Limerick. See 17 June 1921, *The Cork Examiner.*

10. Sergeant Alexander Sullivan, who defended Casement, prosecuted a number of cases brought under the DORA regime. Sullivan was also an outspoken opponent of the insurgency. While on circuit in Tralee, Sullivan was staying at the home of his client, Slattery, when a number of armed men burst in. In a desperate struggle in the darkened hallway Slattery was injured and Sullivan slightly wounded when a bullet singed his eyebrow. It was his view that the shooting had nothing to do with the Rebellion and everything to do with the case he was involved in. He was shot at again when leaving Tralee by train. See Dwyer, R. T. *Tans, Terror and Troubles* (Dublin: Mercier, 2001), p.272. Dwyer has doubted that the first shooting had anything to do with the Rebellion and argued that the second shooting was more a figment of Sullivan's imagination: a lamp on Sullivan's carriage broke loose, flapped and broke a window. A number of men were brought to trial after identifications by Sullivan at Cork Male Prison. When Sullivan gave evidence for the Crown, however, he had a surprising failure of nerve and he was unable to recognise anyone. See Wylie Memoir. Sullivan emigrated to England and the supply of Irish barristers prepared to prosecute cases arising out of the insurgency dried up.

11. Captain Baggally and Captain Newbery were killed.

12. *Record of the Rebellion,* Vol. III, p.18.

13. *Blackwood's Magazine*, 'The Last Days of Dublin Castle', August 1922.

14. In fact MacSwiney was tried under the old DORR because the ROIA Regulations preserved the DORR while the ROIA procedures were phased in.

15. Henry Gover had been in practice in the family firm at Monument Street, London Bridge, since 1911. He had joined the Royal West Kent in 1915 and served in

Flanders for much of the War. He was mentioned in despatches for his service in France.

16. Hannigan, D. *Terence MacSwiney* (Dublin: The O'Brien Press Ltd, 2010), p.47. The government position was maintained in the teeth of opposition from all quarters. *The Guardian* and *The Times* argued that the nature of the charge proved against MacSwiney should not result in his death – however that might come about. *The Times* hinted at the consequences of MacSwiney's death.

    The King was petitioned and privately he argued for clemency and his view became widely known. His conscience dictated the exercise of the royal prerogative of mercy but he privately conceded that this might result in the fall of his government. In public he kept silent. At the Vatican, intense lobbying took place. In private, the Pope expressed the view that MacSwiney's conduct would not amount to suicide because his primary intention was to secure his release. In public, the Pontiff said nothing. It was a triumph of Vatican politics over decency.

17. The other two prisoners were Michael Fitzgerald and Joseph Murray.

18. The Brehon tradition had been revived on the stage some years before by Yeats in *The King's Threshold* in which a man fasts against the King to secure redress. Ultimately, the King declines to observe the demands of Brehon law lest he might be thought weak and *'the very throne be shaken'*. MacSwiney, himself a playwright and a man of letters, was familiar with these concepts. He must have understood only too well that the government could not give way. His final weapon was to evoke ancient law and culture. For this last point I am indebted to the work of John Walsh, *The Irish Cultural Society of the Garden City Area*, 1993. Also, 'Nation Pedagogy and Performance: W. B. Yeats, The King's Threshold and the Irish Hunger Strikes', *Literature and History*, Autumn 2009 Vol. 18, Issue 2.

19. *Blackwood's Magazine*, 'The Last Days of Dublin Castle', August 1922.

20. The first group of prisoners to be tried were the Crowley brothers and Michael O'Reilly from Ballylanders. They had been due to stand trial the preceding September for their part in an ambush on the RIC. At that time, the prison doctor certified them unfit for trial. They were tried in the summer of 1921. At their trial, prosecuting counsel, Major Gover OBE (recently promoted and decorated), reiterated the policy of the Army. Hunger strikes would not be allowed to stand in the way of a trial:
    Anyone in this country who commits a crime and is caught, will be tried and have to suffer for it. That fact cannot be too widely known.The Cork Examiner, 3 June 1921, courtesy of the *Irish Examiner*.

21. *Hansard* HC Deb. Vol. 133, c 909.

22. Churchill, in a letter to his wife, spring 1920. Quoted by Gilbert, M. *Churchill*, Vol. IV(London, 1977), p.449

23. *Thomas Jones, Whitehall Diaries* vol. 3.

24. For the best analysis of Winter's counter-insurgency campaign see Hittle, *Michael Collins and the Anglo Irish War*.

25. 1875–1962. KBE CB CMG DSO. Winter was an artillery officer of exceptional courage and ability. He was a linguist, vet and horse rider par excellence.

Winter later wrote a light-hearted autobiography on the horses he rode, boar he hunted and the women he bedded. His account about his tenure in Ireland contains a number of factual errors. He recounts how two RIC recruits were placed alive into a 'gas retort'. There is no evidence such an event ever occurred. He also recounts that RM Lendrum was buried on the beach up to his neck in sand and drowned when the tide came in. The truth about the murder of Alan Lendrum was shocking enough but Winter's account is not accurate. They do raise a question about the reliability of other assertions made by Winter. But he was plainly a talented officer with an extraordinary range of abilities. After a dull time following the Irish conflict, Winter served with distinction with the Finnish Army against the Soviets in 1940.

26. He was seen once by Wylie heading off to the city centre wearing: 'a long white beard and dark glasses', Wylie Memoir, p.54. According to Wylie, Winter had discovered that Michael Collins had £2,000 deposited at the Munster and Leinster Bank. Winter had decided to go and relieve the bank of exactly this sum. Wylie, the government law advisor, explained that this was stealing, not from Collins but from the bank. Undeterred Winter went into town and demanded and obtained the money. The government was later compelled to return the money to the bank.

27. See Hart, P., *British Intelligence in Ireland.*

28. One was Nancy O'Brien (a cousin of Collins) who was a typist in the civil service with direct access to the correspondence of the most senior civil servants. Also Thomas Markham, a senior civil servant.

29. See BMH WS No. 380, Neligan. Also, BMH WS No. 1284, Broy.

30. Lily Mernin who worked in the intelligence section at Parkgate.

31. Josephine Marchmont Brown.

32. Major J.C. Reynolds of F Company is an example.

33. Billie Beaumont an ex Royal Dublin Fusilier. Drawn to my attention in Hittle, *Michael Collins and the Anglo Irish War.*

34. He used the postal service to provide a drop box address where people could send sensitive information but this netted a hail of abusive letters. The insurgents regularly raided the mail looking for letters to this address and members of the public who wrote in were placed in great danger; it is likely that some were killed as a result. See for instance BMH WS No. 1413, Kennedy. T. Winter also brought a team of fifty bloodhounds to Ireland but these secured only a single capture of a suspect. Winter's plan to use electronic eavesdropping on prisoners also foundered because the equipment was 'ill suited to the Irish brogue', PRO WO 35/214.

35. In his final report, Winter wrote: 'the heads of the rebel organisation are recruited from a low degenerate type, unequipped with intellectual education', PRO WO 35/214.

36. The Auxiliaries were not under the command of General Macready. They answered to their commander Brigadier Crozier who was accountable to the new Police Advisor General Tudor, who in turn was answerable to the Chief Secretary. The Chief Secretary and General Tudor both nurtured unofficial reprisals.

37. Montgomery was awarded the Distinguished Service Order in the Great War and was mentioned in despatches several times. In 1917, he went to the Admiralty as an intelligence officer but he appears to have had no experience as an operative in the field. In the diaries of Mark Sturgis he is referred to as 'Colonel Montgomery of GHQ' which may indicate he was part of army intelligence rather than one of Winter's men. See also BMH WS No. 907, p.208.

38. Winter, O. *Winter's Tale* (London: Richards Press, 1951), p.297.

39. See BMH WS No. 615, Thornton.

40. At Upper Pembroke Street, Major Dowling and Captain Leonard Price were killed and Lieutenant George Murray was badly wounded in the chest. Lieutenant Colonel Woodcock, who had no connection with the Secret Service, was also shot and grievously wounded as he shouted to Colonel Montgomery to warn him of the ambush outside his rooms. Montgomery was gravely wounded. He lingered on for a few days and then died. At Lower Baggott Street a party of Irish Republican Army (IRA) men assembled, including Seán Lemass, later Taoiseach. These men shot dead Captain George Baggally who was a court martial officer not a spy. A few doors away, another group of men broke in looking for Captain Newbury. His wife tried to block the doorway but she was brushed aside and the Captain was shot as he tried to jump from a window. The raiders left him bleeding profusely and hanging from the window. He too was a court martial officer as it turned out, not a spy. These scenes were being played out all over Dublin. At Lower Mount Street, Lieutenant Henry Angliss was living under the pseudonym MacMahon. He was shot and killed. His colleague, 'Captain Peel', heard the shooting and shoved some furniture across the doorway as bullets were fired through the door but he survived.

41. These men included Dick McKee and Peadar Clancy and Conor Clune. These killings attracted a cursory internal inquiry that exonerated the Auxiliaries. See Winter, *Winter's Tale*.

42. BMH WS No. 380, Neligan.

43. See Hittle J. *Michael Collins and the Anglo Irish War*. See also Grant Sturgis Papers.

CHAPTER EIGHT

1. See *Record of the Rebellion,* Vol. III PRO WO 141/94.

2. PRO CAB 24/118 Weekly Cabinet Summary.

3. These four counties were added on 4 January 1921.

4. Hopkinson, M. (ed.) *The Last Days of Dublin Castle* (Dublin: Irish Academic Press, 1999), p.89.

5. For a full account of this trial see Enright, S. *The Trial of Civilians by Military Courts* (Dublin: Irish Academic Press, 2012).

6. See Hopkinson, *The Last Days of Dublin Castle*.

7. CAB/23/2379A.

8. WO 35/ 208.

9. Harte had suffered a severe episode of shell shock on the Western Front in 1917. He was part of the patrol ambushed at Dillon's Cross and he had watched his friend Spencer Chapman die. Whether Harte was actually legally insane is a moot point but his demeanour after the shooting suggests that he was not in control of his faculties. Post-traumatic stress disorder was then unrecognised but seems a likely explanation.

10. See Macready, Sir Neville, *Annals of An Active Life* Vol. 2 (London: Hutchinson & Co, 1925). See also *The Record of the Rebellion*, Vol. I, p.31.

11. See Hopkinson, *The Last Days of Dublin Castle*, p137.

CHAPTER NINE

1. PRO WO 35/66.

2. Ibid.

3. See Macready's memoir: 'Authority was also given for the carrying of prominent Sinn Feiners on military lorries, which, while it afforded some slight deterrent to the outrages, amused the light hearted soldiery.' *Annals of An Active Life* Vol. 2, (London, Hutchinson, 1925) p.503. See Willis and Bolster BMH WS No. 808. O'Malley, E. *On Another Man's Wound*, p.261. Also PRO WO 35/66, order implemented in Dublin by public notice 16 January 1921. Also *Sixth Division Record of the Rebellion*, p.70.

4. Hopkinson, M. (ed.) *The Last Days of Dublin Castle* (Dublin: Irish Academic Press, 1998), p.89: 'Cracking the whip with one hand and holding out the carrot in the other.'

5. See for Instance: *The Record of the Rebellion, Vol. I, Operations, p.39*.

6. See Hopkinson, *The Last Days of Dublin Castle*, p.102.

7. PRO/CAB/23/23/79A.

8. PRO/CAB/24/123, CP2911.

9. See Hopkinson, *The Last Days of Dublin Castle*.

10. The stress and strains of life in the barracks during the insurgency coupled with mental illness or bullying sometimes spilled over into violence and occasionally soldiers shot down fellow soldiers in barracks. See for instance the trial of Private Helmore for the murder of Corporal Yates: *Cork Examiner,* 15 February 1921. RIC Constable Albert Johnson tried at Wexford by FGCM for attempting to murder a fellow officer: *Waterford News,* 7 July 1921. When asked about why he had shot his colleague he replied: 'That's me every time.' If these trials have a significance it is that they added considerably to Macready's astonishingly large caseload.

11. An attempt was made by Professor Campbell to examine this issue of whether courts martial were partial in favour of police officers and soldiers but no clear-cut picture could be established. An insuperable difficulty relates to the fact that there was no political will to investigate reprisals by police officers and most officers kept their silence but suspected insurgents were prosecuted with enthusiasm.

There is, therefore, no comparable database. Secondly, all officers who were prosecuted defended their cases but many of those involved in the insurgency did not. See Campbell, C. *Emergency Law in Ireland 1918–25* (Oxford: Oxford University Press, 1994), p.82.

12. General Tudor, the Chief of Police, continued to incite reprisals and assassination since his appointment: a fact noted by Macready in his private correspondence. In these months there were hundreds of unofficial reprisals against property: burning farms or creameries which put local people out of work. There were also reprisals against men suspected of complicity in rebel action: intimidation, assault and harassment and killings. Extra-judicial shootings of prisoners were also a factor. The Army's own records show that, during the conflict, 193 civilians were shot and killed for 'failing to halt' and another 57 prisoners were shot dead trying to escape. *The Record of the Rebellion Vol. III, Law* p.17.

13. See *Cork Examiner,* 13 April 1921.

14. Constable Mitchell was tried and executed for his part in a botched robbery where a bystander was shot dead. Constable Pearson was convicted for an identical offence and Reeve and Coburn were also convicted of a murder committed during a holdup in a pub. Reeve and Coburn seemed set to hang but their trial came on shortly before the Truce and their death sentences were quietly commuted in the autumn of 1921.

15. A notable exception concerned a squad of Auxiliaries who ran amok in a small shop in Trim, smashing up the premises and humiliating the loyalist shop owner and his disabled sister. The Cadets were dismissed by their commanding officer, Brigadier Crozier. They then sent a deputation to General Tudor threatening to make some embarrassing disclosures to the press. Most were immediately reinstated and Brigadier Crozier resigned in protest. This was Crozier's account. For a full account, see Macardle *The Irish Republic* (London: Corgi Press, 1967), p.393 and BMH WS No. 843, Rice. The account given by the government was also detailed and asserted a mix up between General Crozier, who was in Dublin, and General Tudor, who was in London. See *Hansard* HC Deb. Vol. 138 Col. 738. Eventually five out of twenty-three were tried and three convicted. Throughout this affair General Macready could only look on. In public, he maintained silence; in private, he argued for a unified command which would allow him to exercise control over the police and the Auxiliary Division.

16. Enright, S. *The Trial of Civilians by Military Courts* (Dublin: Irish Academic Press, 2012).

17. Sentence of death was commuted in the cases of Denis Murphy, Timothy Murphy, Edward Punch, Diarmuid O'Leary and Patrick Casey (Milford).

18. John Egan (Ennis) and Patrick Higgins (Cork).

19. The following men convicted by military courts remained under sentence of death until after the Treaty: John O'Sullivan (Abbeyfeale), Michael O'Keefe, Jack Shine, Patrick Loughlin, Thomas Murray, William Daly, Timothy Keohane, John Driscoll, Cornelius Driscoll, Thomas Looby, Denis Driscoll, Peter O'Connor, Frank Morgan, John O'Connor, Patrick Clifford and Michael O'Sullivan.

20. Macready to War Office 1 November 1921, PRO WO 48/148.

21. *The Record of the Rebellion Vol. III Law.*

22. House of Commons Debates, 14 April 1921. Most of these prisoners were interned under statutory powers but about 790 were interned without statutory authority in the martial law area.

23. See JAG Minute Books WO 83/40-41.

24. Edward Punch and Timothy Murphy. Minute Book of the JAG PRO WO 83/41, p.15.

25. Hopkinson, M. (ed.) *The Last Days of Dublin Castle* (Dublin: Irish Academic Press, 1998).

26. This case was tried in Cork after martial law had been declared but before the implementation date. It was therefore a trial under the ROIA. *R v Murphy* [1920] II IR 190. Macready's reasons for commuting sentence of death do not accord with his approach to all other capital cases that he handled in this period. This gives rise to an inference there was another unstated rationale for his decision.

27. WO 141/48.

28. PRO 141/48.

29. *Higgins v Willis* [1921] II IR 383;

30. Regulation 69(5) ROIR. *Whelan v Rex* [1921] 2 IR 310.

31. *R v Allen* II IR 241.

32. For an account of the Dripsey ambush and the trials that followed, see Enright, *The Trial of Civilians by Military Courts*. Murphy had a strong reference from a Dripsey landowner, Major Richard Woodley who was a highly decorated veteran of the Boer War.

33. Cassel wrote that the trial was lawful and the evidence was 'sufficient to convict' but added 'the identification evidence was not altogether clear and satisfactory'. The witnesses contradicted each other on detail. Cassel also pointed out that the evidence suggested that it was a matter of chance whether this taxi driver or some other was asked to take the fare. Also, Cassel noted that the accused had taken no steps to disguise the registration of his cab. Cassel urged General Macready to withhold the death penalty and give careful consideration to the possibility the prisoner may have become involved at a late stage and 'may have been acting under a degree of duress and compulsion'. His doubts may have been misplaced. See BMH WS No. 389, McCorley and WS No. 746, Culhane. According to accounts given by these men, who were involved in the attack, Leonard had been involved. He had voluntarily driven the killers to the scene but never left the taxi at any stage.

34. *Cork Examiner,* 7 March 1921, courtesy of the *Irish Examiner.*

35. O'Malley, E. *On Another Man's Wound* (Dublin: Anvil, 2002), p.299.

36. *Freeman's Journal,* 7 February 1921

37. See Hopkinson, *The Last Days of Dublin Castle.* The civil servant referred to was Whiskard. His report is clear and fair but demonstrates a certain naivety about the criminal process. PRO CO 904/43.

38. *Cork Examiner,* 15 February 1921.

39. Four of the Drumcondra prisoners were executed. The fifth, spared because of his age, later related that they were moved to different cells on the day of the escape. When O'Malley's escape party departed, they bade them good luck but would not stop to release the padlock on their cell doors. See BMH WS No. 508, O'Sullivan, D. This was probably unfair to O'Malley and the other two escapees who did not lack courage. O'Malley's recollection was that the Drumcondra prisoners had been moved as a punishment for some misdemeanour and could not be taken for that reason.

40. One of the reasons for commuting sentence related to the witness Nellie Stapleton who had also identified a fourth man, Healy. She withdrew her statement against Healy on the grounds that she had seen another man just like him since and was no longer confident of her identification. Whiskard's careful review took this to mean that her powers of observation were less than good and, therefore, her testimony against the others might not be reliable. It is far more likely that she had belatedly realised that, by giving evidence in these trials, she had stirred up a hornet's nest for herself and she had simply found a way out.

41. PRO CO 904/43.

42. PRO WO 71/366.

43. BMH WS 843, Rice.

44. See *The King v (Garde and Others) v Major Gen E. P. Strickland* [1921] 2 IR 17 and *The King v (Ronayne and Mulcahy) v Strickland and Another* [1921} 2 IR 333.

45. As can be seen in this chapter, only months earlier, the JAG had successfully argued that all cases in the martial law area be reviewed by him personally. He appears to have abandoned this stance and the records hint strongly at some exchange of views which have not been recorded or if recorded, destroyed. His deputy in Ireland was Colonel Mellors, about whom little is known. The JAG's review fell to him.

46. PRO WO/141/94 *The Record of the Rebellion Vol. III, Law.*

47. PRO WO 71/381.

48. PRO WO 71/383.

49. PRO WO 71/384.

50. After his review the JAG was informed that the main witness had been paid a reward for the evidence she had given. PRO WO 81/ 41, p.124. The documentary trail is incomplete after this point. The prisoners were released in early 1922 when the Treaty was signed.

51. Macready, Sir N., *Annals of An Active Life* Vol. II (London: Hutchinson, 1924).

52. I acknowledge the source for this: Abbott, R. *Police Casualties in Ireland 1919–22* (Dublin: Mercier, 2001), p.181.

53. See Part II, this volume for the Bloody Sunday Trials, Maher and Foley, Carmody and Lenehan.

54. See the case of Bryan Kelley, this volume.

CHAPTER TEN

1. See *The Record of the Rebellion, Vol. III Law*. P.16. The author suggests that the figure may have been slightly more. See also PRO WO 35/208 register of trials conducted under martial law.

2. There was no single document bringing the Truce into effect. Both sides entered into an oral agreement and later published their own versions which are silent on military courts and executions. One of the provisions agreed to by General Macready reads: 'Military activity shall be restricted to the support of the police in their normal civil duties. Cmd 1534 of 1921, Cessation of Active Operations in Ireland.' In the version issued by Sinn Féin there is a footnote which simply reads 'There are other details connected with courts martial, motor permits and ROIR to be agreed later.' The author has been unable to discover whether there were any such discussions.

3. The Register of Trials WO/35/208 shows no martial law trials after 8 July 1921. There are no records of such trials held at the National Archive in London or reports of such trials in newspapers or other contemporary sources.

4. *The Record the Rebellion Vol. I, Operations*, p.48.

5. Preparations for an extension of the powers of the Army had begun some weeks earlier. In late May 1921, Lloyd George reconvened the Irish Situation Committee under the chairmanship of Neville Chamberlain. The Committee met within days and recommended that if the Southern Parliament failed to function, martial law would be extended to the twenty-six counties. The decisive factors were the advantages of unity of command, censorship of the press and a desire to discontinue official reprisals but find an effective substitute. General Macready argued that martial law could be imposed flexibly deploying a light touch where appropriate. In terms of reinforcements this meant another sixteen to eighteen battalions and two or three cavalry regiments. Plans were made to use the navy to blockade ports and act in support of sweeps by the army. The Cabinet considered and approved the recommendations.

   The review of the measures that worked and those that did not gave rise to other changes of strategy. Official reprisals were abandoned. In the course of the previous six months the army had destroyed 194 homes and 20 other properties in the martial law area. The policy had proved counterproductive because the rebels responded in kind and began to burn the homes of loyalists and so many of the finest Georgian homes were burned to the ground in the spring and early summer of 1921. As Hamar Greenwood put it, 'the loyalists own everything that is worth burning, while the Sinn Féiners who are the sons of farmers, shop keepers, publicans, own nothing.' And so official reprisals were abandoned and a more potent response was sought and identified.

   Another key meeting of the Irish Situation Committee took place on the 15 June when Macready's draft proclamation for martial law was considered. Macready's personal view was that coercion would fail and the record shows his reluctance but if it had to be tried then it must be 'all out or get out'. He questioned whether the Cabinet would support the measure: 'There might be as many as one hundred men shot in a week.' This figure was a reference to executions, not casualties.

Anyone found with guns or bombs would be tried by drumhead court martial and 'executed on the spot'. Other proposals included: identity cards, requisition of goods without payment, the closure of fairs markets and race meetings, the closure of ports and a complete prohibition on any person bringing legal action against the Crown without the permission of the Military Governor. These proposals were accepted subject to refinement by the Irish Situation Committee. It was agreed that, unless the new MPs swore allegiance to the Crown, then martial law would be declared in the twenty-six counties. The date for declaration of martial law was fixed for 14 July.

While this was taking place, General Macready's staff continued to refine a series of draft proclamations which extended the scope of martial law to the twenty-six counties. These new proclamations repeated those already in force in the martial law area and added new provisions: Death was prescribed as a punishment for membership of Dáil Éireann, the Irish Republican Army and the Volunteers.

Under the new proclamations, the jurisdiction of the law courts to grant writs of habeas corpus, mandamus and prohibition were prohibited and suspended. The jurisdiction of all courts to make orders in respect of any claim for damage against the Army was to be forbidden without the express sanction of the Military Governor General.

In early August 1921, General Macready issued orders for convening Drumhead Courts. These were to apply to persons captured in action with arms, bombs or explosives or where there was clear evidence that they had possessed such items immediately before capture. These rules, summarised below, were to apply to all combatants whether in uniform or not. Application was to be made at once to the nearest officer of field rank, to convene a Drumhead Court and the Court would be convened at the nearest convenient place. The trial was to take place with the utmost expedition and everything but the most urgent military operations will give way to that need. No adjournments will be allowed and no considerations were to prevent the commencement and conclusion of the trial. Sentence would be confirmed by the nearest officer of field rank on the spot or by the nearest field officer available. Nothing was to be permitted to cause delay in confirmation. There is a note appended to these instructions which states that the instructions only apply to cases where the evidence appears to be clear beyond possibility of doubt.

Other aspects of military planning developed as the year wore on. Macready asked that provision be made to house 20,000 more internees. More detailed plans were submitted to the Cabinet in September when Macready wrote stating that, in the event of the Truce failing, he proposed to take 'immediate and drastic action'. See Enright, S. *The Trial of Civilians by Military Courts* (Dublin: Irish Academic Press, 2012).

6. *The King (Garde and Others) v Major General EP Strickland and Others'* [1921] 2 IR 317.
7. *R v Allen* [1921] 2 IR 241.
8. *The King (Garde and Others) v Major General EP Strickland and Others'* [1921] 2 IR 317.
9. *The Cork Examiner,* 7 July 1921.
10. Counsel for the prisoners were Sir John Simon KC, Michael Comyn KC, James Comyn, J.A. McCarthy and Richard O'Sullivan of the English Bar. For the Crown, Sergeant Hanna, E.S. Murphy and Lipsett.
11. *In re: Clifford and Sullivan* [1921] 2 AC 570.
12. The central argument advanced by the Crown rested on the decision of the High Court in John Allen which itself rested on the decision of the Privy Council in Marais, the Boer War case, which decided: 'where war actually prevails the ordinary courts have no jurisdiction'. This decision was distinguished by the Master of the Rolls on the grounds that a state of war was in existence at the time of the passage of the ROIA, and that the prerogative powers under which the military acted had been invested in that statute. A fresh initiative had to come through Parliament. Therefore, a person charged with a capital crime could only be tried by a court martial convened under the ROIA.
13. Report to Cabinet for week ending 30 July 1921 CAB/24/126.
14. IR [1921] 280. Reproduced by kind permission of the Incorporated Council of Law Reporting for Ireland.
15. *New York Times,* 30 July 1921.
16. PRO/CAB/24/126.
17. See for instance PRO/WO/83/41, 352.
18. ILTR [1921] Vol. LV p202.
19. Report to Cabinet week ending 6 August PRO/CAB/24/126.

CHAPTER ELEVEN

1. Tierney, M. *Eoin MacNeill: Scholar and Man of Action* (Oxford: Clarendon Press, 1980), p.223.
2. BMH WS Thornton, No. 510.
3. Hansard HC Debates 11 May 1916 Vol. 82 cols. 935-970.
4. De Valera Papers, UCDA, Letter to Lord French, 4 May.
5. MacNeill Memoir. See Tierney, *Eoin MacNeill: Scholar and Man of Action,* p.225.
6. PRO WO 32/4307.
7. It has been suggested that MacNeill had secured a tactical victory by ensuring an 'open' trial, that is, open to the public. See Hardiman, *Shot in Cold Blood.* In fact MacNeill was tried in camera.
8. Contrary to Regulation 42 of the Defence of the Realm Regulations.
9. Contrary to Regulation 27 of the Defence of the Realm Regulations.
10. Irish Military Archives CD 45/3/3.

11. Edmund Kimber DSO. Born 1870. Called to the Bar at Lincoln's Inn in 1892. Married 1913, he was then in practice at Pump Court at the Temple. He went to France in 1914 with the 1/13 London Rifles. He was wounded at Fromelles on the second anniversary of his wedding.

12. The officers who tried MacNeill were drawn from the Royal Irish Regiment, the Dublin Fusiliers, the Sherwood Foresters, the Leicestershire Regiment and the Lincolnshire Regiment. All of these regiments had suffered casualties during the Rebellion. The officers sat in contravention of the rule that required an officer to step down where there was a significant conflict of interest.

13. See Wylie Memoir PRO 89/2.

14. Irish Military History, CD 45/3/3.

15. William Partridge was a trade unionist and a Citizen Army man. He was tried a week before MacNeill. He was convicted of rebellion and sentenced to ten years' penal servitude. Partridge's trial record can be found at Irish Military Archives CD 45/3/3.

16. For an account of the countermand and MacNeill's efforts to stop the Rebellion see BMH WS No.217, Keegan, J.J.

17. These witnesses included constitutional Home Rulers such as Lieutenant Tom Kettle who was killed later that summer on the Somme, also Colonel Maurice Moore who had a distinguished record as a soldier, notably during the Boer War when he commanded a battalion of the Connaught Rangers. Moore had been involved in the Volunteers in 1914 but went with the National Volunteers after the Redmondite split. Finally, Creed Meredith.

18. Letter, Irish Military Archives CD 45/3/3/.

CHAPTER TWELVE

1. See PRO/ WO 374/14944/109785.

2. Gibbon, M. *Inglorious Soldier* (London: Hutchinson & Co., 1968), p.44.

3. Ibid., p.43.

4. BMH WS No.707, Noyk.

5. Dixon was alleged to have used his paper to pursue a vendetta against his ex-landlord Joseph Issacs JP.

6. Richard Carroll, an unarmed insurgent, was also killed by Colthurst. In later years, when questioned, Colthurst passed no comment on other killings laid at his door.

7. Sir Francis Vane, quoted in Gibbon, M. *Inglorious Soldier* (London, Hutchinson, 1968).

8. BMH WS No.1,019, Bucknill. This witness was later a Lord Justice of Appeal. He was a legal advisor to General Maxwell and saw the increasingly anxious stream of telegrams emanating from Whitehall and Horse Guards and drafted the replies on instructions from Maxwell.

9. Brought to my attention by Foxton, D. *Revolutionary Lawyers* (Dublin: Four Courts Press, 2008).

10. In private correspondence with his wife before the trial. Brought to my attention by David Foxton's study of this trial: see Foxton, *Revolutionary Lawyers*, p.82.

11. Townshend, C. *Easter 1916: The Irish Rebellion* (London: Penguin, 2005) p.290. Civilian counsel later advised that the current regulations were sufficiently wide to permit the trial of a soldier on active service for murder and the amendment to the regulations was not pursued. See WO 35/68.

12. This account of the trial is taken from PRO WO 35/68.

13. Evidence to the Royal Commission (Cmnd 8376).

14. An opinion shared, for instance, by John M. Regan, then a junior officer with the Royal Irish Rifles. Augusteijn, J. *The Memoirs of John M. Regan. A Catholic Officer in the RIC and RUC 1909–48,* (Dublin: Four Courts Press, 2007).

15. These were Captain George Lawless, Medical Superintendent of the Armagh District Lunatic Asylum, and Major Francis Purser.

16. Archbold, J.F. *Criminal Pleading Evidence and Practice,* 25th Edition (London: Sweet and Maxwell, 1918).

17. Cmnd 8376.

CHAPTER THIRTEEN

1. BMH WS No. 349, Reilly.

2. Martin F.X. (ed.) *Leaders and Men of the Easter Rising: Dublin 1916* (London: Methuen and Co., 1966), p. 178.

3. Ibid., p.175.

4. *Documents Relative to the Sinn Féin Movement,* Cmd 1108.

5. MacManus, F. *After the Flight* (Dublin: Talbot Press, 1938), p.210.

6. De Courcy Ireland, J. *The Sea and the Easter Rising* (Dublin, Maritime Institute of Ireland, 1996).

7. His counsel, Sergeant Sullivan, records that Casement knew the content of the diaries and did not dispute them. Sergeant Sullivan appears an entirely reliable witness. BMH WS No.253, Sullivan.

8. Sullivan held the office of Second Sergeant, an ancient legal badge of seniority and ability. Sullivan led Artemus Jones and John Hartman-Morgan, a constitutional lawyer. Counsel was instructed by George Gavan Duffy.

9. BMH WS, No. 253, Sullivan.

10. *The King v Casement* KB [1917] 98.

11. Ephesian, *Lord Birkenhead* (London: Mills and Boon, 1926), p.80.

12. 25 Edw 3. St. 5. c.2.

13. See de Courcy Ireland, J. *The Sea and the Easter Rising.*

14. Waghorn may have been a little more forthcoming with Constable O'Reilly when waiting to give evidence at the committal proceedings at Bow Street. O'Reilly later recalled that Waghorn told him the *Aud* had been shadowed down the west coast of Ireland for some time.

15. Gearty, C. *The Casement Treason Trial in its Legal Context* (2001) Irish Jurist, 36. At least one distinguished lawyer has suggested that the court could afford to be

fair because the evidence was overwhelming and Casement had no defence. In all other cases of this period, when it really mattered, these judges always favoured the government. Casement's trial, however, was fair and conducted according to law and one cannot go beyond that.

16. PRO HO 144/1636/311643/42.

17. Described by his executioner, Albert Ellis: 'He appeared to me, the bravest man it fell to my unhappy lot to execute.' Casement's companions on U-19 were more fortunate. The Attorney General entered a nolle prosequi against Bailey and he was released. Monteith had escaped capture. He was sheltered for some months by Jesuits before crossing to Liverpool under an assumed name and then to America. The debate about the authenticity of the Diaries has now been revived. See Mitchell, A. *16 Lives Roger Casement* (Dublin: O'Brien Press, 2016), Hyde, P. *Decoding Casement* (2016, unpublished thesis).

CHAPTER FOURTEEN

1. The account of the trial comes from PRO WO 141/72 which contains summaries of evidence and contemporary press reports.

2. Holman Gregory KC and M.W.T. Snell.

3. His continued detention was justified on the grounds that his offences were committed while a soldier in active service during the Great War. HC Debates *Hansard* 1923 Vol. 167, Cols. 13-14.

4. He secured a ban on James Joyce (*Ulysses*) and D.H. Lawrence (*Pansies*).

CHAPTER FIFTEEN

1. Tracing this case has proved difficult and I acknowledge the kind assistance of Seán Hogan.

2. Resident Magistrate Major E. J. Dease, The Rath, Queen's County.

3. BMH WS No. 1,716, MacEoin and WS No. 1,439, Maguire.

4. They were represented by Tim Healy KC and Patrick Lynch KC with Joseph O'Connor.

5. Where a district was proclaimed under The Criminal Law & Procedure (Ireland) Act 1887 50 & 51 Vict, c 20, the Attorney General was entitled to move the trial to another area. Under section 4 of the Act, the defence was entitled to apply to the High Court for a variation or discharge of the order. This is what happened in this case. Where the defence satisfied the court that the cases could be more fairly and impartially tried elsewhere, it was the duty of the court to move the case to that district. This practice was approved by the court the following year in *R v Fitzgerald and others* IR [1920] 428.

6. See for instance McEldowney, J. 'The Queen v McKenna (1869) and Jury Packing in Ireland', *Irish Jurist* Vol. 12, 1977.

7. A nolle prosequi was entered by the Attorney General which prevented any further proceedings against the prisoners.

8. O'Brien confided his part to Ernie O'Malley.

CHAPTER SIXTEEN

1. An inquest was convened the following day and found that the Sergeant had died of a single wound to the chest. The jury expressed their sympathy to Sergeant Brady's widow and six children.
2. This trial was brought to my attention by Mr Seán Hogan, from Tipperary, and I acknowledge that debt with thanks.
3. Wylie Memoir, PRO 30/89/2.
4. Madden also faced a charge of wounding Constable Foley. It was the practice at the time not to add other counts to an indictment charging murder. The prosecution offered no evidence on the second indictment and a not guilty verdict was recorded.
5. BMH WS No. 1323, Needham. One other prisoner in custody was James Carroll. He had played a full part in the ambush. The prosecution against him rested solely on evidence from Gilligan but the case against Carroll was also dropped.

CHAPTER SEVENTEEN

1. For a report see *Freeman's Journal* 23 November 1920.
2. According to local sources the Army ran amok and killed a local man, Thomas Harris, and ten-year-old Patrick Duggan.
3. Comyn J. *Their Friends at Court* (London: Barry Rose, 1973), p.49.
4. The ambush is described: See BMH WS No. 600, O'Hannigan. There is a consensus among Limerick historians that O'Rourke played no part in the insurgency.

CHAPTER EIGHTEEN

1. This account is taken from the *Irish Times* and *Derry News and Donegal People*, 11 December 1920.
2. The full charge read: 'In that she, in Ireland, on divers dates between the 1st day of January 1918, and the 26th day of September 1920, unlawfully and wickedly did conspire, combine, confederate, and agree together with one Eamon Martin and divers other persons unknown, to organise, promote, assist and encourage a certain organisation known as the Fianna Éireann, which said organisation was being conducted between the days aforesaid for purposes of arranging for and securing the perpetration of certain felonies and criminal offences – namely the committing of murders of members of His Majesty's military and police forces and the liege subjects of his majesty, into unlawful drilling of men, the carrying and using of firearms, the furnishing and training of recruits for the Irish Volunteers – an unlawful association duly proclaimed under and pursuant to the Provisions of the Criminal and Procedure (Ireland) Act 1887– the inciting of persons to take part in the proceedings of the said unlawful association known as the Irish Volunteers and inciting the liege subjects of our Lord and

King to become disaffected, and to do actions calculated and intended to cause disaffection to his majesty, and to prevent by force and arms the execution of the laws of this realm, against the peace of our Lord the King, his crown and dignity.'

3. Hopkinson, M. (ed.) *The Last Days of Dublin Castle* (Dublin: Irish Academic Press, 1998), p.46.
4. *Derry News and Donegal People*, 11 December 1920.
5. BMH WS No.707, Noyk.
6. Winter, O. *Winter's Tale* (London: Richards Press, 1951), p.300.
7. Dungan, M. (ed.) *Speaking Ill of the Dead* (Dublin: New Island, 2007), p.94.
8. Wylie Memoir PRO 30/89/2.
9. See Dungan, *Speaking Ill of the Dead*, p.87.

CHAPTER NINETEEN

1. The trial took place on 17 December 1920.
2. BMH WS No. 207, Aloysius, p.16.
3. Brigadier Ormonde Winter asserted in his memoirs that a captured list of Dáil loan subscribers showed a surprising find: 'on that list I discovered the names of several of my personal friends', Winter, O. *Winter's Tale* (London: Richards Press, 1951), p.300.
4. Kathleen Hicks, a shop assistant at Robert Cutler's Hardware and Fancy Store in Waterford, was one of many court martialled. She was charged with having three typed forms inviting subscriptions to the Dáil loan. She made no defence and was convicted and imprisoned. Her case was not unusual.
5. A handful of prisoners were prosecuted for acting as officers of the Dáil. For example, Thomas James Loughlin was prosecuted before a Field General Court Martial in March 1921. He was charged with possessing documents said to emanate from a Minister of the Dáil, being in possession of documents naming him as an officer of the Dáil, while acting as an officer of the Dáil, 'entering the offices of the Town Clerk, Wexford Corporation and examining the books of the said body and taking extracts there from'. See 16 March 1921, *Cork Examiner.*
6. PRO WO 35/124/40. The prosecution of Charles Gavin for acting as a clerk to a Dáil court. Gavin was interned from March to December 1921.
7. Diarmuid Crowley was imprisoned for two years for acting as a judge in the Dáil courts. William McKnight from Longford was prosecuted for acting as a judge but the case was dropped due to insufficient evidence. See also PRO WO 35/118/36, Liam O'Duffy, who had one years' imprisonment imposed.
8. See 18 February 1921,*Waterford News*.
9. This was one of the charges brought against Terence MacSwiney.
10. Evans G. *The Raising of the First Internal Dáil Éireann Loan and the British Responses to it, 1919–1921*(NUI, 2012), p.47.
11. See for instance BMH WS No. 1642, Halley.
12. BMH WS No. 1373, Balfe, p.16.

CHAPTER TWENTY

1. BMH WS No. 1113, Brennock.
2. BMH WS No. 743, Daly. Daly recalled that General Strickland had ordered a 'drumhead' trial, that is one convened under martial law. This may have been what he was told and what motivated his escape but it would not have happened. The ambush took place on 10 December 1920 before martial law was proclaimed. No prisoners were tried by drumhead military courts for acts done before the cut-off date imposed by the Army: 27 December 1920. See Enright, S. *The Trial of Civilians by Military Courts* (Dublin: Irish Academic Press, 2012) and see PRO WO 141/94. Had he been tried, the trial would have been convened under the Restoration of Order in Ireland Act.
3. This account of the trial is drawn in part from *The Limerick Chronicle.*
4. *Cork Examiner,* 18 February 1921.
5. BMH WS No. 325, Reverend Coyle: assaulted whilst in custody.
6. Canon Magner was killed by an Auxiliary, Cadet Harte in December 1920, and Father Griffin was killed by Auxiliaries in November 1920.
7. John Reilly, an ex-soldier was shot dead by masked men in May 1921. He was said to be an informant and he was killed for that reason. *The Limerick Chronicle,* 19 May 1921.

CHAPTER TWENTY-ONE

1. See BMH WS No.1525, Maloney.
2. Ned and Gerard O'Dwyer.
3. The officer who led the operation, John M. Regan reported that two men were killed in this way. Augusteijn, J. *The Memoirs of John M. Regan. A Catholic Officer in the RIC and RUC 1909–48* (Dublin: Four Courts Press, 2007). P164–5.
4. Abbott, R. *Police Casualties in Ireland* (Cork, Mercier Press, 2001) p.167. There is no firm evidence that Constable Reid died.
5. Henry Wade, Ned Moloney, Daniel Sheahan, John Quinlan and Martin Conway.
6. See Augusteijn, *The Memoirs of John M. Regan.*
7. For a comprehensive account of this incident, see: Toomey, T. *The War of Independence in Limerick* (Privately published 2010).
8. Thomas Eastwood, known as Ralph. He was Brigade Major with the Sixth Division until 4th May 1921. Later, Lieutenant General Sir Thomas Eastwood, KCB, DSO, MC. Later he was GOC Northern Command in England and Governor of Gibraltar 1944.
9. BMH WS No 1,525 Maloney.
10. No trial record survives. Curiously the office of the JAG retained a notice posted on the walls of the great house setting out the rules laid down for the evening: 'Don't strike matches on the doors, walls or scratch them in any way. Don't prance your feet while dancing...' By order, The Committee.

11. This account is taken in part from *The Cork Examiner,* 24 February 1921.
12. *The Sixth Division Record of the Rebellion,* Imperial War Musuem.

CHAPTER TWENTY-TWO

1. Ballistic evidence was used in the prosecution of Kevin Barry in November 1921 but not otherwise.
2. Winter, O. *Report on the Intelligence Branch of the Chief of Police, Dublin Castle from May 1920 to July 1921.* PRO WO 35/214.
3. Adolf Beck (Cmnd 2315). In that case the absence of a foreskin provided a prison warder the vital clue that the prisoner had been misidentified. That case was regarded as a freak instance involving the criminal and the innocent lookalike. This failure to understand the dangers of visual identification evidence is abundantly plain from a review of the standard criminal textbook at the time: *Archbold* 25th edition 1918 which makes no reference to the subject. It was not until the 1970s that the courts began to recognise the dangers of visual identification and take a structured approach to the subject. See for instance, *Report of the Committee on Evidence of Identification in Criminal Cases,* 1976, Cmnd 338 134/135. See also *R v Turnbull* [1977] QB 224. And see *Archbold Criminal Practice and Pleading* 2015.
4. The Judge Advocates operating in Ireland during this period included Kenneth Marshall CBE, JAG who was very experienced. The others were Lt Colonel E.H. Chapman OBE, also, Lt Colonel H.M. Meyler of the Border Regiment, Sutherland Graeme CBE and Captain Young the court martial officer of the Sixth Division. The decisions of the last three officers show a very limited ability in criminal law.
5. For a very full account of the trial see *Freeman's Journal* 27 January to 2 February 1921. There was a fourth prisoner Daniel Healy who applied for and was granted a second trial. He escaped trial when the maid, the only witness against him, declined to give evidence.
6. The accused were all represented by counsel. Teeling was represented by Charles Bewley. Conway by Thomas Brown K.C. and Vincent Rice. Potter by Albert Wood K.C. and Samuel Porter. The Crown was represented by Denis Henry, the Attorney General, Travers Humphreys K.C. and Rowland Oliver.
7. Lieutenant Angliss was a Lieutenant in the Royal Inniskilling Fusiliers. He was living at 22 Lower Mount Street under the name McMahon.
8. Rice BMH WS No. 843.
9. James Murphy and Patrick Kennedy. See the trial of Captain William Lorraine King, this volume.
10. See Bonsall, P. *The Irish RMs: The resident magistrates in the British Administration of Ireland* (Dublin: Four Courts Press, 1997).
11. This was done in the case of Michael O'Rourke who was acquitted of murder just after Bloody Sunday. Michael O'Rourke had no connection with the insurgency but his life was under threat simply because of a suspicion held against him.

12. BMH WS No. 445, p.13. Slattery, who recalled the raid vividly. Connolly was what he termed 'an undesirable character' and regretted not shooting him for that reason alone.
13. BMH WS No. 843, Rice, p.12.
14. The reasons for the sentences being commuted are dealt with in *Days of Terror 1921*, this volume.
15. See *Freeman's Journal* 2, 3 and 4 February 1921
16. A reliable account of the trial can be found in *Freeman's Journal* 2, 3 and 4 February, 1921
17. O'Malley, E. *On Another Man's Wound* (Dublin: Anvil Books, 2002) p.298.
18. The President of the court was Lieutenant Colonel Badham of the Worcester Regiment. The Judge Advocate was Kenneth Marshall CBE.
19. Lieutenant Bennett was also killed at that address. But the charges related only to the death of Lieutenant Ames.
20. Edward McGelligott KC leading Farrell for Rochford. Moran was represented by James Williamson KC and Charles Wyse Power, instructed by Michael Noyk. Travers Humphreys K.C. and Roland Oliver appeared for the Crown.
21. BMH WS No. 908, O'Flanagan.
22. References to false alibis are well documented in the literature of the time. See for instance: Healy, M. *The Old Munster Circuit* (Dublin: Mercier, 1986), Comyn, J. *Their Friends at Court* (London: Barry Rose Publishers, 1973) and Augusteijn, J. *The Memoirs of John M. Regan. A Catholic Officer in the RIC and RUC 1909–1948* (Dublin: Four Courts, 2007) and see the trial of Bryan Kelley, this volume.
23. BMH WS No. 706, Noyk.
24. BMH WS No. 499, Kennedy and No. 220, Daly.
25. In 1916 he had been part of the garrison at Jacob's factory and was later interned.

CHAPTER TWENTY-THREE

1. The record of this trial comes from PRO WO 71/366.
2. *The Treason Act of 1351* was applicable to Ireland by reason of *Poyning's Act* of 1494.
3. Instructed for the defence were junior counsel, Charles Power, Nolan Whelan, Charles Bewley. E. A. Swayne KC was instructed at a late stage to argue a novel point of law.
4. Muir prosecuted Crippen and most of the high-profile murder trials of this period. He was senior Treasury Counsel at the Old Bailey and later Recorder of Colchester and a Bencher of Middle Temple.
5. Hopkinson, M. (ed.) *The Last Days of Dublin Castle* (Dublin: Irish Academic Press, 1998), p.102.
6. BMH WS No. 508, O'Sullivan.

7. See Hopkinson, *The Last Days of Dublin Castle*. The dead men were unarmed police orderlies. It appears that they had been mistaken for members of Royal Irish Constabulary undercover squad run by head Constable Eugene Igoe.
8. PRO WO 71/366.
9. Hamar Greenwood, Chief Secretary. *Hansard*, HC Debates 14 March 1921.

CHAPTER TWENTY-FOUR

1. O'Malley, E. *On Another Man's Wound* (Dublin: Anvil Books, 2002), p.273.
2. Ibid.
3. Hardy was suspected of leading a group of military who had been engaged in shooting suspected insurgents in their homes in Thurles and also of killing Tomás Mac Curtain, Lord Mayor of Cork. No evidence has ever been produced in support of these suspicions.
4. BMH WS No. 380, Neligan, p.14.
5. See, for instance, Leeson, D. M. *The Black and Tans: British Police and Auxiliaries in the Irish War of Independence* (Oxford: Oxford University Press, 2011).
6. J.L. Hardy DSO MC, of the Connaught Rangers and Inniskilling Fusiliers. 1894–1958, soldier and novelist.
7. See O'Malley, *On Another Man's Wound*.
8. The charge was laid under Regulation 7 of the Restoration of Order in Ireland Regulations. The report of the trial comes from *The Manchester Guardian*, 13, 14 and 15 April 1921.
9. For centuries a dying declaration was admissible in criminal or civil proceedings where it was proved that the maker of the statement was under a settled expectation of death. The rationale of the rule rested on the idea that a man who knew he was dying would not lie. See for instance *Wright v Littler* 97 Eng Rep 812. In the case of William King it could not be proved that Murphy was under a settled expectation of death and the statement was not admitted in evidence.
10. Hopkinson, M. (ed.) *The Last Days of Dublin Castle* (Dublin: Irish Academic Press, 1998), p.125.
11. PRO CO 904/188.
12. BMH WS No. 1,280, Broy, p.117.
13. King remained with the Auxiliaries until November 1921 when they were disbanded. He later served in the Second World War dying in Gaza, 1942, aged fifty-seven.

CHAPTER TWENTY-FIVE

1. The charge was laid contrary to Reg. 67 of the Restoration of Order in Ireland Act Regulations.
2. The account of this trial is taken from PRO WO 71/366.

3. Another man, Jack Donnelly, was wounded and captured and, although he too was later tried and convicted, the Truce intervened and he was not executed.
4. Abbott, R. *Police Casualties in Ireland 1919–22* (Dublin: Mercier, 2001), p.208. Beard had reached the rank of Brigadier at the age of thirty-two. He must have been a young man of quite exceptional ability.
5. This was a most unfortunate moment for the prisoner which could have been avoided by Nolan Whelan. Defence counsel also witness summonsed General Macready and the Chief Constable of the DMP in the hope of establishing, through cross-examination, that the country was in a state of war and, therefore, the prisoner should be accorded belligerent status. This status had been denied the rebels of 1916 who had fought in uniform by the laws of war and it is hardly likely that the government would grant such status to those who did not fight in uniform and abide by recognised laws of war. The court declined to require the witnesses to attend.
6. He had been a member of the Boland's Mill garrison and was subsequently interned after the surrender.
7. The other indictment alleging the murder of Cadet Beard was not pursued having regard to the conviction for the murder of Cadet Farrell.
8. See Abbott, *Police Casualties in Ireland 1919–22*, p.209.

CHAPTER TWENTY-SIX

1. *The Record of the Rebellion. Volume III, Law.* PRO WO 141/94.
2. For an account of the trial in connection with the Mallow barracks raid, see Enright, S. *The Trial of Civilians by Military Courts* (Dublin: Irish Academic Press, 2012).
3. WO 83/40 Minute Book, Judge Advocate General. And letter JAG to Sir Hamar Greenwood 21 March 1921.
4. Strickland Papers, IWM. *Notes on the Organisation and Methods of Sinn Féin.*

CHAPTER TWENTY-SEVEN

1. These men were Dan Breen, Sean Tracey, Eamonn O'Brien, James Scanlon, J.J. O'Brien, Thomas Shanahan, Seamus Robinson, Edward Foley and Sean Lynch.
2. From an account by Tom Toomey, an historian who interviewed some of the children of the school in their later years.
3. Inquest evidence 22 May 1919, *Freeman's Journal*.
4. PRO WO 71 365. Extensive efforts were made to find Ring. When he was found he was no longer a witness well-disposed to the Crown. He gave evidence favourable to the defence. However, on re-examination he told the court that he heard one of the raiders call out 'Paddy' which may have supported the case against Maher.
5. George McElroy of the Old Barracks, Clarecastle. He died in 1929 aged eighty-nine.

6. Foxton, D. *Revolutionary Lawyers* (Dublin: Four Courts Press, 2007) suggests the men were tried by a jury twice but no verdict was reached. This does not appear to be so. The appeal lodged with General Macready, which was drafted by counsel, explicitly states that the prisoners were sent for trial at Limerick and that change of venue applications were soon lodged by the prosecution and defence. PRO CO/904/41.

7. The Criminal Law and Procedure Act 1887 provided a mechanism for a change of trial venue where the Attorney General believed that a fair and impartial trial could not be otherwise achieved. It also provided a mechanism for the prisoner to challenge the order made by the Attorney General and persuade the High Court that the case could more fairly be tried elsewhere.

8. The ROIA Regulations permitted the Army to assert jurisdiction in respect of any untried indictments. In the case of Maher and Foley, the High Court had made an order sending them for trial at the next Assize. The legal question was whether, in these circumstances, the Army could assert jurisdiction to try the prisoners by court martial. The High Court ruled that the order sending them to the Assizes raised no bar and that the indictment they faced was just an untried indictment which the Army was entitled to try by court martial under the ROIA. The High Court refused a writ of prohibition preventing the Army from trying the men. The trial record shows that the case was remitted for court martial under the ROIA Regulations of 13 August 1920.The central legal issue raised was litigated by a number of prisoners. See *Rex (Rodgers) v Campbell and others* [1921] ILT 192.

9. The evidence against Murphy showed he was on the platform at the station but little more. He secured a separate trial but the trial record does not disclose a reason for his counsel seeking this. He was acquitted at his trial.

10. The President of the Court was Bt. Lieutenant Colonel Powell, CBE DSO 2nd Battalion Welsh Regiment who tried many of these cases. The trial record can be found at PRO WO 71/365 and 365A.

11. Patrick Lynch KC and Richard Best KC with Joseph O'Connor. Instructed by John Power from Kilmallock.

12. The hangings were carried out by John Ellis. This was the largest number of hangings in a single day in living memory. Ellis later wrote a compelling memoir of his work: *Diary of a Hangman* (London: True Crime Library, 1996) but he never wrote about these executions.

13. Toomey, T. *The War of Independence in Limerick 1912–21* (Privately published, 2010).

14. Maher was picked out by Arthur Morris, a soldier of the Shropshire Light Infantry stationed at Fermoy. He was picked out by an off-duty RIC sergeant, Edward Sullivan, and John Farrington, an RIC man who were both passengers on the train. Neither of these officers had come forward to help the party of policemen who were attacked nor did they come forward to give first aid to Sergeant Wallace.

15. See, for example, BMH WS No. 1,647, p.11.
16. See, for instance, accounts given by the participants BMH WS No. 1421, Robinson and also accounts by Breen, D. *My Fight for Irish Freedom* (Cork: Mercier, 2010), p.59. Breen names all the men who took part including Foley but exculpates Maher. See Toomey, *The War of Independence in Limerick*. See also Abbott, R. *Police Casualties in Ireland 1919–22* (Dublin: Mercier Press, 2001), p.30.

CHAPTER TWENTY-EIGHT

1. This was a trial under the Restoration of Order in Ireland Act. The charge alleged 'committing a crime within the meaning of Section 67 of the Restoration of Order In Ireland Regulations, that is to say, murder, in that they, on 20th day of January 1921, at Listowel, in the county of Kerry, feloniously, wilfully and of their malice aforethought did kill and murder Tobias O'Sullivan'.
2. Joseph McCarthy for Lenehan and Devereux. J.N. Fitzgerald represented Carmody and O'Carroll. The name of prosecuting counsel was withheld for his own safety.
3. The dead included Sergeant Thomas Kane and Constable Joseph Morton. Constable Arthur Hoey was seriously wounded. There was a single fatality on the rebel side, Liam Scully.
4. *The Irish Rebellion in the Sixth Divisional Area*, p.25. Imperial War Museum.
5. Augusteijn, J. (ed.) *The Memoirs of John M. Regan, A Catholic Officer in the RIC And RUC, 1909–1948* (Dublin: Four Courts, 2007), p.164.
6. Major Mackinnon of the Auxiliaries in April 1921 and Head Constable Francis Benson in May 1921.
7. Head Constable William Storey in May 1921.
8. He was forty-three years old and left a devoted widow, Mary, and three young children. Abbott, R. *Police Casualties in Ireland 1919–22* (Dublin and Cork: Mercier Press, 2000). See WO 35/157A for inquest evidence.
9. *Record of the Rebellion*, Vol.III, p.18.
10. PRO WO 81/41, p.124.
11. BMH WS No. 968, Lenehan. He had been a Volunteer in the Listowel area from 1914 but as the years passed he took no active part in the Rebellion apart from hiding arms in his workshop when asked.
12. BMH WS No. 1123, Brosnan. BMH WS No. 970, Ahern. There is no reason why they should not tell the truth and the detail of their accounts tally closely with the evidence given in the trial.
13. It was later said that Brosnan came out into the street and and found that O'Sullivan was holding hands with his seven-year-old son. Brosnan hesitated and then fired the first shots and 'regretted it for the remainder of his life'. Dwyer, Ryle T. *Irish Examiner*, 2 April 2011. There is no contemporary evidence that supports this account. See, for instance, Inquest evidence PRO WO 35/157A. Brosnan never spoke in public about this event.

CHAPTER TWENTY-NINE

1. BMH WS No. 1716, Mac Eoin.
2. As recalled in a personal note by Colonel Wilford. BMH WS No. 1716, Mac Eoin.
3. Among the dead was a most distinguished naval officer, Commander Craven DSO, DSC, DSM. Also Cadet George Bush, Harold Clayton and John Houghton.
4. Bewley, C. *Memoirs of a Wild Goose* (Dublin: McCormack, 1989).
5. Macready, Sir N. *Annals of an Active Life* Vol. II (London: Hutchinson, 1924).

Select Bibliography and Note on Sources

Abbott, R. *Police Casualties in Ireland* 1919–22 (Dublin: Mercier, 2000).

Andrew, C. & Dilks, D. *The Missing Dimension: Governments and Intelligence Communities in the Twentieth Century* (London: MacMillan, 1984).

Asquith, C.*The Diaries of Lady Cynthia Asquith* (London: Century, 1987).

Augusteijn, J. *The Memoirs of John M. Regan. A Catholic Officer in the RIC and RUC 1909–1948* (Dublin: Four Courts Press, 2007).

Bayly, Admiral Sir Lewis, *Pull Together!: The Memoirs of Admiral Sir Lewis Bayly* (London: Harrap and Co, 1939).

Bonsall, P. *The Irish RMs: the resident magistrates in the British administration of Ireland* (Dublin: Four Courts, 1997).

Bradbridge, E.U. (ed.) *59th Division 1915–1918* (Chesterfield: Wilfred Edmonds, 1928).

Brennan, R. *Allegiance* (Dublin: The Richview Press, 1950).

Brennan-Whitmore, W.J. *With the Irish in Frongoch* (Cork: Mercier Press, 2013).

Brock, M.&E. (eds) *Margot Asquith's Great War Diary 1914–1916: The View from Downing Street* (Oxford: Oxford University Press, 2014).

Callwell, C. E. (ed.) *Field Marshall Sir Henry Wilson: His Life and Diaries* (London: Cassel & Co, 1927).

Campbell, C. *Emergency Law in Ireland 1918–1925* (Oxford: Clarendon Press, 1994).

Comyn, J. *Their Friends at Court* (London: Barry Rose, 1973).

Crane, C. P. *Memories of a Resident Magistrate 1880–1920* (Edinburgh: T & A Constable 1938).

De Courcy Ireland, J. *The Sea and the Easter Rising 1916.* (Dublin: Maritime Institute of Ireland,1996).

Dungan, M. (ed.) *Speaking Ill of the Dead* (Dublin: New Island, 2007).

Dunn, H.*The Minstrel Boy*: Francis Ledwidge and the literature of his time, including five previously unpublished poems (Book Link, 2006).

Dwyer, T. Ryle, *Tans, Terror and Troubles: Kerry's Real Fighting Story, 1913–1923* (Cork: Mercier Press, 2001).

Ferguson, K. *King's Inns Barristers, 1868–2004* (Dublin: The Honourable Society of Kings Inn, in association with the Irish Legal History Society, Irish Academic Press, 2005).

Ferriter, D. *A Nation and Not a Rabble: The Irish Revolution 1913–1923* (London: Profile Books, 2013).

Foy, M. *Michael Collins's Intelligence War: The Struggle Between the British and the IRA, 1919–1921* (Stroud: The History Press, 2006).

Fox, R. M. *History of the Irish Citizen Army* (Dublin: James Duffy & Co, 1944).

Foxton, D. *Revolutionary Lawyers Sinn Féin and Crown Courts in Ireland and Britain 1916–1923* (Dublin: Four Courts, 2008).

Gibbon, M. *Inglorious Soldier* (London: Hutchinson, 1968).

Griffith, K. & O'Grady, T.E. (eds) *Curious Journey: An Oral History of Ireland's Unfinished Revolution* (London: Hutchinson, 1982).

Hannigan, D. *Terence MacSwiney: The Hunger Strike that Rocked an Empire* (Dublin: The O'Brien Press, 2010).

Hittle, J. B. *Michael Collins and the Anglo-Irish War* (Virginia: Potomac Books, 2011).

Hogan, S. *The Black and Tans in North Tipperary* (Nenagh, 2013).

Hopkinson, M. (ed.) *The Last Days of Dublin Castle: The Diaries of Mark Sturgis* (Dublin: Irish Academic Press, 1998).

Howard, P. & Nichols G. *Past Nichols the Undertakers: Six Generations of a Dublin Family Business, 1814–2014* (Dublin: privately published, 2014).

Jeffery K. (ed.) *The Sinn Féin Rebellion As They Saw It* (Dublin: Irish Academic Press, 1999).

Jenkins, R. *Asquith* (London: Collins, 1969).

Kiberd, D. (ed.) *1916 Rebellion Handbook* (Dublin: Mourne River Press, 1998).

Laffan, M. *The Resurrection of Ireland: The Sinn Féin Party, 1916–1923* (London: Cambridge University Press, 1999).

Leeson, D. M. *The Black and Tans: British Police and Auxiliaries in the Irish War of Independence* (Oxford: Oxford University Press, 2011).

Longford, Earl and O'Neill, T. P. *Eamon De Valera* (London: Hutchinson & Co, 1970).

Macardle, D. *The Irish Republic* (London: Corgi, 1967).

McCarthy, C. *Cumann na mBan and the Irish Revolution* (Cork: The Collins Press, 2007).

MacManus, F. *After the Flight* (Dublin: Talbot Press, 1938).

MacMillan, M. *Peacemakers: The Paris Conference of 1919 and Its Attempt to End War* (London: Joseph Murray Ltd, 2001).

Meakin,W. *History of the 5ᵗʰ North Staffords 1914–1919* (London: Hughes and Harper, 1920).

Middlemas, K. (ed.) *Thomas Jones Whitehall Diary 1916–25*, Vol III (London: Oxford University Press, 1969).

Montgomery Hyde, H. (ed.) *Trial of Sir Roger Casement* (Edinburgh: William Hodge and Co Ltd, 1960).

O'Brien, P. *Uncommon Valour: Easter1916 & the battle for the South Dublin Union* (Cork: Mercier Press, 2010).

Ó Broin, L, *W.E. Wylie and the Irish Revolution, 1916–1921* (Dublin: Gill & Macmillan, 1989).

Ó Broin, L. *Dublin Castle and the 1916 Easter Rising* (Sidgwick and Jackson, London, 1970).

O'Callaghan, J. *Revolutionary Limerick: The Republican Campaign for Independence in Limerick, 1913–1921* (Dublin: Irish Academic Press, 2010).

O'Donoghue, F. *No Other Law* (Dublin: Irish Press Limited, 1954).

O'Duibhir, L. *The Donegal Awakening. Donegal and the War of Independence* (Dublin, Mercier, 2009).

Officers of the Battalions, *The Robin Hoods* (Uckfield: The Naval and Military Press, 2010).

O'Malley, E. *On Another Man's Wound* (Dublin: Anvil, 2002).

Oram, G. *Death Sentences Passed by Military Courts of the British Army 1914–24* (London: Francis Boutle Publishers, 1998).

O'Sullivan, M. and O'Neill B. *The Shelbourne and its People* (Dublin: Blackwater Press, 1999).

Ramsay, D. *'Blinker' Hall, Spymaster: the man who brought America into World War I* (Stroud: Spellmont, 2008).

Ryan, A.M. *16 Dead Men: The Easter Rising Executions* (Dublin: Mercier Press, 2014).

Spindler, K. *The Mystery of the Casement Ship* (Berlin: Kribe-Verlag, 1931).

Spindler, K. *The Mystery of the Casement Ship* (Tralee: Anvil Books, 1966).

Taylor, P. *Heroes or Traitors?: Experiences of Southern Irish Soldiers Returning from the Great War 1919–1939* (Oxford: Oxford University Press, 2015).

Toomey, T. *The War of Independence in Limerick 1912–1921* (Limerick: privately published, 2010).

Townshend, C. *Easter 1916: The Irish Rebellion* (London: Penguin, 2005).

Townshend, C. *The Republic: The Fight for Irish Independence* (London: Penguin, 2014).

Warwick-Haller, A.& S. (eds) *Letters from Dublin, Easter 1916: Alfred Fannin's Diary of the Rising* (Dublin: Irish Academic Press, 1995).

Whitton, F.E. *The History of the Prince of Wales's Leinster Regiment, Volume 2* (Aldershot: Gale & Polden, 1920).

Winter, O. *Winter's Tale: An Autobiography* (London: Richards Press, 1951).

Yeates, P. *A City in Wartime: Dublin 1914–18* (Dublin: Gill & MacMillan, 2011).

Essays and Dissertations

Evans G.*The Raising of the First Internal Dáil Loan and the British Responses to it, 1919–1921* (NUI, 2012).

Oldham C. H.*The development of tillage in Ireland during the World War.*Journal of the Statistical and Social Inquiry Society of Ireland.Vol.XIV, No 2.

Sloan, G. *The British State and the Irish Rebellion of 1916: An Intelligence Failure Or a Failure of Response* Journal of Strategic Studies, Vol. 6, No. 5, 2013.

Wells, A. R. *Studies in British Naval Intelligence 1880–1945* (PhD thesis, University of London, 1972).

Archives

Lancers Archive, Grantham, Lincolnshire
Leicestershire Regiment, Leicestershire County Archive, Wigston, Leicestershire
Lincolnshire Regiment, Lincolnshire County Archives, Rumbold Street, Lincoln
Museum of the Sherwood Foresters, Chilwell, Nottinghamshire
National Maritime Museum of Ireland

Public Record Office Kew

Chief Secretary's List, PRO.CO 903/19
Intelligence Notes CO 903/19
Record of the Rebellion in Ireland 1920–21 and the Part Played by the Army in Dealing With it:
Volume 1 Operations
Volume II Intelligence
Volume III Law
A Report of the Intelligence branch of the Chief of Police, Dublin Castle, May 1920– July 1921 PRO WO 35/214 and CO 904/156B
Trial Records WO 71 344 – et seq.
Trial Register WO 213/8
Wylie Papers PRO 30/89/2
National Library of Ireland
Gavan Duffy Papers
Irish National Aid Association and Voluntary Dependants' Fund Papers

UCDA
De Valera Papers

Bodleian Library
Asquith Papers
Nathan Papers

Irish Military Archives
BMH Witness Statements
Contemporary Documents
Pension Records

Army Publications
Kings Regulations and Orders for the Army 1914
Manual of Military Law, 1907 (6th Edition)

Royal Commissions and Government Reports
The Royal Commission on the Arrest and Subsequent Treatment of Mr Francis Sheehy-Skeffington, Mr Thomas Dickson, and Mr Patrick James Macintyre upon and after their arrest on the Twenty-fifth day of April last, Cd 8376
The Royal Commission on the Rebellion in Ireland 1916, Cmnd 8279
Statistical Tables of the Dublin Metropolitan Police for the Year 1916, Cmd 30, 1919
Criminal and Judicial Statistics, Ireland 1917, Cmd 43
Criminal and Judicial Statistics, Ireland 1918, Cmd 438, Appendix 31
Criminal and Judicial Statistics, Ireland 1919, Cmd 1431 Appendix 31
The Vice-Regal Commission on the Reorganisation and Pay of the Irish Police Forces, 1919
*Documents Relative to the Sinn Féin Movement,*Cmd 1108
Outrages (Ireland) 31st March 1920 Cmd 1431

Statutes

The Treason Act 1351
Poyning's Act 1494
The Appropriation Act No. 3 of 1922
The Compensation (Ireland) Commission 1922
The Petty Sessions (Ireland) Act 1851 XCIII
The Criminal Law & Procedure (Ireland) Act 1887 50 & 51 Vict, c 20
The Criminal Injuries (Ireland) Act 1919 9 Geo 5 c 14
The Defence of the Realm Act 4 & 5 Geo V c.29
The Defence of the Realm (Consolidation) 1915 *Act* 5 Geo V
The Defence of the Realm 1915 *(Amendment) Act* 5 & 6 Geo V
The Firearms Act 10 & 11 Geo 5 Ch 43
The Prisoners (Temporary Discharge for Ill Health) Act 1913 3 & 4 Geo V c.4
The Restoration of Order in Ireland Act 1920 (10 & 11 Geo 5 C.31)

Secondary Legislation

The Military Exercises and Drill (Ireland) Order 1916

Cases

R v Governor of Lewis Prison ex parte Doyle [1917] 2 KB 254
R v Allen II IR 241
Clifford and Sullivan [1921] 2 AC 570
Egan v Macready [1921] 1 IR 265
The King v Fitzgerald and others [1920] IR 428
R v Maher and Others [1920] IR 429
The King v Fitzgerald, Edwards and Hooper. Irish Law Times 9 December 1920
Higgins v Willis [1921] II IR 383 *R v Murphy* II [1921] IR 190 *R (Garde and Others) v Major Gen E. P. Strickland* [1921] 2 IR 17 *R (Ronayne and Mulcahy) v Strickland and Another* [1921] 2 IR 333 *Whelan v Rex* [1921] 2 IR 310

Newspapers

The Irish Law Times and Solicitors' Journal
The Times
The Manchester Guardian

The Irish Times
The Freeman's Journal
The Cork Examiner
The Sligo Champion
The Mayo News
The Killarney Echo
The Waterford News
Le Monde
The New York Times
The Limerick Chronicle
The Limerick Leader

Index